Sex and Revolution

SEX AND REVOLUTION

Women in Socialist Cuba

LOIS M. SMITH
and
ALFRED PADULA

New York   Oxford
OXFORD UNIVERSITY PRESS
1996

Oxford University Press

Oxford   New York
Athens   Auckland   Bangkok   Bombay
Calcutta   Cape Town   Dar es Salaam   Delhi
Florence   Hong Kong   Istanbul   Karachi
Kuala Lampur   Madras   Madrid   Melbourne
Mexico City   Nairobi   Paris   Singapore
Taipei   Tokyo   Toronto

and associated companies in
Berlin   Ibadan

Copyright © 1996 by Oxford University Press, Inc.

Published by Oxford University Press, Inc.
198 Madison Avenue, New York, New York 10016

Oxford is a registered trademark of Oxford University Press

Library of Congress Cataloging-in-Publication Data
Smith, Lois M.
Sex and revolution : women in socialist Cuba / Lois M. Smith
and Alfred Padula.
p. cm.   Includes bibliographical references (p. –) and index.
ISBN 0-19-509490-5.—ISBN 0-19-509491-3 (pbk.)
1. Women—Cuba—Social conditions.   2. Sex role—Cuba.   3. Women's
rights—Cuba.   4. Women—Employment—Cuba.   5. Sex discrimination
against women—Cuba.   I. Padula, Alfred.   II. Title.
HQ1507.S63   1996
305.42'097291—dc20   95-11827

1 3 5 7 9 8 6 4 2

Printed in the United States of America
on acid-free paper

To my mother, Priscilla May,
for her energy and independence

To my mother, Dorothy B. Padula,
and my father, the late Alfred L. Padula Sr.,
whose generosity underwrote this project

Preface

We became engaged in this project in 1983 when the Women's Studies Committee at the University of Southern Maine asked Professor Padula, who had studied Cuba for some years, to give a brief presentation on Cuban women. Soon thereafter Lois Smith became a partner in the project. When our research indicated there was no comprehensive history of women in revolutionary Cuba, we naively decided to write one.

Each of us framed our own central question regarding the project. For social historian Padula the basic question was: How did three decades of socialist revolution change the lives of Cuban women? Social scientist and activist Smith asked: What lessons did the Cuban experience offer regarding the revolutionary model and sexual equality? Overall, we have both approached the question of women and the Cuban revolution as feminists interested in exploring the complex interplay between culture, on the one hand, and economic, political, and social institutions, on the other, in the determination and manifestation of gender roles and values in society. We have tried to view the progress of Cuban women in terms of the ambitious if ambiguous goal of "full sexual equality" set by Fidel Castro, the Communist party, the Federation of Cuban Women, and various leading officials.

The study of Cuban women is a problematic enterprise. Sources are scant. The standard prerevolutionary histories of Cuba hardly mention women beyond a cursory nod to one or two heroines of the wars for independence. Cuban social scientists and historians have resisted writing about the post-1959 period because it is simply too politically sensitive.

Only in the late 1980s did a growing body of work on gender, sexuality, and social relationships begin to emerge from the island's research institutes and universities. Even then there was much that could not be said. Patriarchy, for example, simply could not be discussed. Much of the work on Cuban women by the Cuban press has been of the "everything's fine here" variety. It must be consulted with caution.

Although the Federation of Cuban Women (Federación de Mujeres Cubanas, or FMC) has a very large staff, only a few *federadas* do research, and most of this is for in-house use only. Some of the research enters the public arena from time to time in FMC reports, articles in Cuban periodicals, or speeches by FMC director Vilma Espín. Nonetheless, as of 1995, neither the FMC nor Cuba's own scholars had yet produced a book-length analysis of women's status in revolutionary Cuba.

Cuban statistics pose certain challenges to researchers. Sometimes they are contradictory. Categories and terms are left undefined and change frequently, which complicates efforts to accurately trace trends over time. Furthermore, although the Cuban revolution has published a great deal of data on its performance in certain areas, there has been little or no information on a number of issues of particular interest to women. In some cases the data simply haven't been collected; in others they are inexplicably withheld. For example, there are no data on rape or violence against women, there are very little on single mothers, and there is only the scantiest information on contraceptive use. No data are published according to race or ethnic group, and there are virtually no national survey data that would indicate women's views, as opposed to men's, on issues of national and local import.

The hostility between the United States and Cuba has also affected our efforts to conduct this project. The Cuban revolution has been suspicious of initiatives by foreigners—and North Americans in particular—to investigate its performance. The U.S. economic embargo has complicated efforts to travel and maintain routine communications between the two countries. Although we have been to Cuba on ten occasions since 1978, this account basically relies on Cuban published materials.

We have incurred many debts in the course of researching this project. We owe particular thanks to the staff of the Otto G. Richter library at the University of Miami, which put its splendid collection of Cuban periodicals—particularly *Bohemia* and the Federation of Cuban Women's *Mujeres* and *Muchacha*—at our disposal. We also want to thank the library at Radio Martí in Washington, D.C., for allowing us to make use of its substantial microfilm collection. Thanks also to Vilma Petrash, a graduate student, for patiently searching out materials in the University of Pittsburgh library. We wish to thank Cassandra Fitzherbert at the library of the University of Southern Maine for helping us track down many obscure sources. Eleanor Weymouth patiently guided us through the mysteries of WordPerfect.

As this project developed over the years, we received help and comments from many friends and fellow students. In particular, we would like to thank Nelson Valdés, who has always had a unique way of looking at things. Sandy Halebsky deserves thanks for the support and good company he has provided on this long road. We also appreciate the encouragement and insights offered by Carollee Bengelsdorf. Thanks to Melissa Payson for her characteristically trenchant critiques, and to Eleanor Clark for her decade of support.

On our visits to Cuba we have benefited from the views and assistance of many. In particular, we want to thank Monika Krause, former director of sex education in Cuba, for many hours of insightful conversation. We owe thanks to the Federation of Cuban Women which on many occasions provided us with materials and offered comments, and in particular to its director, Vilma Espín, who assisted us very handsomely in 1986. We want to thank Marta Núñez Sarmiento of the sociology department and a number of other women at the University of Havana. Many thanks also go to Karen Wald for her hospitality and assistance. Although we never had the pleasure of meeting journalist Mirta Rodríguez Calderón, we owe her a special debt; her articles about women's situation in Cuba have been an important source for us. We wish to thank the Center for Cuban Studies in New York, which arranged some of our visits to Cuba; its library and book service have also been most helpful.

Many thanks to Nancy Lane, our editor at Oxford University Press, for her confidence in our project. Our hats are off to the anonymous readers at Oxford who slogged through early drafts and encouraged us to keep going.

Finally, we wish to express our thanks to family and friends who patiently stood by us during this decade-long mania as we proceeded through numberless drafts and revisions. Needless to say, all conclusions expressed here are our own.

Austin, Tex.   L.M.S.
Portland, Me.   A.P.
March 1995

Contents

Abbreviations

ANAP   National Association of Small Farmers (Asociación Nacional de Agricultores Pequeños)

CDRs   Committees for the Defense of the Revolution (Comités para la Defensa de la Revolución)

CTC   Confederation of Cuban Workers (Confederación de Trabajadores Cubanos)

ESBECs   Basic Secondary Schools in the Countryside (Escuelas Básicas Secundarias en el Campo)

FDIM   International Democratic Women's Federation (Federación Democrática Internacional de Mujeres)

FEEM   Federation of Secondary School Students (Federación de Estudiantes de Enseñanza Media)

FEU   Federation of University Students (Federación Estudiantil Universitaria)

FMC   Federation of Cuban Women (Federación de Mujeres Cubanas)

GNTES   National Working Group on Sexual Education (Grupo Nacional de Trabajo para Educación Sexual)

MINREX   Ministry of Foreign Relations (Ministerio de Relaciones Exteriores)

MINSAP	Ministry of Public Health (Ministerio de Salud Pública)
MTTs	Territorial Militias (Milicias de Tropas Territoriales)
PSP	Popular Socialist Party (Partido Socialista Popular)
UFR	Revolutionary Women's Union (Unión Femenino Revolucionario)

Sex and Revolution

Introduction

This book is about the way three decades of social revolution transformed the lives of women in Cuba. It is an examination of one nation's effort to conceptualize, prioritize, and implement sexual equality, and it offers an assessment of the successes, failures, and dilemmas of that process.

As of early 1995, the Cuban revolution was staggering toward a solitary demise, the island's economy was in ruins, and hunger stalked the land. Individualism and the family had replaced the community and the state as the primary forces in society. Market forces were ever more powerful. The U.S. dollar had become legal currency. It is hard to imagine that only a few years earlier Cuba was the champion of socialism in the Americas, the cynosure of intellectuals worldwide. Cuba was then carrying out one of the greatest social experiments in the history of the Western hemisphere. It was trying to make equality in every sphere the basic operating principle of society; equality among the sexes would resolve "the woman question" once and for all.

The Cuban revolution entered the world arena in 1959 when a small group of guerrillas and urban insurrectionists overthrew the dictatorship of General Fulgencio Batista. Thereafter a series of economic and social reforms were launched which indicated that the goal of the revolution was nothing less than the creation of a new social order. The main engine of this transformation was to be the state under the firm and charismatic command of its guerrilla hero, Fidel Castro. In 1961 Castro announced what was already clear: this was a socialist revolution. Within a very few years Cuban capitalism was destroyed, and its defenders had fled to Miami. The economic and political power of Cuban families was crushed, as was the power of the Catholic church. A massive and unprecedented redistribution of wealth was begun. Cuba became one of the most egalitarian societies in the world. Each of these developments profoundly affected women's lives. In this new atmosphere of change certain traditional perceptions of appropriate female behavior were challenged and many formal and informal restraints on women's activities were eased.

Fidel Castro described the changes that were taking place in women's private and public lives as "a revolution within the revolution," and it was very much within the revolution that contemplations of "the woman question" in Cuba were to occur. Cuba had adopted the standard Marxist position that true sexual equality can be established only through socialist revolution, that socialism and women's liberation were one—that "one" being socialism.[1] Feminism was roundly denounced by the revolution for being a bourgeois indulgence and an imperialist tool to divert women from the more important class struggle by tricking them into rejecting men.

The triumph of the Cuban revolution stimulated the hopes of activists and intellectuals throughout Latin America. Many now considered Cuba to be the standard-bearer for the liberation of the region from underdevelopment, exploitation, and U.S. imperialist domination. The revolutionaries expected that the Federation of Cuban Women (FMC), created by Fidel Castro and headed by his sister-in-law, Vilma Espín, would set a much emulated example for women throughout the hemisphere.

The history of the Cuban revolution raises profound questions regarding the interplay between gender, power, ideology, and culture. Certain revolutionary efforts to transform women's lives were extraordinarily successful while others fell short of expectations. Many initiatives produced unanticipated results, both positive and negative.

This book reviews a wide range of revolutionary strategies encompassed in structures, policies, and laws to address sexual inequality and difference. It offers insights into the implications of the way power is organized and managed, examining the limitations of state policies aimed at promoting and managing social and cultural transformations as significant as the changes in relations between the sexes.

In chapters 1 through 3 we identify a number of historical trends in the treatment of women that were carried forward by the revolution, as well as ways in which programs and policies implemented after 1959 challenged established tradition. Chapter 1 finds the circumstance of Cuban women prior to 1959 to be considerably more complex than what has been presented by both the revolution and some of its harshest critics. Chapter 2 explores the underappreciated role of women in the rebellion against the Batista dictatorship and notes ways in which their activities influenced policies adopted after 1959. Chapter 3 finds that the

FMC's early, frenetic activities were essential components in the revolutionary government's attempt to break down the divisions of the old society.

In chapters 4 through 7 we trace how the use of state power has both benefited and hampered the advancement of women. Chapter 4 finds the FMC to have had an ambiguous position in the formal power structure, a position that weakened its ability to be a forceful advocate for women and may have even helped to prevent the emergence of women in the highest realms of party and state. Chapters 5 through 7 examine the use of state power to improve women's condition, opportunities, and security with respect to the health and education systems, the "twin jewels in the revolutionary crown."[2]

In chapters 8 through 11 we find that the treatment of women in the Cuban economy provides insight into the regime's perception of sexual equality and its relative importance in the revolutionary agenda. Chapters 8 and 9 look for the central logic behind Cuban policies regarding women in the economy, cite inconsistencies that emerge, and trace women's movement in the workforce from 1959 to 1992. Chapter 10 explores the way in which traditional ideas in government, in specific policy areas, and in the public sphere have complicated women's work experiences. Chapter 11 looks at the state's effort to provide services that facilitate women's employment, considers ideological and cultural issues, and concludes with an overall assessment of the women's employment program.

Chapters 12 through 14 treat social relations, attempting to gauge whether radical political change can have a lasting impact on those most personal, perplexing, and, some would argue, important aspects of society. Chapters 12 and 13 contrast the way in which many external aspects of the family changed while many internal dynamics continue as before. Chapter 14 shows that Cuban sexuality has defied the efforts of the regime to tame and control it.

In each chapter we try to give a sense of dynamics and chronology in order to illustrate how the circumstance of Cuban women changed over time. It is important to note, however, that while it would be interesting to compare the progress of Cuban women to that of women in other nations, doing so is beyond the scope of this exercise. This is not a comparative history.

In 1977 Mirta Aguirre, one of Cuba's leading Marxist intellectuals, offered her fulsome praise for the USSR's support of Cuba. "Glory to Lenin! Long Live the Soviet Union!," she wrote.[3] Fourteen years later the Soviet Union, whose beneficence had directly or indirectly paid for many of the programs that had such an impact on women's lives in Cuba, was no more.

Yet even if the revolution is now dying, the conduct of three decades of Cuban socialism will remain worthy of study. So, too, will the story of the women whose lives were changed, for good or ill, by this great social experiment in the Caribbean.

1

Women in Prerevolutionary Cuba

*Among nations in which woman is honored, in which her influence domi-
nates in society, there will assuredly be found enlightenment, progress,
and true public life.*

Gertrudis Gómez de Avellaneda, nineteenth-century Cuban poet[1]

*For sale: one black girl, eleven or twelve years old, can sew . . . very
able . . . for 18 ounces of silver.*

Cuban newspaper advertisement (ca. 1848)[2]

*The Cuban woman is the queen of Eden . . . for her gracefulness, her
beauty, and her love of dancing.*

Cuban song (1950s)[3]

*We women had nothing here before the revolution. Years ago they gave
us the vote to shut us up . . . but after that, nothing.*

Estela García, domestic servant (1950s)[4]

What was the situation of Cuban women before 1959? From the perspective of the island's leading social chronicler fresh from the 1958 Red
Ball at the Havana Country Club, their condition was splendid indeed.
What an edifying sight—hundreds of elegant women, the cream of society, dancing the night away in a Havana that proudly boasted that it
spent as much on parties "as any great capital of the world."[5] The Cuban
foreign minister of that era, Andrés Vargas Gómez, observed that his
generation had been brought up to revere women. "She was a sacred
creature and it was her right to have precedence in all things."[6] The
writer Lolo de la Torriente thought women were doing just fine in the
1950s: "There is no doubt that the Cuban woman has reached, in the
course of the present century, great social and political importance. . . .

7

Women have invaded the . . . most significant sectors of social life, acting always as a force for progress."[7]

⟨1⟩ But when a leading journalist of the revolution, Mirta Rodríguez Calderón, sought to portray women's status before 1959, she had an entirely different vision. She recalled not the splendor of the country clubs nor the special consideration extended to women of the upper class, but the misery of poor women in the countryside. To Rodríguez Calderón, the prototypical woman of the old republic was Yina the prostitute. Born to a family of eight with no father and no hope, sold into vice at age eleven to service poor men in backwater towns for forty cents a lay, Yina had "a past that she wanted to erase from memory" but that revolution sought to keep vivid.[8]

Yina reflects one extreme of prerevolutionary Cuba, the ladies of the country club set another. Between these extremes there was a substantial middle class which included a growing number of professional women: businesswomen, lawyers, doctors, journalists, teachers and university professors, poets and musicians. There were women who fought for and achieved feminist legislation; there were women holding political office and women arrested for their political views.

⟨2⟩ The life of women in Cuban society was influenced in no small part by race, class, place of birth, and religion. Even so, there was considerable social mobility in the old Cuba. Indeed, social climbing was the national passion. The melding of Hispanic Catholicism and African pantheism produced gender ideals that were complex and sometimes contradictory.

⟨3⟩ The ostensible role model for Cuban women was the Virgin Mary: Mary the mother, Mary the powerless, Mary without sexual instincts, the servant of men. Men were perceived as impulsive and dominated by sexual drives, and it was women's duty to accept and forgive this moral weakness. Men were sexual, women spiritual. Women's lives were to revolve around the home, where they were expected to remain; the streets were the province of men.

The Cuban version of Mary is the Virgen de la Caridad (Virgin of Charity), whose shrine is located in El Cobre, a mining-town near Santiago. She is the divine mother to whom Cubans pray in times of trouble. Her image was worn by soldiers in the wars of independence. Veterans of the Cuban expeditionary force to Angola in the 1970s left their medals on her altar in thanks for their having survived, and Cuban exiles in Miami built a chapel on Biscayne Bay to honor her.

⟨4⟩ The church's influence on the people was strongest in urban areas and among the middle and upper classes, but the subversive influence of Africa was everywhere. Thus many Cubans perceived the Virgen de la Caridad not as the white goddess of European origin, but as "Oshun," the dark-skinned goddess of pleasure, a hedonist who loved to dance and make love. As sociologist Nelson Valdés has observed, Cubans live comfortably with this paradox.[9]

In addition to religion, demographics had great impact on the destiny of Cuban women. For many years the Spanish crown forbade unaccompanied women to voyage to the New World, so at the end of the sixteenth century, white women constituted less than 10 percent of the Cuban population.[10] Most of the slaves brought from Africa to work the sugar fields were also men. For black women who did arrive in Cuba, the harsh conditions of rural life made pregnancy and childbirth dangerous. One observer noted that during the sugar harvest pregnant slave women were forced to cut cane "practically to the day of delivery."[11]

The balance between white men and women began to improve in the seventeenth century when the crown permitted single women to emigrate to Cuba. The number of whole families going to Cuba also increased. By the end of the eighteenth century, women constituted 43 percent of the white population, but black men still outnumbered black women two to one in some rural areas.[12]

The long-term deficit of women had a profound impact on the family as well as on racial and sexual relations in Cuba. Sexual rivalry between white and black men was fierce. Ironically, while white men enjoyed access to women of color, black men were imagined by whites to be sexual marauders in pursuit of white women. Wide-scale miscegenation between whites and blacks produced a large mulatto population. The shortage of women also contributed to male-to-male sexual activities, and a perception emerged that only the "receptors" in these encounters were homosexuals. In rural areas bestiality was casually accepted.

Interracial sexuality is the central theme of Cuba's most famous novel, Cirilio Villaverde's *Cecilia Valdés*. The novel, set in Cuba in the 1830s, introduces Cecilia as the illegitimate daughter of a plantation owner and a slave. It is María de Regla, another black slave, who raises Cecilia and the white children of the big house. The writer William Luis concludes that Cuba's Marías are the true mothers of the upper class.[13]

For many years Spain restricted interracial marriage out of fear it would give blacks a prestige which might undermine the slave system. Such unions, according to one colonial official, brought "dishonor to white families, upheaval and disorder to the country."[14] In the countryside among the lower classes concubinage was the norm and illegitimacy was rife. Poor people could not afford marriage, and furthermore priests tended to remain in the towns and cities. Often illegitimate children were conceived during sugar harvests, when cane cutters moved from plantation to plantation. The cane cutter Esteban Montejo boasted that on one glorious holiday he made love to no less than twelve different women, but in his decrepitude he could not recall whether he had any children as a result.[15]

Marriage was particularly important to elites as a means of safeguarding family property and honor. Through marriage, patriarchs could protect their family properties from the claims of children sired in casual dalliances. Illegitimate children not only were disinherited but also bore

a social stigma. An illegitimate child born to a poor family was not infrequently abandoned by the father, the responsibility being left to the
mother. The resentments and tensions borne of illegitimacy would taint
Cuban history for centuries and lead to various legal reforms in the twentieth century.

Issues of race and class also influenced women's employment. In the
nineteenth century it was unthinkable for an upper-class woman to work.
To achieve upper-class status, a woman had to avoid manual labor of any
kind, but as the twentieth century advanced, certain jobs became acceptable. More women of the growing middle class became teachers, secretaries, office workers, and bureaucrats. Fathers and husbands did not like
the idea of their women working outside the home. To allay these concerns—and to ease the problem of child care—lower-class women often
brought work such as sewing, laundry, and even factory piecework into
the home. Husbands, anxious to defend their role as providers, would
not not always tell census takers that their wife worked, at home or away.
This attitude continues to pose problems for historians who rely on government census and labor statistics.

Prostitution was another source of employment for poor women. In
1657 the bishop of Havana complained to the Spanish crown that slaves,
in some cases owned by priests and monks, were engaged in prostitution.[16] At the end of the nineteenth century a Spanish public health official, Dr. Benjamin de Céspedes, noted that Havana's prostitutes were so
brazen that it was impossible for honorable women to walk in the streets
to get the exercise they required.[17] Dr. de Céspedes did not, however,
propose the end of prostitution, but rather argued that "by tolerating
prostitution sexual appetites are prevented from getting out of control,
and damaging the honorable family."[18] The only way to deal with men's
"irresistible" sexual instincts, Dr. de Céspedes claimed, was to promote
hygienic prostitution regulated by the state.[19] His recommendations
went unheeded, and prostitution continued routinely and illegally.

During the colonial era the church was mute about prostitution. It
was too thorny a subject. In the twentieth century, women's groups complained about prostitution, but still nothing was done. Houses of prostitution were routinely used to introduce young men to sex. For example,
in the 1920s Desi Arnaz, aged fifteen, was taken by his uncle to be sexually initiated at Santiago's best bordello, the Casa Marina.[20]

Finally, foreign influence had a significant impact on the lives of Cuban women. For centuries the white upper class had looked to Spain and
in some cases to France for cultural models. In the twentieth century,
however, European influence would be challenged by North American
modes. Investments, culture, and technical innovations from the north
changed women's lives. And after 1959 three decades of close linkage to
the Soviet Union and East Europe would have its own unique influence
on the lives of Cuban women.

Women, War, and Exile in the Nineteenth Century

Throughout history Cuba has served as a way station for *conquistadores,* immigrants, and exiles. This transitoriness is reflected in the lives of two writers of the nineteenth century: María de las Mercedes Santa Cruz y Montalvo (the Countess of Merlin) and Gertrudis Gómez de Avellaneda (La Avellaneda).

The Countess of Merlin was born in Cuba in 1789 but sailed off to Spain and marriage to a French count. She would write enchantingly (in French) of her memories of Havana.[21] A visit to Havana in 1940 stirred an intense nostalgia for her youth: the stories of her black nanny, Catalina, a former slave, and the abundance of slave labor, which contributed to the genial life of the Cuban upper class.[22]

La Avellaneda was born in Cuba in 1814. After escaping an arranged marriage and breaking a number of engagements, she left for Europe at age twenty-two. She spent the next twenty-three years in Spain and France, where her career as a novelist, poet, and playwright blossomed.[23] In 1859 she returned for six years to Cuba, where she edited a short-lived magazine celebrating famous women, *The Cuban Album of the Good and the Beautiful.* Her novel *Sab* was one of the first antislavery novels in the Western hemisphere.

Three years after La Avellaneda left Cuba for the second time, the island's first brutal war for independence from Spanish colonialism began. Women served as spies and messengers, nurses and seamstresses, but their most celebrated role was as "heroic mothers" who provided their sons for the struggle. Of all the heroic mothers, the most revered is Mariana Grajales, "the lioness," mother of "the bronze Titan" General Antonio Maceo. Seven of her thirteen children died in the fighting. She is one of the few women to be honored with a monument in Cuba.

If war won certain honors and respect for women, for men it enhanced the "heroic culture" and provided an opportunity for the expression of machismo. The Cuban film *Lucía* (1968) would recreate a charge of the black cavalry, the Mambises, who rode into combat swathed in hog grease. Naked, they were all the better attired for wrestling with the terrified Spanish recruits. To earn rights and respect, one had to dominate, to inspire terror, to kill. That was men's work.

In 1869, in the midst of the war, the rebels held a constitutional convention which sought to end slavery in order to encourage blacks to join the struggle. During the convention Ana Betancourt de Mora, a schoolteacher and a daughter of a cattleman of Camagüey, rose to make a historic plea for women's liberation: "Citizens: The Cuban woman, from the dark and tranquil corner of her home, has waited patiently and with resignation for this sublime hour in which a just revolution will break her yoke, untie her wings. . . ."[24] Her plea for women's equality was not granted. By 1878 the war had ended in a standoff.

In 1882 writer and poet José Martí, who would later be revered as the father of Cuban independence, acknowledged the resourcefulness that women had shown during the war. He suggested that they be permitted to enroll at the university, as they were increasingly doing in Europe and North America. An education, Martí noted, meant that women would be more than "beautiful toys" subject to masculine whim.[25]

But Martí's views on women were ambivalent. He wanted Cuban women to have the vote, access to government jobs, and the right to higher education, but he was also a romantic poet who considered women's principal virtues to be tenderness, simplicity, modesty, and delicacy. Women, he thought, ought to be symbols of love, reflecting that which is most pure. They should reject egoism, vanity, and frivolity.[26]

Martí's own relations with women were problematic. He abandoned his wife, Carmen Zayas Bazan, to continue his struggle against Spanish colonialism from exile in New York. After two years she and her son followed him, but she returned to Cuba in 1884, never to see her husband again. He was consoled by a mistress. Shortly after arriving on a mission to liberate the island colony, Martí was shot dead by Spanish troops in Cuba's Oriente province in 1895.

The writer Diego Vicente Tijera was less intrigued than Martí by North American women. They were too energetic: "Gymnastic exercise with its violent games . . . would ruin the delicious undulations of our women's Venusian bodies," he wrote in 1898.[27] He was appalled by short-haired, bespectacled women in pants walking with "brisk firm steps" and carrying a title of doctor in their handbags. He preferred the Roman woman as model, the *mujer matrona,* a woman "of cultivated intelligence and solid virtues" whose life centered on the home.[28]

While men speculated, women's lives, stimulated by economic need and technological innovations, were changing. In the 1880s Domitila García of Camagüey learned typesetting in her father's printing shop and later established a typesetting academy for young women. She became Cuba's first woman editor and publisher, producing a newspaper intended for women, *El Correo de las Damas.*[29] When it published an article on women's sexuality, the archbishop of Havana issued a pastoral attacking the newspaper.[30]

In 1883 the University of Havana admitted its first woman student, Mercédes Riba y Piños. A student of philosophy and letters, she graduated with high honors, the first woman to earn a college degree in Cuba.[31] A few years later María Luisa Dolz, the daughter of a well-to-do lawyer, received a degree in natural sciences, then went on to become one of Cuba's first feminists and, as an educator, trained generations of Cuban schoolteachers.[32]

In 1895 the second stage of Cuba's drive for independence from Spanish colonialism began. The Spanish attempted to cut off the rebels' source of food, obliging peasants—typically women—to live in fortified villages that were virtual prison camps. Some women fled to the hills with their children. This struggle became known as the "women's war."

Cuban women exiled to the United States formed groups such as the Daughters of the Liberator Club, the Mercédes Varona Club, and the Cuban Revolutionary Club of José Martí's Women to support the rebels.[33] Sugar heiress Marta Abreu of Santa Clara gave most of her fortune to the rebel cause. A few women even participated in the fighting. Adela Azcuy, a university graduate from a well-to-do family, earned the sobriquet *la capitana* for her bravery under fire.[34]

Cuba won its independence—but at great cost. Fifteen percent of the Cuban population died of wounds, starvation, or disease. More than a third of Cuban wives were widowed.[35] A whole generation of revolutionary leaders were dead. Much of the sugar industry was destroyed. Thus women lost homes, husbands, and livelihoods. But slavery was gone and the power of the church—deeply resented because of its close ties to Spain—had been sharply reduced.

Independence and Foreign Influence

The peace of 1898 was followed by three years of U.S. military occupation. For the next half century the United States became the primary model for modes of life and behavior for Cuban women. Frederic M. Noa, an American who lived in Cuba for many years, wrote expansively in 1905:

> To the Cuban woman in general, the American intervention and influence were a godsend indeed; as for the first time in four hundred years, the gates of opportunity were opened to her, and the regenerating forces of modern civilization could freely penetrate the length and breadth of the island.[36]

After the war necessity obliged war widows to go to work. The most common options included domestic service, seamstressing, clerking, and cigarette making. In 1905 a woman who washed and ironed a hundred pieces of laundry—a good day's labor—would make about $2.70 a week, a cook $7.20, a maid $5.40.[37]

Women also found work in the tobacco industry. They sat on wooden benches in small factories, removing the stems and veins from tobacco leaves while Spanish classics and popular novels were read aloud to break the monotony. A cigar factory paid $3.60 a week, the best industrial wage for women. At the turn of the century there were about sixteen hundred women in the industry.[38] By the 1950s, 90 percent of Cuban stemmers were women, nearly half of them Afro-Cubans.[39]

The arrival of technological innovations from abroad brought new opportunities for women. In the late 1850s the Hamel brothers began to import Singer sewing machines, which they sold on credit. From 1869 to 1889 some forty thousand machines were sold, thereafter almost five thousand annually.[40] Sewing became a source of income for many women.

The first typewriters were brought to Cuba in the 1880s by exiles returning from the United States. Emilia de Cordova, became Cuba's first woman typist.[41] The first typing manual in Spanish appeared in 1903. The telephone provided another source of "decorous" employment for women. By 1885 there were a thousand telephones in Havana. Young women were hired as telephone operators by the U.S.-owned Cuban Telephone Company.[42] By 1953 nine thousand women were working for the island's telephone and telegraph companies.

The education of Cuban women gained ground slowly during the twentieth century. In 1899, 42 percent of women over ten years of age were literate,[43] but in some rural areas the level of literacy was much lower, particularly among black women. Instruction there rarely passed the third grade. Virtually all the teachers were women.

The U.S. military government (1898–1902) encouraged education. State responsibility for education was established in the 1901 constitution. In 1903 thirteen hundred Cuban teachers spent the summer studying North American pedagogical methods at Harvard University.[44] By 1919 the literacy rate for females over the age of ten had risen to 61 percent.[45]

During World War I the municipality of Havana inaugurated a music school, most of whose students were women. In 1916 President Menocal founded a teacher's training school for women, and by the late 1920s it had 682 students.[46] Eventually there would be such a school in every province. In 1918 Angela Landa, inspired by a French educational experiment, founded the Escuelas del Hogar, or home economics schools. By the mid-1920s 235 women were studying sewing, embroidery, basket weaving, child raising, cooking, and other domestic tasks. In subsequent years Escuelas del Hogar were opened in many cities and towns.

Women also began to go to high school, often in private Catholic institutions. The nuns of the order of Saint Teresa, who had left Cuba after Spain's defeat in 1898, returned during World War I. By 1926 they had built six secondary schools for young women, one in each of the island's principal cities.[47]

Education gradually reached into the countryside. An example was Julia de la Osa y Sierra, a daughter of former slaves, who grew up on the Isle of Pines in the late nineteenth century. The mother of twelve children, she had but one dress. Crocodiles often lay in wait when she hung out the wash. In hard times she and her family lived on corn and sugar water. Despite her poverty, Julia went to school.[48]

A teaching career became the dream of many young women. María Luisa Campos, one of twelve children in a poor black family in Las Tunas, wanted desperately to become a teacher and worked as a maid to pay her high school tuition. Competition to enter the teachers' college in Holguín was intense; there were about five hundred applications for seventy-five positions. María won a place, but then her dream fell through—she didn't have money for books, clothes, or rent. Instead María opened a "school" in her own *bohío,* (rural hut). Children went free, adults were charged twenty-five cents a month. "In this way," she recalled, "I taught two generations to read and write."[49]

Schools and teachers came to the sugar fields of Oriente province. In 1931 Fidel Castro, aged four, learned to read in a one-room schoolhouse in the hamlet of Birán. Years later he would recall the difficulties he caused his teacher, Miss Felieu: "Whenever I disagreed with something . . . or whenever I got mad, I would swear at her and immediately leave school, running as fast as I could."[50]

Foreign investments in sugar brought a prosperity which created new opportunities for women, particularly in Havana. By 1919 there were eleven thousand women in white-collar jobs. In the 1920s there were twice as many women working in Havana as elsewhere in Cuba. Havana continued to offer women greater opportunities for the rest of the century.

Economic growth, higher educational levels, and foreign examples all stimulated demands in the legislature for changes in women's legal status. The Spanish civil code of 1889, which regarded women as incompetents, still reigned. Husbands had almost total control over their wives' property and earnings. But conservatives argued that an orderly household required male control. Women, said one senator, lacked sufficient education and were too susceptible to masculine blandishments.[51] The reforms passed, however, thanks to the support of a rising bourgeoisie anxious to protect growing family fortunes against men seeking to marry for money and land.

A law to legalize divorce was proposed in 1918. The bill's opponents argued that it would cause promiscuity and destroy the family, and they characterized its proponents as advocates of social revolution. Some legislators, however, saw the divorce bill as a way of punishing the church for its opposition to Cuban independence, a means to help separate church and state.[52] Although the law passed, from 1918 to 1927 only 2,374 couples applied for divorce.[53] Divorce was not socially acceptable. Besides, it was customary for Cuban men to have mistresses. Why upset the "official" family? Wives consoled themselves by spoiling their sons, thus perpetuating the patriarchal cycle.

Activism and Reform

During the early twentieth century, Cuban women began to organize for political and social action. In 1917 the Club Feminino, or Women's Club, was organized in Havana with the goal of aiding the less fortunate, stimulating culture, and promoting healthful motherhood. The club sponsored speakers, conferences, and recitals and established a free night school for women. It found Havana's jails so appalling that it persuaded the city fathers to create a separate prison for women in Guanabacoa.[54]

In 1923 the Club Feminino brought thirty-one women's organizations together for Cuba's first National Women's Congress. The delegates, virtually all from the middle and upper classes, discussed the rights of illegitimate children, protection for single mothers, adultery, prostitution, equal pay for equal work, and women's suffrage. They contended that women's suffrage was vital to improving the nation and that mothers ought to make government respond to the needs of family.[55] As historian Lynn Stoner has noted, the Congress was important for its insistence on a social role for the state. Heretofore Cubans had regarded the church and private charities as the appropriate vehicles for social welfare. Now the idea that the dilemmas of the less fortunate could be resolved by "a few coins dispensed by hands covered with diamonds," as one critic put it, was out of date.[56]

Women who sought a more active role for the state sometimes cited the successes of the public education system in the United States. Others were impressed by revolutionary Mexico, where the state played a powerful role in every sector of national life. Still others were influenced by the Russian revolution of 1917. Indeed, three of Cuba's leading intellectuals of the 1920s and 1930s—Ofelia Domínguez Navarro, Mirta Aguirre, and Mariblanca Sabás Alomá—were socialist feminists.

Ofelia Domínguez Navarro, born in 1894, was interned in a Spanish concentration camp during the war for independence. At seventeen she became a teacher, creating her own school in a friend's house.[57] She earned a law degree by taking correspondence courses. As a lawyer she defended prostitutes, an experience that stimulated her strong belief that charity was not enough.

Mirta Aguirre was born in 1912 into a well-to-do family. By the late 1920s she had begun her career as an essayist, poet, and educator. In 1932 she joined the Communist party (founded in 1923) and became a writer for its daily newspaper, *Hoy*. Later, when she was a professor at the University of Havana, her Marxist views influenced a generation of students.[58]

Of the three, Mariblanca Sabás Alomá had the sharpest pen. She was a daughter of the haute bourgeoisie, but as a newspaper columnist she was sharply critical of upper-class women. They spent their days, she once wrote, gossiping about the divorces and affairs of their friends and relatives, and they cared only about boyfriends, clothes, and dances. Their frivolity, she thought, was the fault of convent educations, "which failed to demonstrate the ample panorama of real life."[59] The objective of the new feminist activism, as Mariblanca Sabás Alomá explained, was to expand women's traditional roles, not to reject them. She grew indignant when critics alleged that a feminist was "a women who had ceased being a woman, who has given up grace and beauty and has a deep voice, a demonic manner, a curse for men always on her lips . . . and, horror of horrors, the shadow of an incipient beard."[60]

Many of the issues that concerned socialist feminists came to a head at the second Congress of Cuban Women in 1925. There Ofelia Domínguez Navarro called for legislation to make all children equal, legitimate or not. Conservatives feared that the acceptance of illegitimacy would threaten the centrality of marriage. Sabás Alomá wanted welfare for single mothers with children. Conservatives accused her of "collusion with the Russians," who, they alleged, were bent on destroying the family and advocating free love.[61] Others, however, argued that if illegitimate children had rights to support and inheritance, then the men who fathered them might be more cautious.

By the late 1920s almost a quarter of the students at the University of Havana were women. Half were studying to be teachers, another quarter were majoring in liberal arts and pharmacy. Some of these women became involved in politics. The Communist party of Cuba attracted young women who thought that Cuban society needed to be radically transformed. Charita Guillaume, a rural schoolteacher who had been active in the Club Feminino, joined the party in 1927. She helped to organize labor unions, worked with children in the party's Pioneer League, and, as a member of the party's Association for the Popular Education of Women, helped to create libraries in sugar communities.[62] On March 8, 1931, Cuban socialists celebrated International Women's Day for the first time. Three decades later these women of the left would play an important role in the consolidation of Cuban socialism.

The 1920s and 1930s also saw the appearance of more conservative intellectuals, such as the writer and historian Lydia Cabrera. Born in 1894, into a well-to-do family, she was living in Paris by 1927, fascinated by African culture and its resonances in her own childhood. In 1939 she returned to Havana with her lifelong companion, María Teresa de Rojas,[63] and began to write about Afro-Cuban culture. One of her twelve books, *El Monte,* a study of Afro-Cuban religion and magic, is considered one of the most important books ever written about Cuba.

Elena Mederos was another talented daughter of the bourgeoisie, one who would become minister of health and welfare in Castro's first cabinet. Born into a wealthy family in 1900, she earned a degree in pharmacy from the University of Havana. In 1929 she and thirteen female collaborators created the Lyceum of Havana.[64] With its night school, lecture halls, and lending library the Lyceum of Havana was a unique institution. Politically it was neutral: Marxists and Catholics felt at home there. Its social programs were progenitors of the School of Social Welfare at the University of Havana.

In the 1920s tourism from the north, stimulated by the Volstead Act and Prohibition, increased dramatically, bringing a new wave of foreign influence. Upper-class Cuban women went to the movies, smoked, danced the Charleston, and had their hair bobbed. The Ziegfeld Follies came to Havana in 1927, the dancers' high kicks and scanty costumes causing an uproar.

The development of the electronic media—radio in the 1920s and television in the 1950s—also had considerable significance for women. The soap opera made its appearance. Improved recording techniques made Cuban music—and musicians—world famous. Women participated in the growing entertainment industry as singers, musicians, and dancers. In 1930 a Havana music critic described a new female jazz band as playing "like a dream." The name stuck and the band became the Orquesta Femenina Ensueño, the women's dream band. Other women's bands such as Las Anaconas, La Renovación, La Social, and Las Hermanas Alvarez continued to play in Havana and the United States.[65]

Did this new age of women's activism and activity portend the ruin of home and family? In a talk at the Cuban telephone company in 1930, Graziella Barinaga, a university graduate and a vice president of the National Feminist Alliance, argued that Cuban feminism was not "the first step" toward the decline of women's interest in marriage and the home. Rather women were seeking a new and better kind of home characterized by intellectual equality and a mutual expression of love and respect, a home where a husband would truly want to spend his free time rather than a place to come to only for eating and sleeping. Women, she thought, had the same mental capacity as men, but they did not want to become men, to *masculinizarse*.[66]

Revolution and Women's Suffrage in 1933

Improvements in women's condition were linked to advances in education and new technologies, to politics, and to the periodic revolutionary surges which have marked the island's history. Gerardo Machado courted women's support in his 1924 presidential campaign by promising them the vote. In 1925, as president, he signed a decree that enabled working mothers to breast-feed infants at work and that also fixed female hiring quotas in certain jobs.[67] The new regulations were in response to the expansion of the female labor force in the 1920s, particularly in textiles. Female labor was cheap—costing thirty to fifty cents a day—as long as the women were single and didn't get pregnant.[68]

President Machado did not give women the vote, but he did manipulate the elections of 1928 to remain in power. With the onset of the Depression in 1929, hunger and deprivation spread through Cuba. In Havana women responded by participating in strikes and demonstrations against the Machado regime. The government replied with strong-arm tactics including an all-woman gang of strikebreakers. Women activists began to see the overthrow of Machado as part of a larger program to democratize the island. They hoped a new regime would give them the vote, which they could use to purify the corrupt political system.

By 1933 revolution was in the air. In the countryside workers were raising red flags over sugar mills. In the cities university women participated in demonstrations. Inés "Nena" Segura Bustamente recalled how she and other student protestors would assemble at the top of the university steps, the famous *escalinata* that sweeps down into Havana, and how they were intercepted by police with truncheons. Inés was arrested twice. She was expelled from the university and spent eight months in prison. Machado opened a special cell block for women on the Isle of Pines.[69]

In August 1933 President Machado abandoned the island and was succeeded by an interim government led by former professor Ramón Grau San Martín. In 1934 President Grau gave women the vote. Women used their new power to elect seven female representatives to the congress and to push for protective labor legislation. One result was the 1934 law obliging employers to provide a twelve-week maternity leave. Also factories and institutions employing more than fifty women were required to provide nurseries for children under age two. Female sales clerks such as those at Woolworth's won the right to sit down whenever their work allowed it. A subsequent law forbade employers to fire women workers upon their marriage in an attempt to avoid future maternity expenses.[70]

There were loopholes, however. The maternity code did not apply to domestic servants, who comprised at least one-quarter of female workers. Nor did it apply to agricultural workers. Furthermore, factories such as the Ariguanabo textile mill, Cuba's largest, decided not to hire women in order to avoid the expenses imposed by government regulation. Other employers ignored the new laws. Woolworth's reclassified many of its female workers as temporaries in order to avoid paying benefits and also ceased hiring married women to avoid the expenses of the maternity law.[71]

From 1940 to 1952 Cuba enjoyed an unprecedented era of democratic politics. Colonel Batista, now turned popular reformer, was elected president in 1940. He would be followed by Grau San Martín in 1944 and Carlos Prío in 1948. As president in the 1940s, Batista helped craft a new constitution that incorporated the feminist legislation of the 1920s and 1930s and added an important new element, namely, a section guaranteeing the rights of illegitimate children. There was also an equal rights article to protect women in the workplace.

In 1944 President Grau attributed his victory to women's votes. "My government is a government of women," he said.[72] But although there were a few new women in the congress in the 1940s, there were no new legislative victories, and much of the extant legislation was ignored.

On the Eve of Revolution

By the 1950s women's participation in the Cuban workforce was relatively high compared with other Latin American nations. According to the 1953 census, women constituted nearly 13 percent of the formal labor force, more than half of them in white-collar jobs, mostly as teachers, social workers, clerks, and public employees.[73] By 1957, 48 percent of the workers in Cuba's service sector were women.[74]

The growth of a substantial middle class after World War II stimulated the demand for domestic help, even as some domestics moved on to become factory workers. In 1953 one-quarter of all working women were domestic servants,[75] many having begun such work before puberty. Some domestics were subjected to economic and sexual exploitation, others were treated as members of the family. Some exiles brought their maids with them to Miami in the early 1960s.

Black women continued to confront discrimination. For the most part they were not allowed to work in front-office jobs such as bank teller, although a few (mostly university students) did get jobs in El Encanto, the most luxurious department store in Havana.[76]

The first lady of Cuba in the 1950s was Batista's second wife, fairer-skinned and more socially presentable than his first. Nonetheless, the grande dame of Cuban society was María Luisa Gómez Mena, the Countess of Camargo. The countess, whose husband was a sugar baron and head of the Havana Yacht Club, reigned over a thriving social industry of canasta and clubs, cocktail parties and Cadillacs. Fur wraps, made possible by the advent of air conditioning, were de rigueur. The capital's social columnists, employing their most flattering language, kept the public abreast of Havana's elegant balls, correct young men, distinguished parents, and splendid weddings.[77]

Upper-class women headed a number of important publications in the 1950s: Clara Clark Pessino owned the English-language *Havana Post,* Esther Hernández owned the magazine *Avance,* and Josefina Mosquera edited the women's magazine *Vanidades.* But for some *Vanidades* was an example of precisely what was wrong with Cuban society. It was a song to consumerism: almost a third of its pages were advertisements, often for the products of North American subsidiaries in Cuba. Another third were fashions, and most of the remainder consisted of gossip about movie stars and short stories drenched in romance.

Changes in technology were bringing Cuba and the United States closer. Speedier airliners made Miami and Havana less than an hour apart. The tourist industry expanded, bringing with it jobs for women in hotels and restaurants. Cheap air travel also made it easier for *cubanas* to go north. An annual shopping trip to Miami was routine for middle-class women. Juliana Flores, the daughter of a janitor in Cardenas, went to a Protestant high school in the United States because her father thought it safer than Havana. Juliana was pleased to get away, tired of the inevitable question of Cuban parents: "When are you getting married?"[78]

The tourist boom in the 1950s was enhanced by Havana's reputation for tropical sensuality. Tropicana, the world's greatest outdoor nightclub, with its chorus girls in feathers and G-strings, was in full swing. Visitors disembarking from steamships in Havana were given "business cards" by young men advertising the availability of their sisters. Santiago's bar girls eagerly awaited the arrival of American sailors on weekend leave from the naval base at Guantánamo Bay. Even so, prostitution remained largely a function of Cuba's own patriarchal society. In the countryside prostitutes made their annual migration to service the cane cutters during the sugar harvest. One out of four births occurred outside marriage, a rate that had remained constant for thirty years.[79]

The women's movement, which had displayed such energy in the 1920s and 1930s, ran out of steam in the 1950s. The middle class hesitated, then accepted with a sigh of resignation the military coup of Fulgencio Batista in 1952. The energies of a new generation of politically conscious young women turned to challenging the new dictatorship. Women had won benefits from previous struggles—but at a high price. What benefits would be won in the struggle that was about to unfold and at what cost?

2

The Struggle Against the Dictator, 1952–1958

We have proven that in Cuba it is not only men who fight. Women also fight.

Fidel Castro (January 1, 1959)

I believe it takes a great effort to be violent, to go to war. But one has to be violent and to go to war when there is good reason. And what you cannot lose in the face of it all is sensibility. You must keep the same human qualities you had before you started killing. It is painful to kill, but if it is necessary, you must do it.

Haydée Santamaría (1967)[1]

The most familiar images of the anti-Batista insurrection are of men: male university students demonstrating in the streets, young guerrilleros in tattered fatigues in the Sierra, the bearded heroes Fidel Castro, Che Guevara, and Camilo Cienfuegos riding triumphantly on tanks into Havana.

This image does not acknowledge the powerful role women played in the rebellion. Without them, Castro never would have succeeded. Years later anthropologist Natalia Bolívar, herself a former member of the underground, observed that women's role had never been fully acknowledged.[2] Even in subsequent Communist party publications the role of women continued to be slighted.[3]

At one level women played their traditional role as helpers—raising money, giving shelter, teaching, nursing. As couriers they exploited the stereotypical image of women as innocent and incompetent and were thus able to foil the dictator's police. But women also played more central roles, occupying key positions in the urban underground and in the Sierra. Women lawyers represented imprisoned revolutionaries. Women made and planted bombs and hurled Molotov cocktails. And some women entered the revolutionary pantheon of heroic martyrs.

Women never pressed their position, however, nor were they properly rewarded, perhaps in part because they themselves underestimated their contribution. Even Vilma Espín, a significant participant in the struggle, thought of herself as "a sergeant, not a leader."[4] When the rebellion triumphed and the task turned to implementing a social and political revolution, its architects were men. Women were expected to be loyal implementers or grateful recipients of the male-determined revolutionary program. Women's concerns were viewed as peripheral. Those women who could not accept this status were rejected by the revolution.

Anthropologist Elsa Chaney observed in her classic study of women in Latin American that "most women prominent in political life—and not only in Latin America—are related to male politicians."[5] Of the women who participated in the Cuban insurrection, the very few who received high government positions—albeit not as high as those given to their male counterparts[6]—were the women closest to Fidel Castro: Celia Sánchez, Vilma Espín, Haydée Santamaría, and Melba Hernández. But the insurrection is also the story of many lesser-known Cuban women who often paid dearly for their political beliefs and their hopes for a better future.

Women of the Insurrection, 1952–1954

Soon after General Fulgencio Batista seized power in March 1952, Fidel Castro assembled a small group of men and women, mostly fellow members of the reformist Ortodoxo party, who were eager to challenge the Batista dictatorship. Castro's general staff consisted of his sister Lidia, Melba Hernández, Haydée Santamaría, and Haydée's younger brother, Abel.

Haydée Santamaría was born and raised at the Constancia sugar mill in Las Villas province, where her father ran the carpentry shop. She and her brother Abel felt compassion for the workers who suffered unemployment between sugar harvests. To escape their "very reactionary" family, the two moved to Havana, sharing a tiny apartment, which in the early 1950s became the original headquarters of Fidel Castro's movement.[7]

In 1952 Melba Hernández was a thirty-two-year-old lawyer whose legal skills would be crucial to Castro's rebellion. Her parents' home became an alternative meeting site for Castro's organization.

Castro planned to start a rebellion against the Batista dictatorship by attacking the Moncada military barracks in Santiago de Cuba on July 26, 1953. Haydée Santamaría and Melba Hernández went by train to Santiago carrying weapons in a suitcase and flower box. In Havana Natalia Revuelta, the wife of a prominent heart surgeon and one of Castro's mistresses, typed and mimeographed copies of a manifesto written by Castro.

At a farm outside Santiago, Melba and Haydée cleaned and set up cots and ironed uniforms for the 120 men who would attack Moncada. Castro would not permit the women to engage in combat, a restriction that infuriated Melba Hernández.

> I protested to Fidel that we were as revolutionary and that it was unjust to discriminate against us for being women. Fidel hesitated; we had made a sensible point. . . . We couldn't believe that we would be left behind after we had considered ourselves an essential part of the group![8]

A compromise was struck; the women would go to Moncada, but as nurses to care for the wounded.

The Moncada attack failed; most of the rebels, including Haydée's brother and her fiancé, were captured and later executed. Melba and Haydée were arrested. Within a week the others, including Fidel Castro, had been caught and imprisoned. Melba Hernández served as Castro's attorney during his trial.

Haydée Santamaría and Melba Hernández were sentenced to seven months in prison. Haydée recalled:

> The Supreme Court wanted to free us. It was not the custom for women of so-called decent families to go to jail. I belonged to a rural family of position and culture, not of the street. But . . . we were part of it [the rebellion], and what would I have done when I got out? I couldn't get a job. I would have had to go home.[9]

Although Moncada failed militarily, the publicity catapulted Castro into national prominence and won his movement new recruits. One of those was a young engineering student named Vilma Espín Guillois. Her father was the vice director of Bacardí rum in Santiago, and her mother the daughter of the French consul in Havana. At twenty-two, Vilma, a chemical engineering student at the University of Oriente, had already participated in protests against Batista's coup and had written and distributed antigovernment pamphlets throughout Santiago: "It seemed easier for us because we could carry papers under our skirts."[10] In May 1952, a year before Moncada, she joined the newly formed National Revolutionary movement, where she met Frank País, a seventeen-year-old student. He soon organized his own action group, with Vilma in charge of finance.

Following the Moncada attack, Vilma continued working with País's organization until she graduated from the University of Oriente in 1954. She then left Cuba for a year to study chemical engineering at the Massachusetts Institute of Technology. When she returned in 1955, Frank País's group had fused with Fidel Castro's 26th of July Movement (M-26-7).

Organizing, 1954–1956

During Castro's imprisonment, the M-26-7 Movement had been managed largely by women: Melba, Haydée, Castro's sister Lidia, Natalia Revuelta, and to some extent his wife, Mirta.[11] They printed and distributed ten thousand copies of Castro's justification for the Moncada attack, entitled "History Will Absolve Me." Early in 1955 an amnesty committee was formed at the prompting of the mothers of the imprisoned rebels. Lidia Castro was one of its leaders.[12] Delia and Morelia Darias Pérez, sisters who had helped distribute "History Will Absolve Me" in Oriente, helped gather twenty thousand signatures on amnesty petitions, which were then presented to the Cuban Senate.[13] In April pro-amnesty demonstrations were held throughout Cuba. In May Batista yielded, signing an amnesty decree "in honor of Mother's Day."[14] Freed, Castro went to live with his sister Lidia in Havana.

Castro ordered his followers to establish his 26th of July Movement in every Cuban province. He formed a national directorate, which included Melba Hernández and Haydée Santamaría. Castro planned to travel to Mexico, prepare a guerrilla force, and return to Cuba.

In June 1955 María Antonia Figueroa, a former legal associate of Melba Hernández, became head of the M-26-7 national finance committee. She also brought Frank País and Gloria Cuadras to the Movement. Gloria Cuadras had served in the student activist group, the Revolutionary Directorate, at the University of Oriente in 1930.[15] After Batista's 1952 coup she organized a group called the Association of United Cuban Women to support antigovernment activities. Gloria now took charge of M-26-7 propaganda in Oriente province.

Another Oriente woman, thirty-five-year-old Celia Sánchez Manduley, was to become a key figure in the Cuban insurrection. The daughter of the doctor at Media Luna sugar mill, Celia had sent food and encouragement to the Moncada survivors during their imprisonment at the Isle of Pines. She worked with the amnesty campaign, distributed copies of "History Will Absolve Me," and helped organize the movement's units in Oriente. Soon after Castro's release from prison, Celia came to Havana to meet with the movement's national directorate. Upon Celia's advice Media Luna was chosen as the landing site for Castro and his guerrillas. She obtained coastal charts of the area from the Cuban navy.

Castro left for Mexico in July 1955. There he was aided by fellow Cubans María Antonia González and Teresa "Tete" Casuso. "Tete" Casuso's Mexico City apartment was used to store arms for Castro's forces.[17] It was at María's apartment that Fidel Castro met the peripatetic young Argentine revolutionary Ernesto "Che" Guevara in the summer of 1955.

In July 1955 Vilma Espín passed through Mexico, where she picked up messages from Castro for Havana. In August Castro's "Manifesto No. 1 to the People of Cuba," smuggled into Cuba by another young woman, outlined a program for radical social and political change including "adequate measures in education and legislation to put an end to every vestige of discrimination for reasons of race or sex."[18]

In September 1955 Castro wrote to Carmen Castro Porta, a leader of the Women's Martí Civic Front. The Front, founded after Batista's 1952 coup, was composed of a few hundred women of various classes in cities throughout Cuba, a heterogeneous group including communists, *ortodoxas,* and others of no particular political affiliation, all dedicated to the overthrow of the dictatorship and to free elections. Front members distributed propaganda and raised funds; their literature said nothing about women's condition. In 1953 they urged the archbishop of Santiago to aid political prisoners, but he replied "that we were very young and that we really ought to be thinking of marriage and babies."[19] The archbishop gave the young women some pamphlets on marriage. Instead the women planted bombs, set white phosphorous fires in department stores, and burned cars belonging to foreign firms.

Carmen Castro Porta was no novice to political activism. In the 1930s she had been arrested for protesting the Machado dictatorship; in the 1950s she was detained seven times and imprisoned twice for terrorism and "disrespect for authority."[20] In his letter Castro told her that the Women's Front's collaboration with the M-26-7 had been "decisive" and that the women should join his organization: "As you see, we lack an important component: a feminine arm. This is the function that we have reserved for the Women's Martí Civic Front [to] convert it into the feminine apparatus of the 26th of July Movement."[21] Castro got his way. Thereafter Carmen Porta disappeared from public prominence in Cuba.

In December 1955 more than a hundred women from the Women's Front demonstrated in the streets of Havana in support of a peaceful resolution of Cuba's political crisis. The women chanted: "We want peace, not blood. Liberty is the essence of life."[22] Scores of women were beaten and arrested by the authorities. Such spectacles garnered sympathy for Batista's opposition.

The Sierra and the *Llano,* 1956–1959

Castro's invasion force left Mexico for Cuba in the yacht *Granma* at the end of November 1956. There were no women on board. In Santiago Frank País's M-26-7 forces prepared an uprising to distract the dictator's attention. Gloria Cuadras asked no questions. "I didn't want to know [the details], I just complied. That's how we were."[23]

Back from MIT, Vilma Espín aided Frank País's preparations for Castro's landing, practiced using arms, and organized a program to train women as medical aides.[24] Celia Sánchez also prepared for Castro's arrival, sending men into the Sierra Maestra mountains and arranging for trucks to transport Castro's invasion force. At her command the phone lines in the region would be cut.[25] The planning was of no avail, however. Castro's boat was slowed by bad weather, then discovered and attacked by Batista's arm. Castro and a small band of survivors made their way up into the mountains, where they found refuge with a friend of Celia Sánchez. In the ensuing weeks, women played a vital role as messengers and arms runners.

In February 1957, when *New York Times* correspondent Herbert Matthews indicated his desire to visit Castro in the Sierra, Castro called a meeting of the national directorate, which consisted of Haydée Santamaría, Celia Sánchez, Vilma Espín, Frank País, Armando Hart, and Faustino Pérez. Never again would women comprise so large a percentage of the top revolutionary leadership. The meeting was Castro's first encounter with Celia Sánchez, whose organizational skills and peasant contacts had saved his rebels after the *Granma* landing.

Herbert Matthews and his wife were transported from Havana to Oriente by M-26-7 member Liliam Mesa. Matthews described Liliam as "young, attractive, from a well-to-do, upper-class Cuban family . . . a fanatical member of the 26th of July, typical of the young women who risked—and sometimes lost—their lives in the insurrection."[26] Vilma Espín served as interpreter for the Matthews interview.

In March 1957 the urban cadre of the M-26-7 organized the Civic Resistance, a broad anti-Batista front that provided money, medicine, and supplies to the guerrillas.[27] Women played a decisive role in this group. The owner of a Santiago beauty parlor that became a center for women's activity in the rebellion later commented that without women "there wouldn't have been a revolution."[28] Vilma Espín remarked that clandestine life in the cities was more dangerous than being a guerrilla: "It wasn't like the Sierra where one could say, 'If I die, I die fighting.' You were like a hunted animal. And death came after torture and prison. . . . Many wanted to go to the Sierra but couldn't because there weren't enough arms."[29]

In April 1957 Haydée Santamaría and Celia Sánchez brought a CBS television crew up to the Sierra, and Castro posed for them in front of a bust of José Martí that Celia and her father had brought up there four years earlier. Haydée and Celia remained in the Sierra for two months.

The Santiago police had by now identified Vilma Espín as a member of the M-26-7, and she was forced to go underground.[30] In May she narrowly escaped arrest. Then Frank País was arrested. The Civic Resistance and Women's Civic Martí Front organized demonstrations protesting his detention and also sought aid from the archbishop and various embassies to win his release. Frank was finally let go.

In May, during a battle with Batista's forces, Celia Sánchez, armed with an M-1 carbine, became the first woman to participate in combat. Thereafter Celia returned to the *llano,* or urban lowlands, to continue her work as supply master. Castro's brother Raúl called her "our helping hand," adding, "we are going to have to name you the official mother of the detachment."[31] Fidel Castro told her:

Your absence has left a real vacuum. Even when a woman goes around the mountains with a rifle in hand, she always makes our men tidier, more decent, gentlemanly—and even braver. And after all, they are really decent and gentlemanly all the time. But what would your poor father say?[32]

Batista's police knew that Celia's detention would be a severe blow to the M-26-7. On one occasion they mistakenly reported that Celia had been captured. Afterward a relieved Castro wrote that "if you . . . are well, all goes well and we are at peace." Raúl Castro called Celia our "beloved little mother."[33] Soon thereafter Celia was indeed captured, but she managed to escape "in a hail of bullets."[34] The news caused consternation in the Sierra. Che Guevara wrote in his diary that Celia was "our only known and safe contact . . . her detention would mean isolation for us."[35]

The guerrillas in the Sierra gained another valuable recruit in June 1957 with the arrival of twenty-one-year old Clodomira Acosta Ferrales from Manzanillo. A former farm worker and maid, Clodomira carried messages between various M-26-7 units in the Sierra, and later in the *llano*. Detained on a number of occasions, she always managed to talk her way to freedom. After each detention Clodomira would mock the "featherbrains" who released her.[36]

In July 1957, political prisoners began a hunger strike backed by demonstrations by the Women's Front and the women of the Civic Resistance Movement. The women brought water and medicine to the strikers, they visited the families of prisoners to offer support, and they informed journalists of the atrocities committed by prison authorities. A former prisoner recalled that "there wasn't a night or day in which the prison halls were free of women; they were there constantly."[37]

On July 20 Frank País made Vilma Espín coordinator of all activities in Oriente province while he drafted an ideological program for the movement. Ten days later he was shot dead by the police.[38] His death triggered a spontaneous strike that brought Santiago to a halt. Vilma and other M-26-7 leaders organized a demonstration of mourning women in Céspedes Park to greet U.S. Ambassador Earl Smith and his wife during their visit to Santiago. A scuffle broke out between the women and the police, and the police turned water hoses on the women. Vilma later recalled, "The ambassador's wife, who was not accustomed to witnessing these things at such close range, was affected by seeing police hit women while the women shouted, 'Assassins!' "[39] The day after the killing, Castro asked Celia to assume many of Frank's responsibilities.

September brought the guerrillas another valuable courier, forty-one-year-old Lidia Esther Doce Sánchez. Born into a poor rural family, Lidia had worked as a maid in Havana, sending part of her pay home to her three children in Oriente. In 1957 Lidia moved back to Oriente and joined Che Guevara's column as a messenger.

In late 1957 Celia Sánchez went up into the Sierra and remained there until Batista's defeat. She took charge of communications and correspondence. When not filing papers, fighting, or accompanying Castro, Celia carried out projects to beautify the rebel encampments.

The Path to Victory

Early in 1958 momentum was building in favor of the guerrillas. Batista responded with ever greater repression; women could now expect to be treated as harshly as men. Throughout the Sierra the rebels began organizing educational and health services for the peasants. Asela de los Santos arrived from exile in Miami to establish schools. Isabel Rielo and her sister Lilia were sent from Santiago, Isabel serving as an assistant in the guerrilla hospital and Lilia as a teacher of peasant children. In the Sierra Maestra, Violeta Casal became the first female announcer on Radio Rebelde, the guerrilla radio station.

In March 1958 Vilma Espín was preparing the Santiago M-26-7 to participate in an April national strike, which Castro hoped would bring Cuba to its knees. Emergency medical posts were organized by M-26-7 women. Pastorita Nuñez was in charge of a group of women who fabricated hundreds of Molotov cocktails to be used during the strike.[40] When the strike failed, the morale, effectiveness, and credibility of the urban resistance was destroyed. The Sierra forces were now clearly dominant. Haydée Santamaría was sent to Miami to take control of the M-26-7's fund-raising in the United States.

Encouraged by the strike's failure, Batista launched a "final" offensive against the guerrillas and increased repression against the urban resistance. Among the first to fall were the Giral sisters, Cristina and Lourdes, who had sold bonds, distributed revolutionary propaganda, carried messages, and transported explosives. The Civic Resistance's directorate had met in their apartment. They were gunned down by police in June.[41] Cristina was twenty-eight, Lourdes twenty-two.

Margo Aniceto Rodríguez, a forty-four-year-old lawyer who had frequently defended M-26-7 members, denounced the death of the Giral sisters and was promptly arrested. The other women inmates joked, "Margo is such a good lawyer that if she cannot free us she at least comes to stay with us in prison."[42]

On June 21 Isabel Girodana, a twenty-six-year-old student, was detained in Havana with three other activists for carrying out "subversive acts" in Oriente province. She was interrogated for four weeks but refused to disclose any information. Estela Lorenzo González, Cira Tudela Muñoz, and Zobeida García Ricardo were arrested in June along with twenty other Movement members. Cira, who was pregnant, was threatened but not tortured by authorities. Estela and Zobeida were tortured for two weeks but refused to yield. Fellow women prisoners nursed them back to health.

In the Sierra the women mothered Castro's guerrillas during the army's summer offensive. At rebel headquarters women "often had meals ready and waiting for the guerrillas returning from battle." They washed the men's clothing and "continued to do the tasks traditionally done by women while the men slept."[43] Che Guevara found that women were valuable in guerrilla camps because they could perform duties that "are scorned by those [men] who perform them; they [the men] are constantly trying to get out of those tasks in order to enter into forces that are actively in combat."[44] On occasion Che permitted women to take up arms, as in the case of Oniria Gutiérrez, who had hiked up to his camp in the Sierra the previous summer. Oniria argued that if Celia Sánchez could fight, she could too. After considerable discussion, Che yielded.[45]

To prevent Batista's air force from bombing the Sierra, Raúl Castro kidnapped forty-nine Americans and brought them to his camp. Vilma Espín served as interpreter in the subsequent negotiations with U.S. officials. She remained in the Sierra for the remainder of the war.

The Revolutionary Directorate, comprised largely of students from the University of Havana, opened a guerrilla front in the Escambray mountains. They also attempted to educate the peasants, organizing a study group to discuss changing attitudes toward women, but the peasants boycotted it. Changes in rural attitudes would come only slowly and with great effort.[46]

In the summer of 1958, M-26-7 women in the Sierra officially became active combatants. According to revolutionary legend, one day Castro observed the Rielo sisters arriving from the *llano* carrying heavy packs of supplies. Women of such endurance and determination, he decided, should also be allowed to fight. He organized an all-female combat platoon called the "Mariana Grajales" brigade in honor of the heroic mother of the wars of independence. Isabel Rielo, the best shot in the group, was appointed captain. All together there would be some fourteen women, hardly a "brigade" but nevertheless a new role for the women in the Sierra. Castro told them: "You girls have seen how hard I had to argue so that you can fight. You can't let me down."[47]

Inexplicably, the Mariana Grajales brigade was divided into squads assigned to different sectors of the Sierra. The women, armed with M-1 carbines because they were "light and easy to handle," took part in at least ten encounters with the army.[48] After the women's first skirmish a guerrilla commander wrote to Castro:

> I must tell you that after being one of the main opponents to having women in our troop . . . I congratulate you once again because you're never wrong. . . . I wish you could see if only on film . . . the behavior mainly of Teté [Puebla] and also of the other women comrades who when ordered to advance, while some of the men lagged behind, were out in front with a degree of courage and coolheadedness worthy of the respect and recognition of all the rebels and everybody else.[49]

Isabel Rielo later recalled that, even after becoming combatants, the Marianas continued to perform more traditional tasks such as cooking and sewing in the rebel camps.[50]

Urban actions intensified in late 1958, and more women were arrested. In September couriers Clodomira Acosta Ferrales and Lidia Doce Sánchez were discovered at a Havana safehouse. They were tortured and killed by the police, who threw their bodies into the sea. In October Teresa Abreu Manegal, a twenty-six-year-old shoemaker, was picked up by police along with nineteen-year-old María del Pilar Sá Leal. Teresa had ammunition, dynamite and radio parts hidden in her house. They were interrogated for twenty-seven days before being transferred to the women's prison where Teresa's two sisters were already incarcerated. Angelina Nodarse Alvarez, a thirty-two-year-old nurse, was detained in Artemisa and transferred to the military intelligence headquarters for a month's interrogation. Her cousin had been killed by police the previous January.[51]

In November the Mariana Grajales brigade participated in the battle of Guisa. One member, Bella Acosta Pompa, disarmed two soldiers and took them prisoner. In a Radio Rebelde report broadcast after the battle, Castro praised by name each man who had fought well and mentioned that "the squad of the Mariana Grajales brigade also fought bravely . . . enduring bombing by planes and the attack of the enemy artillery."[52]

By the end of 1958 Che Guevara and Camilo Cienfuegos were advancing rapidly across the *llano*. They captured the key railhead of Santa Clara in late December and were poised to take Havana. A little after midnight on New Year's Day dictator Fulgencio Batista fled Cuba. To avoid alarming his wife, he neglected to inform her of their departure until the last moment.[53]

The rebels were also taken aback by the dictator's sudden flight. At the town of Dos Ríos, where José Martí had died many years before, the women of the Mariana Grajales brigade helped to organize an impromptu celebration. Castro arrived. Three pigs were roasted to celebrate the victory. The group then prepared for the long march to Havana.

The first stop was at Bayamo, where a huge reception awaited them. Angelina Antolín of the Mariana Grajales brigade recalled it as "the most emotional moment of my life."[54] The group then proceeded to Holguín, where the women joined other brigade members.

In Matanzas the rebel caravan was reorganized, and the women rode atop several captured tanks as the caravan entered Havana. The entire city was in the streets. The tanks and trucks advanced under a rain of flowers. As the *Marianas* swept past, men yelled up to them, "Look! Here are the most beautiful women in Cuba!" *Mariana* Rita García found the women's comments the most moving: "The women asked, 'You fought? You shot?' And when we said, 'yes,' many of them embraced us, crying. I tell you that those hugs conveyed an emotion and affection that I will not forget."[55]

The Aftermath

The significance of women's participation in the Cuban insurrection was not lost on its male leaders. In 1960 Castro created the Federation of Cuban Women (FMC) to harness the political enthusiasm, talents, and energy of Cuban women for the revolution.

At the same time, all other independent women's organizations were disbanded. Most of the women who participated in the guerrilla struggle disappeared from public view after 1959. A few went on to hold modest positions.

Isabel Rielo, leader of the Mariana Grajales brigade, founded the Lidia Doce School for Militias in 1961. In the 1980s she was head of pharmaceutical services at a leading Havana hospital and served an internationalist mission in Vietnam. She died in 1989.

Haydée Santamaría founded Casa de las Américas, an important public relations and literary organization. She married fellow M-26-7 member Armando Hart, who became minister of education and then minister of culture. She committed suicide in 1980 on the twenty-seventh anniversary of the Moncada attack.

Melba Hernández went on to serve as a founding member of the Federation of Cuban Women and was chairwoman of the Cuban Committee of Solidarity with Vietnam, Cambodia, and Laos.

Vilma Espín and Raúl Castro married soon after the triumph of the rebellion. Fidel Castro appointed Vilma director of the FMC in 1960, a position she still held in 1995. For many years she was an alternate member and briefly a full member of the Politburo of the Communist party. In the 1980s her marriage crumbled, but she continued to serve as the unofficial "first lady" of Cuba at official functions.

Celia Sánchez remained Castro's closest personal confidante for many years. As overseer of Castro's personal schedule Celia wielded significant power. She also served as a kind of national benefactress, a socialist Eva Perón, who through the years responded to personal appeals for assistance and investigated complaints of injustice from thousands of Cubans. She died of lung cancer in 1980. A hospital and a textile factory bear her name. Celia was the first woman of the revolutionary generation to have a monument built in her honor—and the only revolutionary woman to approach the postmortem status of Che Guevara and Camilo Cienfuegos.

3

Making Social Revolution: The Federation of Cuban Women

This unification of all sectors of women within the revolution constitutes a force, an enthusiastic force, a force in numbers, a large force and a decisive force for the revolution.

Fidel Castro (1960)[1]

The basic function of the Federation of Cuban Women is to incorporate women into the construction of socialism, elevating the general political, cultural, and technical level of the nation. All of the FMC's activities are designed precisely to mobilize women, organize them, and improve their condition.

Vilma Espín (1971)[2]

It was [Fidel Castro] who pointed out the tasks our women's organization would undertake and outlined its objectives. . . .

Vilma Espín (1975)[3]

The first months of 1959 gave no hint of the changes in store for Cuban women. In Havana the revolutionary army crowned its carnival queen as "the Queen of Liberty" in the salon of mirrors at City Hall. The French film *Be Beautiful and Keep Quiet* was playing at the Arenal theater on La Rampa. Lingerie ads flitted seductively through the pages of the newspaper *Revolución*. Nevertheless change was coming. Women's support for the insurrection had been critical to the defeat of the dictator; it would now be equally important for the survival of the new regime.

The government sought first to unify the various women's groups into a single organization, the Federation of Cuban Women (FMC), which would eventually become the largest women's organization in the history of Latin America. The FMC would extend women's traditional caretaking role into the social life of the nation. It would also guide women to support and implement revolutionary policies determined by male decision makers. Many of these policies would benefit women of the lower classes and bring confusion and defeat to women of the middle and upper classes.

Activism and Agitation

The precursor of the FMC was the Revolutionary Women's Union (Union Feminino Revolucionario, or UFR), organized by a small group of women in March 1959. The UFR, dedicated to peace, democratic liberties, and economic improvement, was one of many new groups to emerge in 1959. Its members went from door to door explaining, cajoling, and pressuring women to support the revolution. This time-consuming but effective process of face-to-face persuasion would become a characteristic technique of mass organizations in revolutionary Cuba. The UFR raised money for the agrarian reform of May 1959 and for antiaircraft defenses. It published a magazine called *Blanca*.[4]

The most prominent organizers of the UFR were not the women of Castro's 26th of July Movement (M-26-7) but members of the Popular Socialist Party (PSP), the Communist party of pre-Castro Cuba. Prominent among them were Elena Gil, Clementina Serra, and Rosario Fernández.

Elena Gil was the daughter of a lower-middle-class family. In 1920, at age fourteen, she went to work as a secretary. Later she joined the Cuban Telephone Company and became active in the telephone workers' union. Fired for participating in the strike of 1934 and accused of being a communist, she in fact did not join the party until 1945. In 1959 she became chief of "women's improvement" in the UFR.[5]

Clementina Serra attended teacher training school in the 1930s, one of the few respectable ways for young women to gain independence. "I am a daughter of the working class. . . . my parents were revolutionaries," she once told an interviewer.[6] In 1960 she became head of Cuba's day care program.

In 1959 Rosario Fernández, a former servant and shoemaker, was asked by the Popular Socialist party to recruit women for the UFR. She brought 500 women into the organization. Years later she became chief of women's employment in Cuba.[7]

In the fall of 1959 Rosario Fernández helped organize a Cuban delegation to the Congress of Latin American Women in Santiago, Chile. It included Castro supporters, communists, and Catholics and was headed by Castro's sister-in-law, twenty-nine-year-old Vilma Espín. The sixty-five-member Cuban delegation—the largest sent by any nation—caused an uproar at the Congress. Santiago's conservative newspaper *El Mercurio* warned of the Cubans' communist influence. Conservatives tried to exclude the Cubans but failed.[8] Espín told the conference that "the enemies of the Cuban revolution are the enemies of the progress of Latin America."[9] When the Cuban delegates returned to Havana, they were greeted as heroines of the revolution.

By 1960 the UFR was getting housewives to participate in meetings, conferences, and political rallies. When the UFR marched by, bourgeois women would shout, "There go the prostitutes!" and the revolutionaries would answer, "Viva Cuba libre! Viva Fidel!"[10]

In February 1960 Rosario Fernández led UFR women to help defend visiting Soviet Deputy Foreign Minister Anastas Mikoyan against demonstrators from the Catholic University. When middle-class women demonstrated against the arrest of their sons for counterrevolutionary activities, the UFR "forced them to disperse."[11] When bourgeois women tried to organize a pot-banging demonstration in the town of Cardenas to protest food shortages, they were confronted by UFR activists.

Meanwhile upper-class women were fleeing the island. María Luisa Gómez Mena, the Countess of Camargo, departed for Switzerland, leaving behind her sugar mills, her Marie Antoinette furniture, and her reputation as a great hostess. Her Havana mansion, the "House of the Forty Doors," would become the Museum of Decorative Arts. Elena Mederos, minister of welfare under Castro's first government, quit in May 1959. Mercedes García Tuduri, a philosophy professor at the Catholic University, went into exile in 1962.

Some women of the middle and upper classes chose to remain in revolutionary Cuba. The internationally renowned dancer Alicia Alonso returned to Cuba and was rewarded with control of the National Ballet. Other women were propelled into new and sometimes dangerous activities. Albertina O'Farrill, the Marquesa of Montoro, was one who stayed behind—for a while. The Marquesa had spent her youth at Havana's Sacred Heart Academy and the Havana Yacht club, surrounded by a protective web of family, friends, and attentive servants. Andrés Vargas Gómez once observed that his aristocratic cousin was "born to live in beautiful palaces and to entertain in luxurious salons."[12] But in 1959 her family, which had been close to the Batista regime, was in trouble. She began to help her friends find asylum in Latin American embassies in Havana and helped to transport children out of Cuba. Her income was reduced to nothing. In the mid-1960s she was arrested and spent thirty months in prison before going into exile.

Some middle-class women joined the counterrevolution and were arrested and imprisoned. In the early 1960s there were some twelve hundred in the Guanajay women's prison alone.[13] Prison conditions in the 1960s were grim, and sentences for women were far harsher than those that had been meted out by the Batista dictatorship. Ana Lara Rodríguez, a medical student at the University of Havana, imprisoned in 1961 for protesting against the communization of the revolution, was incarcerated for nineteen years at the New Dawn Prison. Dr. Martha

Frayde, after having served as Castro's representative to UNESCO in Paris in the early 1960s, attempted to flee the island in a raft and was imprisoned for three years.[14]

The Federation of Cuban Women

In 1960 mass organizations were created in order to integrate Cubans into the revolution. In July it was the Committees for the Defense of the Revolution (Comités para la Defensa de la Revolución, or CDRs), neighborhood groups responsible for organizing and monitoring local residents; in August it was the Federation of Cuban Women (FMC). The FMC was reportedly Fidel Castro's idea. FMC chief Vilma Espín once observed that during the M-26-7 insurrection women didn't talk about "inequality or discrimination" or about "feminine emancipation."[15] When Castro created the FMC, Espín remembered thinking: "Why do we have to have a woman's organization?I had never been discriminated against. I had my career as a chemical engineer. I never suffered. I never had difficulty."[16]

But the purpose of the Federation of Cuban Women was not simply to address sexual discrimination. The FMC was designed to mobilize and monitor an important sector of society. Or as Vilma Espín explained: "We had to organize and train the enthusiastic, firm and powerful mass made up of our women. . . . Our work was aimed at winning over more and more women, uniting them and—with them—building a conscious force on behalf of the revolution."[17]

Fidel Castro founded the Federation of Cuban Women on August 23, 1960. The UFR and other women's organizations were disbanded; Cuban women were at last united. Gone were "the false differences of focus and concepts that separated us."[18]

The FMC was organized into neighborhood, regional, munipical, provincial, and national units. Its two magazines, *Mujeres* and *Romances* (later renamed *Muchacha*), helped to spread the word by publicizing its objectives and activities. At its first congress, in September 1962, it had almost four hundred thousand members. By its fifth congress in 1990 the FMC had some three million members, more than 80 percent of all Cuban women between fourteen and sixty-five years of age.

In the 1960s and 1970s the local FMC committees met once a month. Members were encouraged to take part in educational programs and neighborhood projects. The FMC was particularly important for housewives who, for various reasons, were not able to go "out into the streets" to seek employment or participate in volunteer labor. It also gave women an opportunity to socialize away from their husbands.

Evidence of a woman's participation in a mass organization like the FMC was an indicator of her "integration" into the revolution. This in turn was taken into account when she sought any benison from the state such as housing or a promotion at work.

The rapid growth of the FMC was the result of patient legwork by recruiters who went house to house. Sometimes they were accompanied by military escorts to protect them from counterrevolutionaries, or from spouses who did not approve of the revolution's intrusion into their households. When Flora, an early FMC organizer in a remote town, agreed to recruit her neighbors, she said, "I'll do it, but give me time because [my husband] doesn't understand."[19] But years later Flora was head of the municipal FMC and the women of the town were literate, some having gone on to college.

When the great literacy campaign was launched in 1961, thousands of volunteers from the FMC joined in. They delivered mail to literacy workers, provided housing, did sustitute teaching, and served as "loving mothers" to the seventy thousand literacy workers who were awarded secondary school scholarships.[20]

The FMC also took the lead in developing a national day care system. On April 10, 1961, Clementina Serra inaugurated the first three day care centers in Cuba, all in Havana. By December there were thirty-seven.[21] FMC president Vilma Espín noted that the day care program was the effort "closest to our hearts."[22] To help finance day care, FMC members sold coffee in workplaces and on the street. "Drink your coffee and give two cents to the day care centers," read one FMC poster.[23] FMC members sewed children's clothes, made dolls to sell at craft fairs, and held dances. In 1963 they raised over a million dollars for day care.

The government pledged that every town that wanted a day care center would have one. Sometimes the government contributed a building or a house abandoned by the fleeing middle class. Neighbors would pitch in to fix it up. When nails and boards were rationed in 1961, FMC members had to line up, like everyone else, at hardware stores to buy them. When wheelbarrows to carry cement were lacking, children's wagons were pressed into service.

In addition to its role in literacy and day care, the FMC created a number of innovative programs to help ordinary women: the Ana Betancourt Schools for Peasant Women, schools for maids, sewing academies, and popular schools of health.

The Ana Betancourt Schools for Peasant Women

Fidel Castro's guerrillas had received substantial help from the peasants of the Sierra. In 1960 Castro returned the favor by creating the Ana Betancourt Schools for Peasant Women. This program, controlled by the FMC, brought tens of thousands of peasant women from the countryside to Havana for training. The first of the schools' directors, psychiatrist

Elsa Gutiérrez, recalled that "it was all a great discovery. . . . none of us had ever done anything like this before."[24]

The citadel of the Ana Betancourt program was Havana's National Hotel, a center of tourism since the 1920s. A former student recalled looking out her hotel window one morning and shouting for joy. There was the sea! "It was truly a dream."[25] Some of the students were put up in abandoned mansions in the Vedado and Miramar districts.

FMC representatives told rural parents that the Ana Betancourt program would teach their daughters useful skills such as sewing and clothes making. Many fathers were reluctant to let their daughters go to Havana, thinking they would become maids or prostitutes, but the FMC assured them that their daughters would be safe.

Many of the *Anitas,* as the young women were called, were from the Escambray mountains of Central Cuba. This was not so by chance: one aim of the program was to undercut a peasant counterrevolution in that region. Peasants would think twice about making trouble while their daughters were in the revolution's grasp in Havana.

In 1961 the FMC's director of women's improvement, Elena Gil, told her aides to prepare for three thousand *Anitas,* "But at the railroad station more and more trains filled with country girls kept arriving, and eventually there were 11,000."[26] At the National Hotel in Havana the girls spread out their sewing on the gambling tables of the hotel's casino. When they eventually returned home, they brought hand-sewn clothing for their male relatives.

Upon arrival in the city the *Anitas* were examined by doctors. For some it was the first medical attention they had ever received. They took courses in physical education, dancing and singing, hygiene, and first aid. Political indoctrination included the study of Fidel Castro's speeches. The *Anitas* learned to refute rumors that Cuban children were going to be taken away from their parents and sent to the USSR, or that Castro was going to prohibit religion.

Teaching the *Anitas* was an adventure. There was so much to explain: "We had to make sure they brushed their teeth; we taught them to listen to music and to eat properly."[27] The students had beliefs that startled their young, middle-class teachers. Some were convinced that eating pineapple brought on menstruation. Others would not eat fish. Some thought the light of the moon was dangerous and kept their shades drawn in the evening. Some had never eaten bread or ridden on an elevator. The drains in the bathtubs caused great anxiety. Where did the water go? The telephone was a great mystery: "the little string that talked," one girl called it.[28]

Many of the country girls practiced the Afro-Cuban religion Santería. Under their school blouses they wore the necklaces of the African gods. Sometimes the teachers would be alarmed to find the *Anitas,* hand in hand, in a trance. "We would break up the rite," they recalled, explaining to the girls that such behavior was irrational and uncouth.[29]

Homesickness was a problem for many *Anitas*. But Havana had many diversions: movies on the weekends; trips to the beach; and on Mother's Day, visits from their families. From time to time Fidel Castro himself would visit; the young women were encouraged to embrace him and call him "Papá."[30]

Finally, after a year's work, an *Anita* would graduate, returning home with a diploma certifying that she was a *profesora* of dressmaking. Graduates were given sewing machines and instructions for teaching ten other women what they had learned. Parents and neighbors welcomed the *Anitas* back with fiestas. They found the young women transformed—healthy, their teeth fixed, their dysentery cured. Back in their small towns the *Anitas* helped to establish local sewing and dressmaking programs. Some founded FMC delegations. Vilma Espín later observed that the *Anitas* became "the first political leaders in the countryside."[31]

When the Ana Betancourt program ended in 1976, it had trained nearly a hundred thousand young women.[32] The Cuban school system had now spread throughout the countryside, and the guerrillas of the Escambray had long since been crushed.

In the 1960s the FMC created a nationwide network of dressmaking academies. Located in abandoned homes and stores, the academies were designed for housewives who might have time for an hour or two of instruction a week. In 1968 there were 1,543 academies with 23,950 students. By 1974, 445,299 women had graduated from the academies.[33] Using methods developed in the Ana Betancourt Schools, the academies were machines for socialization. They allowed Cuban housewives to escape patriarchal control—at least for the afternoon. Graduates received diplomas which served as passports to full-time work in the clothing industry.

Domestic Service and Prostitution

Domestic service and prostitution were two fundamental pillars of pre-revolutionary society that the FMC helped to sweep away. In doing so, however, the government and the FMC avoided questioning the patriarchal structures and habits that engendered such practices.

Maid service had enabled many middle-class women to hold jobs and participate in public life, but the revolution viewed domestic service as degrading and exploitative and sought to eliminate it. In 1960, as tensions between the bourgeoisie and the revolution intensified, Fidel Castro organized a school for domestic servants. Its objective was, as one FMC official put it, to "get those maids away from the bourgeoisie" and to "capture them for the revolution."[34] The government press began to describe maids as slaves who were exploited by long hours of work, abusive treatment, and low pay. Critics noted that domestic servants were not protected by Cuban labor law.

The first night schools for domestics were opened in April 1961 under the direction of Elena Gil. The maids studied mathematics, Spanish, and revolutionary history and were trained for a variety of jobs, from secretary to day care worker. The instructors were young women who had participated in the literacy campaign and then attended the Conrado Benítez schools of ideological training. The maids studied the agrarian reform, the rent reform, and the urban reform. "We armed them with solid arguments, with irrefutable truths," said Elena Gil.[35] In 1961 there were seventeen schools for domestics; within a few years thirty thousand maids were studying at a hundred schools, seventy of them in Havana.

Sometimes it was not easy for the maids to attend school. Gaining permission to leave their jobs in time for the eight o'clock evening class could be a battle. The bolder servants told their señoras to dine early—if they wished to be served! In some cases an FMC delegation would visit the señora to request her cooperation. Some maids were given monthly stipends, housing, and clothing to encourage their attendance.

Graduates of the schools for domestics were given the jobs of bank and telephone workers who had gone into exile. Others became day care and health workers, technicians and bureaucrats. Sometimes the former maids were looked down upon at their new workplace. One recalled being insulted by a bourgeois matron "for her odor of cheap powder."[36] It didn't matter. They were enjoying a new life. In 1968 the schools for maids closed after having retrained thousands of Cuban domestics.

The revolution's attack on prostitution was an earnest attempt to improve the lives of thousands of women as well as a symbolic gesture to end Cuba's role as carnal playground of the Caribbean. Although there had been periodic hand wringing over prostitution by Cuban politicians, little had been done to check what was, after all, an important feature of *machista* society. The revolution portrayed prostitution as a shameful legacy of Cuba's colonial and neocolonial past. By claiming that North American visitors were the principal exploiters of Cuban women, the revolution avoided any serious analysis of sexuality and social power. In truth the principal clientele of Cuba's sex industry was Cubans themselves. Indeed the euphoria of the revolutionary triumph of 1959 reportedly brought a boom in business for Cuba's thirty to forty thousand prostitutes.[37]

Law 993 of 1961 outlawed any form of prostitution and stipulated that anyone associated with it could be identified as socially "dangerous." Authorities had three options in sentencing: therapy, reeducation, or imprisonment.[38] Pimps were sent to prison or to work farms. The government at first did not treat prostitutes harshly. It viewed them as hapless victims of the old system and sent them to schools to be rehabilitated. These schools provided ideological and vocational training and taught the women basic etiquette, table manners, and how to avoid "overly ornate" hairstyles and clothes.[39] Prostitutes with families to support were given stipends, and FMC volunteers minded the children while their mothers attended classes.

Many, but not all, of Cuba's prostitutes were grateful for the opportunity to study. Although the rehabilitation program was at first voluntary, it soon became compulsory. Some prostitutes left the country. Those who refused to give up their profession were ultimately imprisoned.

As the FMC's early programs faded into history, they were replaced by more routinized activities, which would continue through the 1980s. These included ideological training of members through "study circles" and Friendship Brigades, and programs in health, education, and agriculture.

Ideological Education and International Links

In order to bring revolutionary values to the grass roots, the FMC inaugurated a program of "study circles" in each of its neighborhood groups. The study circles were linked to lessons that appeared in the FMC's monthly magazine *Mujeres*. The level of the lessons, particularly in the early 1960s, was elementary. For example, Lesson 2 of 1963 instructed students to read a few pages in a primer on Cuban geography.[40]

By 1964, however, women were studying World War I and the transition from capitalism to socialism. In January 1970, FMC members were studying "Lenin and the Emancipation of Women." In the mid-1970s, lessons focused on the resolutions presented at the second FMC congress. In 1983, study circles focused on Cuban history.[41] Lessons often included a list of discussion questions. Thus in Lesson 20 readers found: "Capitalism is characterized by the exploitation of man by man. In socialism this exploitation is eliminated. Explain this great difference."[42]

The study circles were a mixed success. Vilma Espín complained of a lack of "activists" to lead them. By 1980 more than a third of FMC members were avoiding the circles entirely.[43] Espín admonished members to "keep in mind that the ideological education of women is the fundamental task of the federation."[44] In 1980 an adjunct to the study circles called "Study Teams for History Activists" was founded. By 1984, 98,662 women, about 3 percent of FMC membership, were studying and writing about Cuban history.[45]

The Friendship Brigades were another example of the FMC's role in political education. They were designed to interest women in foreign policy and to demonstrate their good fortune in living in socialist Cuba. Each group studied a particular country. Between 1977 and 1985 membership in the Friendship Brigades more than doubled to 185,000 *federadas* (members).[46]

The FMC's international interests were also reflected in its links with the Soviet-controlled International Democratic Women's Federation

(Federación Democrática Internacional de Mujeres, or FDIM). Vilma Espín once served as the FDIM's vice president. The FMC also developed close ties with various United Nations entities and attended major international UN conferences during the "Decade of Women," 1975–1985. Cuba became a member of the Commission on the Legal and Social Condition of Women and was the first signatory of the United Nations Convention Against All Forms of Discrimination Against Women.

But the FMC was reluctant to participate in the more ample social and political debates provoked by feminism. On occasion its leaders denounced feminism for misleading women into blaming men, not capitalism, for their woes. The FMC did not actively participate in the first three feminist Encuentros, or meetings of Latin American women, which began in the 1980s. In 1988 the FMC sent four representatives to the meeting in Taxco, Mexico. In 1990, at the fifth Encuentro in San Bernardo, Argentina, a Cuban representative rejected as "impossible" a proposal by the assembly to hold the next meeting in Cuba.[47]

Social Work, Agriculture, and Education

The FMC's social work programs enlisted women's assistance in combatting a range of social problems. In 1967 the FMC began working with juvenile delinquents referred to it by the national police and the Ministry of Interior. The FMC monitored delinquents' school attendance and discussed their behavior with parents. According to Vilma Espín, delinquency reflected families' failure to "develop their children's collectivist sentiments and love of the revolution, work, the nation and the school."[48] In 1972 the FMC created a national school for social workers to train volunteer "specialists" to oversee the FMC's social work. Over the next six years 12,754 *federadas* graduated from the program.[49]

One aspect of the FMC's social work is illustrated by the case of the illicit sandwiches. In September 1977, when all private vending was illegal, a twelve-year-old boy was arrested for selling *empanadas* (sandwiches) on the street. Since the miscreant was a minor, he was passed on to an FMC social worker, who determined to "win his confidence, to make him my friend."[50] The social worker maneuvered her way into his home and found a household in riotous disorder: cats, dogs, and pigeons under foot, and "promiscuity, bad vocabulary, and vulgar gestures" rampant among family members.[51] The father was a "counterrevolutionary" with a prison record, and the older brother neither worked nor studied. The illicit sandwich business was run by the mother.

The family eventually agreed to stop selling sandwiches and to send the younger boy to school. The unrepentant older brother was removed to the home of a relative. The house was subdivided so that the father could live apart from the rest of the family, a common solution to family strife in housing-short Cuba. Cats, dogs, and pigeons were evicted. Over time the family was transformed and finally came to be regarded as a "model household" by the FMC and CDR.

In 1980, as social work was increasingly professionalized in Cuba, the FMC's role in working with delinquents was reduced, and the keeping of records on minors with behavior problems was passed back to the police. However juvenile delinquency would only get worse in subsequent years. In 1985 the FMC had 18,000 volunteer social workers, and there were at least sixteen different studies underway of juvenile delinquency.[52] By 1990, as disaffection and delinquency among the young increased, the number of FMC social workers rose to almost 24,000.[53]

In addition to doing traditional social work, the FMC has organized Cuban women for volunteer labor, particularly in agriculture, health, and education. One of the most ambitious of these projects was the FMC–ANAP Mutual Aid Brigades, formed in 1966. The Brigades' women volunteers replaced male agricultural workers during emergencies and assisted during harvests. The women also picked vegetables and tended chickens, freeing men for more strenuous tasks. Between 1970 and 1974 the number of women in FMC–ANAP Mutual Aid Brigades grew to 101,273. Many of these women subsequently joined salaried production, and the overall number of *brigadistas* leveled off at about sixty thousand in the 1980s.[54]

A typical project of the mid-1970s found FMC–ANAP brigades in Camagüey harvesting tomatoes, onions, and garlic. *Brigadistas,* mostly housewives, worked four to five hours a day. The local FMC chief observed that her objective was not only to harvest foodstuffs but to engender "a love of work." She boasted that "we do anything they ask of us."[55]

The FMC's Militant Mothers for Education *(madres)* was an effort to link parents more closely to the schools. The school system was itself expanding rapidly and was shorthanded. The new rural boarding schools needed women to comfort homesick students.

The Militant Mothers were given a trial run in 1970 when forty-six *madres,* many of them mothers of students, were placed at the Enrique Hart primary school in Colón, Matanzas. They visited the homes of truant children, cleaned the school, and substituted for absent teachers. In other schools the *madres* cleaned dormitories, made the students' beds, worked in the school kitchen, sewed uniforms, visited sick students in their homes, planted flowers, and gave motherly advice. They also protected school property against vandalism and issued passes permitting students to leave the school grounds. This policing function was not always appreciated; some students considered it spying. The Militant Mothers program was eventually introduced throughout the island's school system; by 1985 there were 1.7 million militant mothers organized in twelve thousand brigades.[56]

FMC president Vilma Espín lauded the Militant Mothers for assisting school administrators in the battle against "academic fraud, individualism, ostentation, extravagance, and accommodationism."[57] In 1985 Espín underscored the *madres'* importance in fighting negative attitudes that were being expressed by some young people through their clothing and conduct.[58]

In short, in 1960 Fidel Castro replaced all other autonomous women's organizations with the Federation of Cuban Women in order to promote sexual equality, to win women's support for the revolution, and to take advantage of women's considerable energies. This was the first time a Cuban government had specifically appealed to women for support and assistance. Women of the FMC became agents of social change. The FMC developed and directed a host of creative programs to address social ills, at the same time overseeing the political education of Cuban women. Thus while the FMC was an enthusiastic participant in the development of the "new" Cuban society, it was also an effective arm of social vigilance for the Castro regime.

Many of the early activities of the Federation of Cuban Women represented a blend of cultural tradition and political change. Thus young peasant women were brought to the big city without chaperones, a startling notion made more palatable by the fact that they would be learning a traditionally female skill: sewing. In program after program this pattern was repeated. A new social mobility among women was emerging. This early blend of tradition and change worked brilliantly; as time went by, however, it became more problematic.

4

The Federation of Cuban Women: Activism and Power

We will always strive to be worthy of Fidel's confidence, of the hopes he has placed in Cuban women, of his permanent encouragement and of his faith . . . that women be a firm pillar of our Revolution.

FMC Draft Thesis (March 1985)[1]

I think women should be promoted more at the state and party level, I honestly do. It is our duty, our moral obligation, and all the more so when I think that our party is still largely a party of men, and our state is still largely a state of men.

Fidel Castro (March 1980)[2]

With its three million members, the Federation of Cuban Women (FMC) might have been a formidable advocate for Cuban women. The FMC's principal task, however, was to defend a revolution whose interests were defined by a male elite. The FMC and Cuban women in general participated very little in the making of policies that governed their lives and the lives of their children and families. When it came to power, the ideas, perspectives, and experiences of Cuban women simply did not count.

This absence of women in positions of power raised fundamental questions about revolutionary Cuba's political culture and institutions. What were the structural paths to power and how did they function? What were the obstacles to women's advancement? How important was the attainment of high rank and national policy-making positions to the women of Cuba? How did the FMC fit within the Cuban system?

These questions are difficult to answer, precisely, because the revolution never created clearly understood channels of power. Much depended on the whims of Fidel Castro and on informal power brokering. For years there was no systematic research regarding women's progress, or lack of it, among the power elite.

Some clues to the view of women among the Cuban leadership can be found in the Cuban constitution. The Constitution of 1976, the first constitution instituted under the revolution, subtly relegated women to beneficiary status. Articles 12 and 13 condemned racial but not sexual discrimination, while article 14 granted women equal rights "as men." Article 53 gave women the "right" to their own organization, a courtesy not offered to men and other groups such as Afro-Cubans. The constitution also allowed women's participation in the labor force to be restricted in order to "protect" their reproductive capacity.[3]

In 1992 Cuba ratified a new constitution, which stated clearly and simply in article 42 that discrimination based on "race, skin color, sex, national origin, religious belief, and any other affront to human dignity is proscribed and sanctioned by law." Article 44 stated unequivocally that "men and women have equal rights in the economic, political, cultural and social realms and in the family."[4] After nearly a hundred years of Cuban independence, women were finally granted full constitutional equality. Their participation in the halls of government, however, lagged far behind.

The Record

The Communist party, the reigning institution in revolutionary Cuban society, set a dubious example for women's participation in power. At its first congress, in 1975, women represented only 13 percent of party membership. This percentage increased slightly to 18 percent at the second party congress in 1980 and to 21 percent at the third congress in 1986. There were never any women among the nine members of the Communist party's Secretariat. Of the 150 full members of the Central Committee in 1983, sixteen (10.7 percent) were women, and there were twelve women (14.6 percent) among the eighty-two alternate members.[5]

The minority status of women in the party was clearly an embarrassment to Cuba's "revolutionary" leadership. At the third congress in 1986 Fidel Castro expressed concern over the party's overwhelmingly white male profile. He stipulated that women's representation must be "in keeping with their participation, and their important contribution to the building of socialism in our country must be ensured."[6]

Despite Castro's words and an ensuing shakeup in the top party lineup in 1986, however, the figures did not change dramatically. FMC chief Vilma Espín was promoted to full membership in the Politburo after having served many years as an alternate. Of the 141 full members of the Central Committee in 1988, nineteen (13.5 percent) were women, and there were twenty-one women (26.6 percent) among the seventy-nine alternate members.[7]

The much-postponed fourth party congress, in October 1991 introduced further changes to give the party a more youthful image. The Politburo was expanded to twenty-five permanent members, and a number of "historic" members including Vilma Espín were removed. Three new women were appointed. One was a party official from Santiago de Cuba; the other two, a biochemist and a sugar industry expert, represented Cuba's new technocratic class. Still, women constituted only 12 percent of the Politburo membership.[8] The new Central Committee consisted of 225 full members, of whom 38 (17 percent) were women.[9]

Typically, organizations with a younger membership featured more women in positions of authority. For example, there were always more women in the Union of Young Communists than in the party itself. In 1988 six of the twenty-four members (25 percent) of the Secretariat and Executive Bureau of the Union of Young Communists were women. Women also comprised 25 percent of the 152 full members of the National Committee of the Young Communists, and 39 percent of the alternate members.[10]

Women were somewhat better represented in the Confederation of Cuban Workers (Confederación de Trabajadores Cubanos, or CTC) than in the Communist party. In 1975 women comprised 25 percent of the workforce and 24 percent of municipal labor leaders, but at the national level only 7 percent of union leaders were women. By 1983, 45 percent of municipal labor leaders were women while only 14 percent of the CTC's national paid staff were women. In 1990 women constituted 22 percent of the National Council of the CTC.[11]

Women were also significantly underrepresented in the top state structures. In the Council of State as of December 1989 there were twenty-five men and four women (13.8 percent). In the forty-five-member Council of Ministers there were two women, Sonia Rodríguez Cardona, minister president of the State Committee for Labor and Social Security, and Rosa Elena Simeón, president of the Cuban Academy of Sciences.[12]

This pattern continued in Cuba's legislative branch, the People's Power. Established in 1974 in part as a response to international criticism that Cuba lacked elective bodies, the People's Power consisted of municipal and provincial councils with limited local powers. Its members were elected every two and a half years. In the 1981 elections only 8 percent (843) of the 10,735 delegates elected were women.[13] The figure increased to 11.5 percent in 1984, and 17.1 percent in 1986.[14] In 1989 the number of women elected in municipal elections declined slightly to 16.8,[15] with less than 5 percent (8 out of 169) of the presidents of municipal councils that year being women.[16] None of Cuba's fourteen provincial presidents was a woman.[17] In the 1992 municipal elections women's overall representation declined to 13.6 percent.[18] Women constituted 7 percent of those elected president of a municipal council that year, and 3 of the 169 municipalities were headed by women presidents and vice presidents.[19]

Women fared better in the National Assembly, the highest organ of the People's Power. The National Assembly met twice a year for three- or four-day sessions to provide a forum for the discussion and approval of laws, but it had no real power. The 1981 National Assembly had 113 women (22.6 percent) among its 499 members. By 1986 that figure had risen to 33 percent.[20]

Women's representation was lowest at the municipal level of the People's Power, where nominations and elections were the most direct. Women's poor showing in local elections reflected the same dilemma that kept them from advancing in the workplace: the double day. Municipal People's Power delegates were not paid; most had regular jobs, and so much of their work had to be done at night and on weekends. Surveys showed that most women, already juggling paid employment and household duties, were not interested in assuming extra responsibilities.[21] Both men and women concluded that a female delegate would not have sufficient time to do a good job.

A similar pattern of underrepresentation was found in Cuba's foreign policy establishment. In 1988 Cuba had diplomatic relations with 125 nations, but only twenty of the ambassadors or chargés accredited to those nations—16 percent—were women. Furthermore few Cuban women were assigned to Cuban embassies abroad. Of the seventy-two members of the Cuban embassy in Moscow in the mid-1980s, two were women. Similarly, not one of the twenty-one officials of the Cuban Interest Section in Washington were women.[22]

This absence of women in the front ranks of Cuban diplomacy was all the more striking in view of the ample opportunity to appoint women, given that virtually the entire prerevolutionary diplomatic corps went into exile or were purged, imprisoned, or retired after 1959. Young men without experience were given the opportunity. Women were not.

Women did fare better in the communications sector. In 1989 there were five women (26 percent) among the nineteen editors of Cuba's four national and fifteen provincial newspapers. Ten (38 percent) of Cuba's twenty-six magazines had women editors. Five (33 percent) of Cuba's fifteen publishing houses and one (17 percent) of Cuba's six national radio stations were headed by women.[23]

Women were also scanted in receiving national honors and medals. In 1982 the Félix Varela Medal, Cuba's highest national honor, was awarded to thirteen Cubans and non-Cubans. None was a woman.[24] In 1982, fifty-three Cubans received the Alejo Carpentier medal, the revolution's highest reward for cultural activity. Of these, ten (19 percent) were women. There was one award reserved for women, the Ana Betancourt medal, and its recipients included Haydée Santamaría, Alicia Alonso, and Angela Davis.

In 1990, when the Ministry of Higher Education honored the nation's best university researchers, four (18 percent) of the twenty-two persons selected were women—this despite the fact that women constituted more

than half of the university students and nearly half of the Cuban researchers. In 1992 only one (5.6 percent) of the eighteen awards went to a
woman.[25]

Finally, women were notably absent in the upper ranks of the most
prestigious institution in Cuban society, the military. Women's primary
military role was to fill the ranks of the voluntary Territorial Militias
(Milicias de Tropas Territoriales, or MTT), Cuba's civilian force. In 1990
half a million women of all ages belonged to the MTT. Women were
also allowed to volunteer in the regular armed forces, but they were ex-
empt from Cuba's obligatory national military service. Between 1984 and
1990 more than 10,000 women enlisted in the professional military.[26]
While at least three women attained the rank of colonel, there were no
women generals. In 1984 Major (later Lieutenant Colonel) Mirtha
García Lorca became the first woman commander of regular troops, in
charge of an all-female antiaircraft artillery regiment which later served
in Angola.[27]

Structure of the FMC

Since relatively few women were in positions of national influence, the
FMC served as the locus of women's power in revolutionary Cuba. The
FMC developed a multilayered structure like that of the Cuban Communist party. Below president Vilma Espín and the national command in
Havana were FMC units at the provincial, regional, and municipal levels,
and below that were blocks and delegations. The neighborhood delegations initially included from 20 to 200 members, but in the mid-1960s
they were restructured so that 50 was considered optimum. Each delegation had a secretary general elected by its members, plus secretaries for
each of the operating divisions.[28]

At the FMC's highest level was a national council and a secretariat
composed of the chiefs of the eight operating divisions: production, organization, finance, education, social services, ideological orientation, political studies and solidarity, and foreign relations. These chiefs were in
effect FMC cabinet ministers. In 1962 the FMC's National Council had
fifty-nine members, including Espín, Celia Sánchez, Haydée Santamaría,
and Aledia March (Che Guevara's second wife), as well as longtime communists such as Elena Gil and Clementina Serra. There were also notable
personalities such as the ballerina Alicia Alonso.

During the FMC's early years much of its local and national leadership,
including the president and the national council, was chosen through
direct elections by the membership. In 1974 the statutes were changed
to have the president and secretary general chosen by a national committee.[29]

In 1970 there were 27,370 FMC delegations in Cuba. Fifty-eight percent were urban and 40 percent rural, and 20 percent were located in

factories and work centers.[30] Over 130,000 women held official positions
in the organization. For many it was their first—and often only—experience in administration and organization. While this experience was supposed to train women for leadership in other spheres, in reality it may
have done the reverse by absorbing the energies of women who might
have otherwise found positions in the CTC (Confederation of Cuban
Labor), the party, or the state.

A visitor to a seventy-five-member delegation in Camagüey in 1974
found that a third of its members were activists, that is, they contributed
substantially to the FMC's work. The delegation's production secretary
kept a data book listing the delegation members, the number of children
they had, whether or not they were employed, and if not, why not. The
data books were helpful in planning not only social activities but also the
construction of schools and day care centers.[31]

The FMC received no government funding, and rather was financed
by members' dues. In the 1970s dues were three dollars a year, deducted
automatically from members' paychecks. FMC members (*federadas*)
sometimes complained that the collection of dues seemed to be the
FMC's principal concern. The FMC routinely donated surplus funds to
the state.[32]

The ideological role of the FMC became more rigorous over the years.
To become a *federada* in the early 1960s, one had agree to abide by the
FMC's objectives and regulations, get the support of two members, be
accepted by the local delegation, and pay the dues.[33] By 1974 the "five
minimum responsibilities" of a *federada* were to attend the monthly
meeting, participate in study circles, pay the quarterly dues, raise one's
children according to socialist precepts, contribute to the local delegation
and to the political development of housewives, and aid the local school
through the Militant Mothers for Education.[34]

Not all FMC members maintained a high level of involvement. Of 1.3
million *federadas* in 1970 there were only 89,169 "activists."[35] The rest
simply attended meetings. Over time, activists tended to be elected leaders, to be appointed to positions of responsibility, or even to be hired as
staff. During the 1960s almost all of the FMC's staff were full-time volunteers, but in 1974 the staff—now numbering fourteen thousand
women—began receiving salaries.[36]

The FMC was an intensely hierarchical organization. Until the late
1980s all its units were obliged to adhere to an annual work plan designed in Havana. Local and regional units were not permitted to determine their own activities. With its top-down lines of command and its
use of military terminology, the FMC—like all mass organizations in
Cuba—had a certain martial aura. Activities were perceived as battles,
struggles, campaigns; members were organized in brigades and detach-
ments. Uniformity was the watchword. In 1974 the FMC launched a
campaign to encourage proper sleeping habits in children, which included a contest "to select a figure and a melody that will be used every
day at a specific hour [on radio] to urge the children to go to sleep."[37]

FMC Congresses

The FMC held its first national congress in September 1962. Over the next twenty-eight years there were four more congresses: 1974, 1980, 1985, and 1990. These congresses offered Cuban women their best chance to influence policy, because Fidel Castro and other high-ranking policy makers inevitably attended. As much as a year prior to a national congress the FMC began reviewing its activities. Local officials and congress delegates were elected, one delegate per thousand *federadas*. "Red Sundays" of collective volunteer labor were scheduled. A congress "thesis" or set of principal issues and concerns was drawn up in Havana, then discussed by local delegations. A list of recommendations to policy makers was drawn up.

FMC congresses offered a forum for debate and letting off steam. Over the years topics included discrimination, the inadequacy of services such as day care and laundromats, inadequate shop hours, logistical problems presented by school vacations and insufficient boarding school slots, and whether men should be permitted to witness the birth of their children at maternity hospitals. Delegates voted on various congress resolutions by raising their hands. Approval tended to be unanimous.

The FMC congresses dealt only with practical issues. No *federada* would raise a question that challenged national policy on nuclear power plants, African adventures, or economic initiatives. Doing so would invade the realm of male elites. Each congress closed with a unanimously approved statement of support for the revolution and its leadership.

The profile of congress delegates did not reflect overall FMC membership. For example, while housewives constituted 70 percent of the FMC's membership in 1974, they constituted only 19 percent of the 1,932 delegates to the 1974 second FMC congress. The vast majority of delegates (78 percent) were working women.[38] Almost half of the delegates were members of the Communist party at a time when housewives were not allowed party membership.[39]

The FMC congresses would typically end with presentations by Vilma Espín and Fidel Castro which reviewed the state of the FMC and laid out its programs for the next five years. Castro spoke last, his addresses many times longer than those of his sister-in-law. Espín always made a fulsome salute to Fidel as the FMC's inevitable guide. "His words constitute a mandate," she said at the fourth congress in 1985. She concluded that "every member of the FMC will know how to fulfill her commitment of honor with the Party, to the Revolution, to Fidel."[40]

The first FMC congress, in September 1962, enabled the FMC to review its remarkable achievements. Under FMC guidance women had taken leading roles in an array of projects: the literacy campaign, the Ana Betancourt Schools, the schools for maids and prostitutes, the day care centers, the health brigades, the schools for the educational improvement of housewives, and the volunteer work brigades. The congress also considered problems. The FMC leadership was concerned about the failure of some of its leaders to consult the "collective directorate" in Havana. These tactics "cut off useful initiatives and alienated enthusiastic members."[41]

The congress revealed the FMC's cultural aspirations for Cuban women. It wanted them to read, and to appreciate music, dance, and theater. Delegations were urged to create minilibraries of selected great books. It also wanted women to engage in sports and asked for an end to bias against gym clothes for women.

The FMC directorate found its own magazine, *Mujeres,* to be doctrinaire, boring, and too difficult for the average Cuban woman. It was failing to provide an image of Cuban women as "filled with tenderness with a great love of humanity, of truth and beauty, and with profoundly firm political convictions."[42]

The second FMC congress, in November 1974, was a celebration of twelve years of progress. It was bracketed by events of great significance: the maternity law (1974), trial elections for the People's Power (1974), the first congress of the new Cuban Communist party and the party's release of its thesis on women's equality (1975), and the promulgation of a new constitution (1976).

The final report of the congress noted that housewives and peasant women were to be educated in Marxism-Leninism, exhorted to combat individualism and male chauvinism, and urged to foster an attitude of "conscious discipline and a love of work."[43] The FMC was to ensure that girls were integrated into socially useful activity and was to educate them "on the proper use of fashions" in socialist society.[44]

The FMC called on women to make sure their sons understood the importance of the military draft and the honor of military service. This idea was important in the mid-1970s as Cuba edged into a major military venture in Angola. FMC women played a traditional mothering role with the armed forces, holding good-bye parties for draftees, visiting them at isolated bases, helping to take care of their families if they were killed.

The dais at the FMC's second congress was dominated not by women but by men: Fidel Castro and several ministers. Cuban women aired their concerns to these decision makers and, in turn, were lectured by them. Castro saluted the many foreign delegates—there were representatives from fifty-five nations—and saw the progress of women as a global phenomenon. Cuban women themselves were advancing nicely. Women, he said, were "an impressive political force."[45]

The third congress, held in the Karl Marx Theater in Havana in March 1980, marked the twentieth anniversary of the FMC. Membership had reached 2,262,559. There were 51,912 delegations and 10,381 blocks.[46] Paradoxically, however, as the FMC grew in numbers, its national importance seemed to diminish. Programs once run by the FMC were now being taken over by others. The sewing academies, so important to the FMC's early history, had been turned over to the People's Power, as had the FMC's sports programs and Plan Jaba, the shopping bag plan (see chapter 8). The Ministry of Education ran the day care program.

Indeed, the congress revealed a growing concern about the FMC's vitality. "The work of the delegations and blocks is not satisfactory," the report to the congress noted. "On many occasions the meetings are not sufficiently prepared and their quality is low."[47] Attendance was slipping. Members found the meetings, with their heavy emphasis on ideological education, boring and irrelevant. In 1979, 90 percent of the delegations had held their required monthly meetings but only 64 percent of their members had attended. A few delegations had ceased to exist.

There were also problems within the "base." In 1980 only one of every seven FMC members was an "activist." The leadership was annoyed. It understood that students and working women sometimes couldn't participate, but the majority of FMC members were still housewives "who could do anything assigned to them."[48]

The gap between the congress delegates and FMC membership continued. In 1980, when only a small fraction of FMC members belonged to the Communist party and women constituted less than a third of the workforce, 55 percent of the delegates were party members and 69 percent were workers. While most FMC members were still housewives, only 23 percent of the delegates were.[49]

The FMC membership was aging. In 1975, 44 percent of congress delegates had been over forty years of age, but in 1980 that figure increased to 54 percent, this at a time when Cuba was experiencing a demographic surge of young women.[50] Efforts to encourage these young women to participate more would become an important priority in ensuing years.

ᴄ The third congress was marked by complaints about discrimination in the workforce and the lack of adequate services. For the first time, the FMC directly criticized another mass organization, the Confederation of Cuban Labor (CTC), for adopting gender-based resolutions which limited women's access to jobs (see chapter 10).[51] In ensuing years the FMC became increasingly outspoken in its criticism of policies and practices that hampered the advance of Cuban women.

The fourth congress, in March 1985, found the FMC both confident and vociferous. More issues and problems were discussed than ever before. There were major complaints against the CTC for its insensitivity and indifference to the problems and interests of working women. The FMC insisted that each workplace with female employees have at least one woman union representative. It demanded that women workers be given special consideration for receiving household appliances that were distributed to the public through work centers, and that mechanisms be established to sanction employers who violated women's rights. It asked that women's employment commissions be given more authority to hire women workers, and it called for affirmative action programs to allocate a specific percentage of leadership positions to women.[52]

The FMC protested that child support laws were inadequate and recommended that support payments be increased. It took on the media, urging that television programming for children be improved and that "disagreeable" music videos not be shown. It called for increased emphasis on sexual equality in the media and more attention to men's participation in the home. It urged that every newspaper dedicate a page a week to women's activities.[53]

The congress also celebrated many encouraging developments. Women were now entering the workforce at a higher rate than men and were staying in one job longer than men. Castro now appeared to agree that day care centers were of concern to men as well as women.[54]

The fifth FMC congress, scheduled for March 1990, came at a time of growing uncertainty. Cuba's great benefactor, the Soviet Union, had collapsed. There were disturbing signs that the new generation of young women, the best educated in Cuban history, was becoming alienated from the revolution. Changes had to be made. One important step was to give local FMC units more autonomy so they could respond to local needs and interests. The number of meetings was cut, and FMC dues were scaled back.[55]

There were disturbing signs that the FMC was becoming irrelevant. A random survey of a hundred women, taken a week before the fifth congress, revealed widespread indifference to the FMC. More than 70 percent of the respondents did not know that a congress of "their" organization was about to occur.[56]

The fifth congress focused on national unity. At the behest of the party, a number of agenda items were scrapped. The ominous slogan "socialism or death" became the congress theme.[57] Some delegates expressed concern for Fidel Castro's spirits, given current problems, and cited the need to prevent him from being overburdened by worries.[58] Vilma Espín reminded the fourteen hundred delegates of the achievements of the revolution and of their debt to socialism. The women replied by holding up picture placards of Celia Sánchez, heroine of the revolution. By the end of the congress Castro would be declared, by unanimous vote, "the son of all Cuban mothers and guide to all Cuban women."[59]

In 1960 Fidel Castro established the Federation of Cuban Women, a classic patron–clientelist maneuver which offered women a place in the new system in exchange for their loyalty and support. The basic ideological concepts that guided the FMC were determined by male elites, as was the overall revolutionary goal of "sexual equality" based primarily on a program of equal opportunity (with certain restrictions). Sharing power with women, however, was not a government priority.

Perhaps because most initiatives for "sexual equality" in revolutionary Cuba came not from women themselves but from male elites, women through the years showed more interest in obtaining state assistance to ease family duties than in increasing female representation in power. That the government might be more responsive to women's needs if it contained more women in policy-making positions appeared not to be a widely held view.

Cuban leaders argued that while male bias and traditional household responsibilities were a large part of the problem, many women were too passive. Women must become "more combative" in order to achieve leadership positions, said Esther Velis, FMC secretary of foreign relations.[60]

The FMC did achieve a number of advancements for Cuban women, including the Family Code of 1975, the development of affirmative action programs and job quotas to guarantee work for women in new industries, and a national sex education program. In the 1980s FMC lobbying became more public. Its tenacity paid off in generating attention and some support for paternity leave, in gaining permission for male relatives to attend to hospitalized family members, and in improving health services in day care centers so that mothers would not have to leave work to care for ill children.

Yet FMC concerns were not infrequently swept aside by "larger" considerations. In 1985 the FMC praised the peasant free markets as a boon to women and called for their expansion. In 1986 Castro shut them down.[61] In 1985 the FMC declared the new housing law "undoubtedly one of the greatest satisfactions that the people have received."[62] Two years later it too was rescinded.

The FMC was hobbled by the fact that there were no clearly established and universally understood mechanisms through which the organization might exercise its influence. By establishing the FMC as an "independent mass organization," the Cuban government gained access to and support from millions of women without having to concede specific powers in return. The FMC became a convenient means of ghettoizing women's concerns, of siphoning their energy and influence from other, more genuinely powerful institutions such as the Communist party and the upper ranks of state.

It appears, however, that the FMC was often the best of imperfect routes for women to influence real decision makers in Cuba. At a 1989 conference in Halifax, Nova Scotia, a representative of the FMC noted that a third of the members of the National Assembly of the People's Power were women, in her view a significant achievement. Yet when asked how women brought about changes in policy, she spoke of Fidel Castro's attendance at the FMC congresses. "He comes and listens to what needs to be done," she said.[63] However, FMC congresses occurred only once every five years, and Castro had consistently failed to address concerns voiced at earlier congresses. Women of the National Assembly could do little to influence policy, because the assembly was merely a rubber stamp for elite initiatives. Most interesting—and painful—was the FMC's acceptance of a formula by which every five years women pleaded their needs before the great patriarch. Everything was to be gained through and owed to the great chief.

The history of the FMC paralleled that of the revolution. At the beginning there were years of frenetic and innovative activity. Then as the revolution stabilized in the 1970s, innovation was gradually superseded by bureaucracy, routine, and a certain measure of boredom. By the end of the 1980s a new generation of women had grown to maturity under the revolution, and many were too highly educated for the FMC's simple formulas and "Havana knows best" mentality. This new generation did not have the time or inclination for FMC activities. They had outgrown the FMC. In part to rekindle women's belief in the FMC as a viable and relevant institution, the organization became increasingly outspoken on issues such as discrimination against women workers.

· Ironically, just when the FMC emerged as a more forceful advocate for women, public discussion of disbanding the FMC began to be heard. There was some speculation that the removal of a number of leading FMC members from the central committee at the fourth Communist party congress in 1991—members such as Dora Carcaño Araújo, secretary general of the FMC; Asela de los Santos Tamayo, former vice minister of education; Rosario Fernández Perera, national leader of the CTC; and Elida Valle Fernández, member of a special team of advisors to Fidel Castro—was an effort of the party to distance itself from a waning institution. Others suggested that because women—especially housewives, the bulk of FMC membership—were particularly sensitive to the realities of economic crisis, the party wished to forestall any potential for public criticism from within its own ranks.[64] The FMC was becoming moribund and irrelevant because it had neither the freedom to find its own voice and explore varied interests and policies nor sufficient power to pursue them.

5

Women and the Health Revolution

Society is moved to compassion upon hearing of the kidnapping or mur-
der of one child, but it is criminally indifferent to the mass murder of so
many thousands of children who die every year, in agonizing pain, due
to a lack of facilities.

Fidel Castro (1954)[1]

Our health indicators are the best in Latin America, the best in the
Third World, and among the best in the world.

Fidel Castro (1992)[2]

The transformation of Cuban health care is one of the principal achievements of the revolution. Medical care was made free and universal. The
new health system emphasized prevention, education, community
involvement, research, and the use of modern technology. As a result, the diseases that are usually found in Third World countries virtually disappeared. There were great advances also in maternal and child
health services, and—at least until the late 1980s—substantial improvements in nutrition. Routine access to good-quality health care transformed the condition and future prospects of millions of Cubans and
was an important source of popular support for the Castro government.

A key feature of Cuba's health revolution was the enormous growth
in the number of trained health care providers. Between 1953 and 1992
the number of doctors in Cuba grew by a factor of eight to nearly
50,000, and the number of nurses increased more than fifteen times to
some 70,000.[3] Women were important participants in this growth. From
1953 to 1990 women's representation among doctors rose from 6 to 48
percent and among dentists from 18 to 69 percent, and the amount of
women increased from 68 to 88 percent of all nurses.[4] Tens of thousands
of women volunteers augmented the services offered by professional

57

medical personnel, and women researchers played a major role in the island's growing medical research effort.

Interestingly, the increased presence of women in medicine did not lead to its devaluation as a vocation. Rather, medicine continued to be the most prestigious career in Cuban society.

Cuba's health revolution also had its problems. Health was politicized. Health information was delivered to the Cuban public on a "need to know" basis. Health care was physician oriented and offered few alternative approaches. Quality was inconsistent, some medicines were in scant supply, and corruption was not unknown. While great strides were made in the reduction of many contagious diseases, others defied revolutionary efforts. Furthermore, the economic decline of the early 1990s brought severe shortages of food and medicine and threatened to undercut many of the system's earlier achievements.

Prerevolutionary Health Care

Health services designed specifically for women began in the late nineteenth century with the opening in Havana of a maternity hospital for homeless women. Women's role in medicine was limited to that of caring helper, providing comfort and attention to patients. Cuba's first female physician, a French immigrant, found it necessary to pose as a man in order to practice. When she was found out in 1824, she was imprisoned.[5]

Cuba graduated its first woman doctor in 1889. The U.S. occupation (1899–1902) brought the establishment of a dental faculty at the University of Havana and a school of nursing with American nurses serving as instructors. Women's participation in the health sector gradually increased. Even so, by 1943 only thirty of Havana's one thousand doctors were women.[6]

By the 1950s Cuba's health facilities had grown substantially. Care was provided through three different mechanisms. First, mutual assistance societies served immigrants and prosperous workers in the cities. By 1959 they employed about half of all physicians on the island.[7] Second, private clinics, which began appearing in urban areas in the 1920s, increasingly became the choice for Cuba's growing middle class. To be attended at a private clinic was an important indicator of social status. Third, for the poor there were state hospitals. In 1956 less than a quarter of Cuba's practicing physicians and only 4 percent of its dentists were working for the state.[8]

Poor women and children could also seek help from charitable organizations. *Casas de socorro,* or alms houses, offered maternity care to poor women. Havana's most famous poorhouse, the Casa de Beneficencia, had a miniature swinging door through which parents could leave unwanted babies; this establishment remained in operation until 1963.[9]

Medical care was largely an urban phenomenon. In the 1930s half of the nation's physicians and more than half of its hospital beds were in Havana.[10] In the 1950s Cuba produced some three hundred medical students a year, but many emigrated to the United States. Cuba's one dental school produced forty dentists a year, far too few to address the island's needs. Three of Cuba's six nursing schools were located in Havana, and trained nurses were employed primarily in the mutualist and private sectors. There were no training programs for other health practitioners. The state health service relied largely upon self-trained practical nurses who often had no more than a third-grade education.[11]

Peasants usually relied on folk healers: herbalists, midwives, and priests of the Afro-Cuban religion Santería.[12] Folk medicine in prerevolutionary Cuba reflected deeply rooted gender views, including a subtle deprecation of women. For example, many peasants believed that women's menstrual blood contained a virulent parasite that could attack men's nervous systems and cause madness. Widespread fear of unwanted pregnancies was reflected in the number and variety of abortives prescribed by rural healers.[13]

Life expectancy in the 1950s was fifty-eight years; in the countryside it was less. The leading cause of death was infectious diseases. The maternal mortality rate was 120 per 100,000 live births.[14] The infant mortality rate was alleged to be 36 deaths per 1,000 live births, a figure some consider suspiciously low.[15]

A New Health System

The health revolution which shook the Cuban medical establishment to the core was launched in 1960. In January the Law of Rural Medical Service initiated the construction of hospitals and clinics in the countryside. All medical school graduates were now obliged to practice one year in a rural zone to repay the government for their education. Mortified by the specter of socialized medicine, nearly half of the island's doctors, including virtually the entire medical teaching staff at the University of Havana, went into exile. In addition, the island's medicine chest was depleted by the U.S. economic embargo of 1962. For years the island suffered shortages of even basic items such as aspirin and contraceptives.

In 1961 all extant health institutions were folded into the newly formed Ministry of Public Health (Ministerio de Salud Pública, or MINSAP). Health care was now the right of all citizens and the responsibility of the state. By 1962 Cuba's state health budget was four times that of the Batista era.[16] All medical school graduates after 1965 would be state employees. Cuba's long tradition of private medicine had ended.

Preventive medicine was given new emphasis. There were aggressive health education programs and nationwide campaigns to inoculate the public against infectious diseases. The new system encouraged community participation, particularly through the mass organizations. The Association of Small Farmers helped establish rural clinics. The Committees for the Defense of the Revolution carried out polio immunizations. The Federation of Cuban Women (FMC) worked to reduce infant and maternal mortality through various outreach programs and helped educate women on fundamental health issues and practices. The FMC's magazines, *Mujeres* and *Muchacha,* became important sources of health information for Cuban women.

It was an exciting time for medical idealists. In 1960 Dr. Edith González and her husband established the first rural medical clinic in Mayarí, a small town in eastern Cuba. They found residents who had no names and who were unsure of their children's ages—people "living on the margins of civilization." [17]

The medical revolution undercut the livelihoods and prestige of traditional folk healers. Thousands of midwives were replaced by young university-trained doctors whose services were free. Although the midwives had aided in the birth of countless Cubans, the new doctors scorned them for their ignorance.[18] Eventually an effort was made to engage midwives, healers, and herbalists in revolutionary programs. Some were retrained and employed in the rural health centers.

In the early years of the revolution, local outpatient centers called polyclinics were introduced throughout Cuba. These polyclinics offered dental care, obstetrics and gynecology, pediatrics and internal medicine. Patients with serious or chronic illnesses were referred to regional hospitals for treatment. In 1987 there were 422 polyclinics throughout Cuba.[19]

One of the key issues addressed by the health revolution was the nation's diet. Malnutrition affected more than a third of the Cuban population prior to 1959, and fully two-thirds of those living in rural areas. In 1960 a program of "nutritional recuperation" was begun for malnourished children up to age five: for approximately three months mothers stayed with their children in special residences and were taught food preparation, basic hygiene, and proper infant care. The program continued for twenty years.[20]

Rice, beans, and root vegetables were the primary foods for most Cubans prior to the revolution. After 1959 meat became more widely available. In 1962 rationing was introduced to ensure equal access to basic foodstuffs. Prices for basic items were subsidized. A "parallel market" was created to sell unrestricted items at higher prices. As time passed, some products such as eggs became plentiful and were removed from the rationing system. The daily caloric content of the Cuban diet increased from 2,500 calories in 1956 to 2,967 in 1987.[21] Pregnant women received special meat and milk allowances, and children under five received an extra liter of milk a day. In 1987 it was estimated that 67 percent of daily calories consumed came from rationed foodstuffs.[22]

In the 1990s, as the breakup of the Soviet Union devastated the Cuban economy, many food items again became scarce. Cuban families were urged to plant victory gardens and to volunteer for agricultural work on state farms.[23] The Cuban media began to stress the use of local products as substitutes for imports.

Despite the problems, by 1992 Cuba's health statistics rivaled those of the developed world. Infant mortality had dropped to 10.2 per 1,000 live births. Vaccinations against eleven childhood diseases and infections reached 95 percent of the targeted population, contributing to the 98.8 percent survival rate of Cuban children during the first five years of life. Maternal mortality was at 3.2 per 10,000 live births. Overall life expectancy in Cuba had reached 77.22 years.[24]

Women Volunteers: Brigadistas and Acompañantes

Many Cuban women began their participation in the health revolution as volunteers. The FMC provided volunteer health workers during emergencies such as the Bay of Pigs invasion and the Cuban missile crisis. In 1964 the FMC organized the Sanitary Brigades, a nationwide program of women health volunteers. Participants, called *brigadistas,* would play a vital role in education and preventive medicine. *Brigadistas* inoculated their neighbors against polio, tetanus, and diphtheria; conducted community discussions about issues such as sanitation, contraception, and cancer; encouraged pregnant women to keep doctors' appointments; and reminded women to have their yearly Pap smear. After the mid-1970s the number of *brigadistas* leveled off to about sixty thousand women nationwide.[25]

Women from all walks of life became *brigadistas,* attending a thirty-one-hour course conducted by the Cuban Red Cross. Ideally, thirty *brigadistas* were assigned to each "health sector" of three thousand to five thousand inhabitants. In areas of low population density the *brigadistas* established first aid stations. Civil defense brigades were also organized to give aid during war or natural disasters.[26] The Sanitary Brigades gave many women the opportunity to participate in an activity in which they had an interest but no formal training. Some women who began as *brigadistas* went on to professional medical careers.

A typical *brigadista,* Nelda Pacheco, working in 1973 in Pinar del Río, was looking after five pregnant women, three premature infants, four people with muscular dystrophy, and one diabetic in her assigned microsector. During her visits to the patients' homes, Nelda recorded the answers of the pregnant women on a standard questionnaire: "Are your feet inflamed? When is your next doctor's appointment? Have you been to the dentist? Are there animals living in the house? . . ."[27]

Occasionally the volunteers' constant solicitations were resented, but the *brigadistas* persisted. They advised pregnant women on proper food and clothing, encouraged them to participate in natural childbirth classes, and reminded them of the virtues of breastfeeding. At local polyclinics *brigadistas* helped keep patients' obstetric records.[28]

The FMC also sponsored "health debates" on selected topics at monthly block meetings. The "debates" focused on articles on specific health themes published in the FMC's *Mujeres* magazine. In 1975 half a million women a month participated in these debates.[29]

During the 1960s the FMC health debates provided basic sanitary education, such as the proper method of constructing a latrine, safe food preparation, and elementary personal hygiene.[30] The first topic specifically related to women, breastfeeding, appeared in 1962. Women were encouraged to nurse their children and to shun prepared infant formulas. They were assured that nursing during menstruation was safe and did not cause a woman's breasts to lose their firmness.[31] In the 1970s the health debates focused on reproductive health matters, including menopause, menstruation, puberty, and ovulation.

In 1970 a "mother companion" program was begun to assist small children during hospital stays. "Mother companions," typically female relatives, were given a special uniform and were encouraged to feed, bathe, and entertain the children. The practice was so successful in reducing children's stress that it was introduced even in intensive care units.[32]

In 1985, women at the fourth congress of the FMC argued that the mother companion rule, which allowed mothers but not fathers to accompany their children in hospitals, was unfair. Husbands ought to share in this process, they felt. Castro agreed that keeping men out of hospitals is "really reverse discrimination,"[33] and so over the next few years the companion program was opened to fathers and other male relatives.

The Family Doctor Program

In 1983 the Ministry of Public Health established the family doctor program, an ambitious new initiative designed to replace the polyclinic as the primary community health unit. Each family doctor team consisted of a general practitioner and a nurse. After graduation, family doctors were assigned for two-year stints to areas where their services were needed. By 1990, 64 percent all family doctors were women.[34]

The first priority of the family doctor program was to bring professional (as opposed to volunteer) medical care to the mountainous Sierra Maestre region. In some cases there were no roads and materials had to be carried in by mules or helicopter.[35] By fall 1988 the family doctor target for mountainous areas had been met. Family doctors were also assigned to day care centers, schools, factories, homes for the elderly, the Ministry of the Interior, and the armed forces. By 1992, family doctors were attending to 68 percent of all Cubans.[36]

One such doctor, twenty-four-year-old Dr. Blanca Gómez Pérez, in

1987 was attending to the health of 933 people in a remote village in Guantánamo province. Her patients included 91 children under age four, 14 pregnant women, and 40 residents over age sixty-five. She counseled local residents to replace dirt floors in their homes with concrete, to build better latrines, and to come to the clinic when they were sick. She had electricity for only four hours a day. Although she found her experience rewarding, Dr. Gómez Pérez hoped to eventually work in a hospital.[37]

The FMC's *brigadistas* worked closely with the family doctor program. *Brigadistas* kept track of area residents, helped to organize exercise programs for the elderly, and performed clerical duties. It was not uncommon in some neighborhoods for the entire health team—doctor, nurse, and volunteers—to be female.

General Health Programs

In the first decade of the revolution diseases such as hepatitis, measles, and malaria were significantly reduced. By the 1970s the leading causes of death in Cuba were the same as those of the developed world: heart disease, cancer, and stroke. These diseases could be fought, at least in part, through changes in public behavior. Women could help avoid heart disease by losing weight, preparing more healthful meals, and exercising more. Women could lessen the risk of cancer by cutting back on their smoking, which had increased significantly after 1959.

Weight was a tricky issue in Cuba. A foreigner living in Cuba during the 1970s found that Cuban mothers believed that a fat child was a healthy child. Some mothers even stimulated their children's appetite with antihistamines or wine. Cuban standards of beauty favored ample curves. The exclamation, "How fat you are!" was a compliment meaning, "You look terrific!"[38]

Complicating this enthusiasm for food is Cubans' affection for fried foods high in saturated fats. Cubans also add sugar to meats, bean soups, cocktails, appetizers, salads, and coffee, let alone desserts. By the early 1980s Cubans were consuming one kilo of sugar per capita per week.[39] The result was widespread obesity. In the late 1980s Cuban officials estimated that approximately 30 percent of the residents of Havana and 25 percent of all Cubans were obese.[40] More than two-thirds of those considered obese were women. Indeed at the fourth national congress of the FMC Fidel Castro peered over the podium and noted that "some of you here are a bit rotund."[41]

A major educational campaign was launched to encourage Cubans to eat better and exercise more. Public service messages in magazines and on radio and television advised Cubans to eat more vegetables, fish, and fruit and to reject "sedentary living."

The antiobesity drive was complicated by Cubans' abhorrence of unnecessary physical activity. One observer noticed that Cubans would "wait in the sweltering heat for a crowded bus rather than walk a few blocks."[42] Physical exertion in Cuba's tropical climate produced perspiration, offensive to Cuban fastidiousness. Nonetheless a campaign to encourage exercise was begun, with women being its principal targets. The FMC opened exercise centers all over Cuba.[43] Exercise classes were also offered through the FMC Schools for Sewing and Dressmaking, and aerobics were introduced in schools and at work. The beauty-enhancing and antiaging aspects of exercise were stressed. The women's magazines featured monthly sections on exercises that target specific problem areas such as "love handles" or "spare tires." A television exercise program for women was broadcast each Saturday afternoon.[44]

The government also tried to combat smoking. In 1976 the World Health Organization ranked Cuba twelfth in the per capita consumption of cigarettes and cigars. By the early 1980s Cuba had advanced to third place. As men reduced their smoking—led by Fidel Castro, who gave up his beloved cigars—smoking among women was on the rise. Thirty-five to 40 percent of Cuban women and 43 percent of adolescent girls smoked. Authorities were concerned that the gap between women's and men's death rates due to heart disease (164.1 per 100,000 for women versus 203.3 per 100,000 for men in 1989) would continue to shrink as more and more women lit up. Smoking also threatened to increase the incidence of lung cancer in women, which, at 11.5 per 100,000 in 1979, was already high.[45]

The Ministry of Public Health therefore launched an antismoking campaign. One ad featured a handsome young woman who asked: "Do you want to be beautiful and healthy? Then don't smoke." It warned that smoking causes bad breath, yellow teeth, and premature aging.[46]

The Cuban medical establishment was also concerned about breast, uterine, and cervical cancer. A national program of Pap smear testing was begun in 1967. Women in the high-risk group, that is, "married women of any age and single women over thirty," were to be tested every two years.[47] Surprisingly few women took the test. In 1987, 700,000 women, roughly one of every six, were tested, and eight hundred cases of cancer were detected. Of those, 89 percent were at an early stage, which, according to Cuban health experts, guaranteed successful treatment.[48]

Breast cancer is the leading cause of cancer death among Cuban women. Between 1979 and 1989 the annual number of such deaths doubled from 400 to 800.[49] All women over age twenty were urged to practice monthly breast self-examination, and an annual physical examination was prescribed for all women over forty. Both ultrasound and mammograms were used for diagnosis and detection.

Several pilot programs for the early detection of breast cancer were implemented in the late 1980s. In 1989 the World Health Organization provided fifteen mobile units to conduct mammograms. Each van featured ultrasound machines and computers and could complete up to a hundred examinations daily.[50] Cuba also imported a linear electrode accelerator for the treatment of tumors, thereby, according to one doctor, raising Cuba "to the world level in the field of current radiotherapy."[51]

Until 1980 all women diagnosed with breast cancer received radical mastectomies. After 1980 modified radical surgery, which leaves the large pectoral muscle intact, began to be employed. In 1988 segmental surgery, which removes only 25 percent of breast tissue, was being used for women with small tumors. Breast reconstruction using either abdominal tissues or the implantation of silicone prostheses was available for mastectomy survivors.[52]

Modern surgical techniques were evident in other spheres of Cuban health as well. By the 1990s transplant surgery—kidney, liver, heart, and lung—had become almost routine in Cuba.[53] In 1988 Cuba became the third nation to complete a neurological tissue transplant to combat Parkinson's disease. The operation was directed by neurosurgeon Dr. Hilda Molina Morejón, the first woman in the world to direct such an operation.[54]

Cuba's health revolution increased the longevity of the island's population. Indeed, by the early 1990s the increased life span posed a growing social dilemma as the island's facilities for the elderly were insufficient, and housewives who at one time looked after aging family members now had jobs and careers outside the home.

Aging, and its impact on beauty, remained of great concern to Cuba's women. Revolutionary heroine Haydée Santamaría admitted to an interviewer in 1977 that for years she lied about her age. To defy time, she was planning to dye her hair blond and have a face-lift "when I get over the fright of the operation."[55]

The stresses introduced by revolutionary change created considerable need for psychological counseling for many Cubans. According to Cuban psychiatrists, counseling was needed to deal with the extraordinary changes in the roles of men and women. Stress was also generated by generational conflicts over child rearing, frustrations over housing, and other problematic factors in daily life.[56]

While Cuban officials recognized the existence of tensions within the family, they insisted, sometimes very vehemently, that Cuba did not suffer from domestic violence. Thus there were no shelters for battered wives, no stories in the media about child abuse or violence in the home. Domestic violence and rape were portrayed as problems that plagued capitalist countries.[57] Neither was mentioned in government statistics of crime in Cuba, nor in public addresses by the minister of the interior.[58] When one of the nation's leading obstetrician/gynecologists, Dr. Ada Ovies, was asked about the procedure for assisting rape victims, she dismissed the issue as "a matter for the police."[59]

The Cuban media did not recognize the existence of domestic violence until 1992. Journalist Mirta Rodríguez Calderón blamed the long silence on the Cuban custom of "washing dirty laundry within the family." A

prominent prosecutor concurred, saying that in Cuba "self-respecting
people refuse to bring such matters before a judge." A second prosecutor
estimated that only one of every hundred cases of domestic violence in
Cuba ever reached the courts. A third prosecutor reported that in his
municipality 75 percent of the victims of domestic violence were women,
while 10 percent were children or the elderly.[60]

Although Cuba has produced little data on male violence against
women, there has been some documentation of women's violence against
themselves. In 1970—the last time suicide statistics by gender were publicly reported—Cuban women between fifteen and twenty-four had a suicide rate twice that of men. In contrast to international trends, married
persons in Cuba were the most likely to commit suicide, while those who
had never married were the least likely.[61] In 1978 suicide ranked as the
sixth leading cause of death in the country (after accidents).[62] The 1981
annual report by the Cuban Ministry of Public Health indicated that, at
27.5 deaths per 100,000 inhabitants, Cuba had one of the highest suicide
rates in the world.[63] When Haydée Santamaría, one of the leading
women of the revolution, committed suicide in 1980, she was buried
with full honors. Nonetheless, Cuban officials announced that suicide
"would never be acceptable in a revolutionary society."[64]

Sexually Transmitted Diseases and AIDS

According to the Cuban media, Cubans became more sexually promiscuous in the 1970s and 1980s. One result was a significant increase in
sexually transmitted diseases. By 1985 syphilis was twice as prevalent as
in 1965, and the gonorrhea rate had increased fortyfold.[65] Infection
seemed to be more common in the cities than in the countryside. Some
speculated that this situation was due to a resurgence of prostitution;
others linked it to the overseas service of some 400,000 Cuban soldiers
in Angola in the 1970s and 1980s. The promotion of stable relationships
became a major tenet of the government's sex education programs in
the 1980s.

Almost all those who sought treatment for sexually transmitted diseases in Cuba were men. Because women are asymptomatic in four out
of five cases, many were unaware of their illness. Men who admit they
have a venereal disease face considerably less social stigma than women
in such circumstances. Polyclinic nurses were encouraged to inquire into
the sexual history of individuals who sought treatment, in order to find
and cure their female partners.[66]

The Cuban government reacted to the AIDS threat with great energy,
implementing a series of unprecedented policies to contain the disease
and its carriers. Cuba's AIDS policies reflected a traditional view that
men are incapable of sexual restraint and that women who engage in sex
with different partners are "promiscuous." Yet despite the revolution's

past mistreatment of homosexuals, the Cuban media was restrained in its portrayal of the homosexual aspect of AIDS transmission.

One of the first major public discussions of AIDS in Cuba came in a full-page newspaper article in April 1987.[67] Soon thereafter there began a massive testing program of blood donors, pregnant women in the first trimester, and patients admitted to hospitals. Others who were routinely tested included hemophiliacs, persons seeking treatment for sexually transmitted diseases, and those returning from extended stays abroad.

In June 1988 the Ministry of Public Health reported that almost all AIDS victims in Cuba were members of high-risk groups, that is, male homosexuals, bisexuals, and those who engaged in sex with foreigners. Lesbians had been publicly identified as low risk.[68] Only 4 of the 166,359 pregnant women tested to that date proved HIV positive. Three had contracted the virus from their steady partners, while the fourth was "a promiscuous young woman who frequently had sex with foreigners."[69] By mid-1992 more than twelve million HIV tests had been administered and 772 HIV positive Cubans (554 men and 218 women) had been identified, 67 of whom died from the disease.[70]

Despite the Cuban medical community's acceptance of therapeutic abortions for genetic fetal abnormalities (see chapter 6), some HIV positive women have been allowed to carry their pregnancies to term, although they are reportedly "counseled" to have abortions.[71] In 1990 all sixteen of the early-term pregnant women who had been found to be seropositive had reportedly "sought" abortions.[72]

Most controversial, at least among foreign observers, was Cuba's policy of quarantining HIV carriers in special sanitariums. The first AIDS treatment facility, Los Cocos, was opened in April 1986. The "patients" were allowed visits by family members and friends but were not allowed to leave without supervision. Residents from Havana and environs were allowed a weekly leave on Sundays, and those who lived farther away were allowed four days every month and a half. The "patients" were chaperoned by paramedics to prevent any sexual contact with persons outside the facility. In 1989 Los Cocos director Dr. Jorge Pérez Avila claimed that a chaperon was necessary because "our responsibility doesn't end at the doors of the institution, we must see to the health of everyone."[73]

Cuban officials defended the policy of quarantine as necessary given that Cuban men could not be trusted to restrain themselves sexually.[74] One chronicler of Cuban AIDS policy has asserted that this lack of confidence in the ability to change male behavior has "led to the general exclusion of recommendations to use condoms" as a means of preventing AIDS transmission.[75] Nevertheless, she reports, condom sales rose dramatically (38 percent) during the first five months of 1988.

There was significant public support for the sweeping measures taken in response to the AIDS threat. Respondents to an internal 1988 Cuban Communist Party survey on public health care in Holguín province revealed overwhelming public approval for current policies. Of those who offered suggestions, 27 percent urged that "measures be taken with homosexuals" *(que se tomen medidas con los homosexuales)*, while 11 percent called for compulsory AIDS tests for "women who change sexual partners frequently or who go out with foreigners."[76]

6

Reproductive Health

Woman is nature's workshop where life is forged.

Fidel Castro (1974)[1]

Sound children assure the magnificent heredity of our revolution.

Dr. José González, obstetrician and author (1985)[2]

We fervently defend the right and choice of all women to be mothers, of all men to be fathers, but we energetically refuse to echo the "pro-life" campaign that in these times is undergoing an unusual boom in the capitalist world.

Dr. Monika Krause, sex education official (1987)[3]

Is it logical that abortion is used as a contraceptive method when the other methods are one hundred times cheaper and ten thousand times less offensive?

Mirta Rodríguez Calderón, journalist (1989)[4]

Abortion is a matter for townspeople. Here in the countryside women give birth and that's that.

Roberto Hernández, oxcart driver (1989)[5]

The improvement of maternal, infant, and child health has been among the principal goals of Cuba's health revolution. Cuban women came to have free access to high-quality prenatal and postnatal medical services, contraception, and abortion. By 1992 infant mortality had declined to 10.2 deaths per 1,000 live births, and maternal mortality stood at 3.2 per 10,000 live births, the lowest figures in Latin America.[6] These achievements were a source of great local pride and international prestige for the revolution.

69

Education played a major role in improvements in reproductive health in Cuba. Basic information on reproduction was brought to citizens through the schools, mass organizations, and the media. In 1985 the first comprehensive woman's health guide was published by the Ministry of Public Health to give women "in a simple, readable and easily understandable form all information regarding their sex."[7]

Menstruation and Menopause

In the past, women's reproductive power had been the object of myth and misinformation. Some Cubans thought menstruation was a fearful and shameful event which unleashed mysterious forces capable of a wide range of phenomena from curdling milk to driving men to madness. Menopause was traditionally viewed as ending not only a woman's reproductive capacity but her sexual life as well. Interestingly, menopause often brought Cuban women wider mobility and status in the family and community.

After 1959 Cuba's health education program attempted to dispel commonly held myths regarding women's reproduction. However, a tension emerged in Cuba, as elsewhere, between educational efforts to establish reproductive cycles as normal and legal tendencies to recognize their abnormal effect. For example, the 1979 Cuban criminal code stipulated that "the upheavals that are produced by menopause, pregnancy, the menstrual period, or a pathological state following birth" could be a factor in crimes committed by women.[8] In some cases these conditions were deemed sufficient to exonerate a woman of criminal responsibility. In 1983 a University of Havana penal expert confirmed that "women during these periods, and above all during menopause, present an irritable emotionality, an emotional instability, that inclines them to commit crimes, and above all, crimes of passion."[9]

The government was not always attentive to the practical needs associated with women's reproductive cycle. For example, for thirty-five years there were simply not enough sanitary napkins in Cuba. In 1988, 30 million packages a year were produced, a number that *Granma* considered "still very inadequate."[10]

Tampons were not available in revolutionary Cuba, although some women made their own out of cotton. Officials claimed that no tampons were produced because of concern over toxic shock syndrome, low demand from Cuban women, and traditional taboos about women touching their genitalia.[11]

Contraception

Cuba's health revolution accelerated a historic trend toward smaller families. In the 1920s Cuban women had an average of six children; in the

1950s they were having slightly fewer than four.[12] Cubans in urban areas had access to intrauterine devices, diaphragms, condoms, and spermicides. Diaphragms were used primarily by educated women. Condoms were associated with prostitution and were thus spurned by "respectable" women. Many Cubans in the countryside still relied on herbal remedies. Withdrawal and vaginal irrigation were other common, if unreliable and even dangerous, means of avoiding pregnancy.

The early years of the revolution were marked by great confusion in the contraceptive realm. As a Cuban demographer later remarked, the revolutionary government "made the prevention of births difficult."[13] It began rigorously to enforce existing antiabortion laws. In addition, the U.S. economic embargo of 1962 cut Cuba's links to its traditional supplier of contraceptive devices. These developments, plus a wave of revolutionary optimism, all contributed to a baby boom.[14]

Contraceptive materials remained in short supply throughout the first decade of the revolution. Condoms from China were of poor quality, and imported birth control pills were too expensive. Given the dearth of birth control options, the government made female sterilization available free of charge to anyone who wanted the operation.[15]

Cuba began producing intrauterine devices in the 1960s. IUDs were already a popular form of birth control, and they cost little to manufacture. Volunteers from the Federation of Cuban Women (FMC) fashioned intrauterine rings from nylon fishing line. These IUDs, which remained in use into the 1980s, reportedly provoked fewer side effects than did the rigid plastic IUDs Cuba had previously imported and would later import again.[16]

The revolution was at first reluctant to promote family planning. Some Latin American nationalists perceived family planning as an imperialist plot to hinder population growth. During the 1960s doctors were authorized to respond to specific birth control questions by patients, but they did not offer unsolicited information or contraceptive devices.[17]

As the 1960s drew to a close, there was growing concern that better public education about contraception was needed. Statistics showed that not only was teenage pregnancy on the rise, but women were continuing to use abortion as a means of birth control. By the 1970s Cuba's improving economy allowed for the importation of various birth control devices.

Improved contraception was designed to help reduce Cuba's high rate of abortion. However, medical officials failed to make public information on the risks associated with various birth control methods. Articles in the popular press made no mention of the potentially dangerous side effects of the IUD and the birth control pill. One 1978 article even stated that there was no evidence that contraception poses health risks to women.[18]

While Cuban officials urged more contraceptive use, they failed to develop national statistics on that subject. As of 1983, for example, such statistics were collected only at the hospital or clinic level and were not computed nationally. Thus the Ministry of Public Health could not determine the pattern of contraceptive use or the incidence of side effects. From time to time medical officials even neglected to order contraceptive devices, causing shortages.[19]

In the late 1980s the Cuban Society for the Development of the Family issued a pamphlet on contraception which for the first time discussed the advantages and disadvantages of available methods. Curiously, however, no health risks were listed for the IUD. Nonetheless, sex education officials admitted elsewhere that complications from IUD use proved to be one of the most common causes of female infertility in Cuba.[20]

Beginning in 1973 condoms were promoted by the Cuban government as the best all-around contraceptive because they required male participation, presented no health risks, and provided protection against sexually transmitted diseases. Condoms were seen as particularly well suited to teenagers, given their irregular sexual activity and the inadvisability of IUD and pill use at an early age.

As of the late 1980s the IUD continued to be the most widely used birth control device in Cuba among adult women, while birth control pills were the first choice of Cuban teenagers. The pills were available without a prescription, although a doctor's visit was encouraged before their use.

In the 1980s Cuba began offering a contraceptive injection which protected against pregnancy for up to three months. In 1988 a five-year injection became available. The only reported side effects were dysmenorrhea, spotting, and cramping.

Female sterilization was authorized only for women who had three or more living children or for whom pregnancy might be life threatening. The husband's written permission was required.[21] Cuban health officials promoted vasectomy as a safe, easy, and progressive method of contraception. It was "more convenient" than female sterilization because it could be done on an outpatient basis. Men did not have to get their wives' consent for a vasectomy.

Though contraceptive devices were widely available in the 1980s, they were not always used. A 1989 study of three hundred women seeking abortions revealed that while virtually all knew about birth control, 80 percent had failed to use it even though none of the women wanted to become pregnant.[22] Yusemi Cabrera, a twenty-three-year-old woman with a degree in naval construction, indicated her resentment of government meddling in contraceptive decisions. Unable to take birth control pills because they made her sick, she opted for the IUD, which also proved to be unsatisfactory. Interviewed as she prepared to have her fifth abortion, Cabrera complained that her requests for sterilization or the five-year injection had been denied: "Do you think it's right that I have to go through this because they don't want to understand me? . . . If I regret it [sterilization] later, that's my problem."[23]

Confusion and misinformation regarding contraception, even within the health profession, continued to be a problem well into the 1980s. Thus in a survey of a thousand health care workers in 1986, birth control pills were identified as the best contraceptive option for adolescents, followed by the IUD and then the condom. Incredibly, Cuban gynecologists identified the IUD as the best birth control method for teenagers.[24]

Abortion

Health officials in Cuba had long been distressed by the population's dependence on abortion as a means of birth control. They blamed this habit on the public's lack of a "contraceptive consciousness."[25] Men traditionally preferred abortion because pregnancy—even if unwanted—affirmed their virility, and women's use of contraception implied a lessening of men's sexual control over them.

Abortion had been illegal in Cuba since the imposition of the Spanish penal code in 1879. Under the 1938 criminal code, which remained in force until 1979, abortion was allowed in only three circumstances: to save the life of the mother, when the pregnancy was the result of rape, and to avoid birth defects due to hereditary sickness or contagious disease. A decision to abort had to be approved by two physicians, but in practice this stipulation was rarely complied with.[26]

Before 1959 contraception was not included in the medical school curriculum. In the cities the widespread availability of abortion kept prices within reach of working-class women. The variety of abortive rites, rituals, and potions prescribed by rural folk healers indicated the importance of abortion in rural areas as well.[27]

For reasons that have never been fully explained, the Castro government actively opposed abortion for several years. A former prostitute recalled that in order to get an abortion after 1959, one had to be accompanied to the clinic by a friend of the doctor or "he wouldn't have dared take the risk."[28] Officials later claimed that the hostility of the government to abortion in the early 1960s did not represent a specific revolutionary policy to limit access to abortion. In 1985 Cuban researcher Luisa Alvarez Vásquez wrote that postrevolutionary limitations on abortion were due "to the reorganization of the public health system and the adaptation of the population to new norms of medical attention."[29] Asked to why abortion legislation was not amended for twenty years, one official blamed "the international political situation, which was characterized by the hostility of the Western world toward Cuba and, above all, toward Cuba's legal measures."[30] Interestingly, until 1988 most abortion statistics were not released publicly but were circulated only as "internal documents."

In addition to increased enforcement of antiabortion legislation, women's access to abortion after 1959 was limited due to the flight of virtually all of Cuba's obstetricians and gynecologists in response to the nationalization of the Cuban health system. In desperation, many women resorted to self-induced abortions or untrained practitioners. The maternal death rate increased dramatically. Something had to be done. In 1965 health officals decided to use the existing law, which permitted an abortion to save the life of a mother, as a legal basis for the institutionalization of abortion. The Ministry of Public Health adopted a policy validating abortions in all cases.[31]

Still, some doctors remained reluctant to perform abortions. One doctor in Mayarí in 1967 complained, "It is not our job to do an abortion."[32] Some anesthetists balked at giving anesthesia to abortion patients, arguing that abortion should be painful so as to discourage promiscuity. The requirement that women get their husbands' written permission encouraged women to seek private solutions to their pregnancies. A study of neonatal and obstetric services in 1970 disclosed a high morbidity rate from self-induced abortions. Public education on abortion was begun.[33]

In the early 1970s the legal abortion rate rose sharply, then leveled. By 1979, 40 percent of all pregnancies ended in abortion.[34] In that year a new penal code officially decriminalized abortion performed according to "established health regulations."[35] Criminal penalties were levied for abortions performed for profit, abortions done outside official institutions, or abortions done by anyone other than a physician. The new law decriminalized self-induced abortion and increased the penalty for the distribution of abortives.

In 1980 twenty-one women died as a result of abortion procedures; thirteen of the procedures were illegal. Alarmed by this figure, the Ministry of Public Health attempted a twofold program of discouraging abortion while at the same time making abortion services safer and more accessible. A minimum postabortion stay of three to four hours at a hospital or health center was established. Women who had had three or more abortions were to be counseled about the health risks. In 1988 a revised penal code increased the minimum sentences for unintentional abortion through violence and the unauthorized prescription of abortives.[36]

In the 1980s abortion was available to Cuban women without charge through the tenth week of pregnancy. Each early-term abortion cost the Cuban government about nine pesos. Second- and third-trimester abortions required the approval of hospital directors. In 1989 there were 160,000 abortions and some 200,000 live births. The abortion rate had held steady for nearly fifteen years despite public education and significant improvement in the availability of contraception.[37]

This high abortion rate became a national issue. Fidel Castro complained that it reflected sexual irresponsibility and not medical necessity. If Cubans didn't act more responsibly, he said, it might be necessary to begin charging for abortions. Other officials contended that better public education, not restrictions, was necessary. Everyone agreed, however, that something had to be done.[38]

The public was ambivalent about abortion. Psychologist and researcher Irasema Alvarez Salabert found in 1989 that half of the one hundred abortion patients she studied felt substantial guilt and moral pain. Cubans interviewed at random on the street expressed a general disapproval of abortion.[39] The medical community was similarly uncertain. A 1986 survey of health officials revealed that 14 percent of those interviewed thought it was too easy for a woman to obtain an abortion. In 1986 a doctor who reportedly refused to perform abortions for religious reasons was dismissed and sent to practice in a remote rural area. In 1987 Dr. Monika Krause, coordinator of Cuba's sex education program, complained that there was an increasing trend among physicians to resist abortions because of "anachronistic" religious ethics or a bourgeois moral double standard. This led Dr. Krause to underscore in a special bulletin for family doctors that "the right to abortion is inviolable."[40]

The Cuban media began warning women against abortion. One nineteen-year-old told a Cuban journalist in 1989 that an abortion she had had four years before caused her such psychological trauma that she was henceforth unable to lead a full sexual life.[41] The director of the National Association of Obstetrics and Gynecology warned that women were lulled into false security by Cuba's lowered abortion mortality rate but that there were many other dangers, such as uterine perforations and fallopian obstructions, associated with abortion.[42]

In the 1980s the medical profession began to recommend the advantages of "menstrual regulation," a kind of mini-abortion that could be done up to fourteen days after a menstrual period is missed. Menstrual regulation removes endometrial tissues, including any fertilized ovum that has not yet adhered firmly to the uterus wall. Heralded as an innocuous means of avoiding abortion and its risks, by 1988 menstrual regulation was available in all obstetric/gynecological hospitals and in a number of polyclinics.[43]

The surge in the Cuban birth rate after 1959 peaked in 1965 and then declined in every age group but one: teenagers.[44] In 1982, 35 percent of births in Cuba, and half of the births in eight of its fourteen provinces, were to adolescent mothers. Teenage pregnancy was highest in rural areas, where the tradition of early marriage and motherhood was strongest. A study of 1,725 births in one eastern province revealed that more than a third of the mothers were under fourteen.[45] The island's high rate of teenage pregnancy worried Cuban officials. These young mothers were undermining Cuba's efforts to raise the national level of education and health.

Ignorance among teens was a major contributor to adolescent pregnancy. A 1982 study found that many teenagers simply could not imagine that sexual experimentation could result in pregnancy. A 1988 study of more than two hundred pregnant teenagers revealed that three-quarters had not used any contraception even though none of the young women wanted to become pregnant. More than half of those interviewed had never sought or received birth control information. One-fifth had had a previous abortion.[46]

Cuban officials were concerned that careless sexual behavior was symptomatic of alienation and rebellion. One young woman who had had nine abortions had never used contraception because it wasn't "natural." Although she "felt bad" each time she aborted, she asked, "Who wants to have a child when you live in a *solar* (tenement)?" The young woman was not "ignorant"; she had a diploma in mechanical drawing but could not get a job in her field. "All they offered me was sewing or cleaning," she said, "and I'm not going to do that, sister."[47]

By 1989 the proliferation of sex education in the media and in school (see chapter 14) had helped to lower teen births to one in four. A prominent sexologist urged doctors to counsel pregnant teenagers to have an abortion, but many doctors didn't welcome this role.[48] Consequently there was considerable enthusiasm in health circles for menstrual regulation, which was seen as perfect for teenagers, who, according to leading obstetrician Dr. Ada Ovies, could "avoid the trauma because they'll not be sure that they are really pregnant."[49]

Until 1983, teenagers as young as sixteen could obtain an abortion without parental permission. Then the Ministry of Public Health stipulated that parental permission "should be" obtained when any potentially life-threatening medical procedure is performed on a patient under eighteen. According to sexologist Dr. Monika Krause, parental permission was never sought for routine operations such as appendectomies, but, she said, "With abortion I believe it is a manifestation of *machismo*. All too often our doctors consider a girl who gets pregnant to be 'easy,' and punish her by denying the operation."[50]

Teenage abortion became a source of contention between parents and officials. Some parents believed their daughters should keep their babies, and some even sued doctors who performed abortions without parental consent. Health officials fretted that many young women delayed telling relatives or medical authorities until it was too late. The result was unmonitored pregnancies, risky late-term abortions, or worse. Rural areas witnessed a resurgence of infanticide, a routine practice prior to 1959. In 1987 FMC president Vilma Espín called for changes so that once again pregnant teenagers could obtain abortions without informing their parents.[51]

In debates on teenage pregnancy and abortion the old double standard about sex being good for boys and bad for girls often came to the fore. Why, one journalist wondered, must girls who sought contraceptive devices "confront the moral and verbal sanction of others?"[52] Parents were also criticized, and fathers in particular, for failing to prepare their children for responsible sexuality: some kept their daughters ignorant while encouraging a conquest mentality in sons; others calmly marched their daughters into abortion clinics as if to a dental appointment.

Childbirth

Prior to 1959 only about half of the births in Cuba took place in hospitals, and in rural areas most births took place at home. The maternal mortality rate was 120 per 100,000 live births, and the infant mortality rate was estimated to be as high as 60 per 1,000 live births. Many young children succumbed to diarrhea, parasites, and other infections.[53]

Maternity care was a priority for the rural hospitals and clinics established in the early 1960s. In 1971 the number of rural medical clinics offering obstetric care had swelled to nearly two hundred. Nationally 87 percent of births were taking place in hospitals, and by 1992 the number rose to 99.8 percent.[54]

Mass organizations contributed greatly to improved maternity and child care. When a woman was found to be pregnant, neighborhood health mechanisms sprang into action. Appointments were made with the family doctor or area polyclinic. Local CDR and FMC cadres made sure the mother kept her prenatal appointments and got to the hospital on time. They also reminded the woman not to smoke, drink, or engage in other unhealthy behavior.

Getting a woman to the hospital in rural areas could be difficult, particularly during the rainy season, when roads were often impassable. This problem led to the creation of a new health service, the maternity home. Women went to the homes, located near regional hospitals, during their eighth month of pregnancy and remained there in safe proximity to the delivery rooms until labor began. Husbands were not always happy about being separated from their pregnant wives,[55] and in such cases FMC or CDR cadre had to persuade the couple that it was for the best. The typical maternity home, serving fifteen or twenty mothers-to-be, was regularly visited by a doctor and an obstetric nurse. By 1985, 105 homes were in operation in rural Cuba.[56] Maternity homes offered women a relaxing hiatus from the demands of the household. There were few restrictions on their activities, and visitors were welcome. Informal classes were offered in child care, nutrition, and contraception; the importance of breast-feeding and vaccinations was stressed. There were books, radios, television, and various recreational activities, and many maternity homes also had a beauty parlor and manicurist. Some of the women had never been so pampered in their lives.

The maternity homes were integrated into Cuba's network of maternity hospitals. Each maternity hospital contained a milk bank for mothers unable to breast-feed their child. Freezers stored fresh placentas, which were used to produce medicines, vitamins, and cosmetics.

In 1986 more than 85 percent of Cuban women were getting regular prenatal care during their first trimester of pregnancy. The first doctor's visit included a review of their entire reproductive history, a complete physical examination, and a dental checkup. Thereafter they were supposed to visit the doctor once a month until the seventh month, twice a month from the seventh to the eighth month, and then weekly until birth. In 1992, women were visiting their doctor an average of fifteen times per pregnancy.[57]

Doctors and health educators gave Cuban women detailed instructions for proper behavior during pregnancy. Expectant mothers were encouraged to eat well but moderately. They were told that sex was fine during pregnancy "only if a woman is willing," but that it should be less frequent and accomplished with *mayor suavidad* ("the greatest gentleness"). They were warned that under no circumstances should women smoke, wear high heels or tight clothing, or read disturbing books. Women were urged to stop housecleaning at seven months and leave their jobs at eight months. They were advised to have an interval of at least two years between pregnancies so that they would be up to the rigorous task of child rearing.[58]

Maternity hospitals and polyclinics gave classes on pregnancy and childbirth. The psychoprophylactic method of abdominal and breathing exercises used in Cuba was similar to that used in the United States. In 1989 a pilot program in Havana allowed men to accompany their partners into the delivery room, and over the next year 124 couples shared the birth experience. Plans were underway to expand this program to all maternity hospitals.[59]

New Birth Technologies

The "technification" of birth, which was rejected by some feminist critics of Western health care systems, was enthusiastically pursued in Cuba. By 1975, Cuban hospitals were routinely using estrogen measurers, ultrasound, and fetal monitors.

In the 1980s research in genetic diseases, study of infertility, and an improvement in prenatal diagnoses were the focus of the maternal health system.[60] A wide range of prenatal testing was offered, including diagnosis of hemophilia A and B, toxoplasmosis, and the alphafeto protein series. All women between the sixteenth and nineteenth week of pregnancy were to be tested for fetal development and advised of the implications of continuing a problematic pregnancy. Abortions were performed through the sixth month, and the aborted fetuses were used for research on congenital defects. A final test for infant allergies would be performed upon birth, with blood taken from the umbilical cord. In 1987, tests done on approximately 90 percent of the island's more than two hundred thousand pregnant women identified about a thousand defects.[61]

Prenatal testing raised difficult ethical issues. Should a fetus with a congenital disease that meant agony for the child and the parents and great expense for the state be aborted? Fidel Castro was sure that every mother would like to know the condition of the fetus and have the option of terminating the pregnancy:

> I don't want to get into matters of religious dogma on this topic. In my opinion this has nothing to do with religion. It has to do with the most elementary common sense and human compassion, because we've seen the tragedy this means to the family.[62]

Cuban officials insisted that they would not pressure women to terminate problem pregnancies, however. In 1986 the president of the Cuban Obstetric-Gynecological Association, Dr. Ada Ovics, indicated that while medical personnel would point out all the difficulties of raising a child with a particular deformity, women would never be forced to terminate their pregnancy. In 1987 Castro stated that "of course, nobody is compelled to undergo an abortion."[63]

Still, some women seemed to be uncomfortable with Cuban medicine's high-tech approach. In 1988 the Mariana Grajales Hospital in Santa Clara lost its title as a model medical facility because of complaints that doctors "had forgotten that the modern equipment was there to back them up, not to represent them."[64]

The treatment of infertility in Cuba has also advanced, and attitudes have changed, if slowly. In 1966, men were reminded that, despite the popular belief that women were responsible for infertility, one-third of infertility cases involved problems with the male. In addition, men were chided for being hesitant to submit to the simplest test while women, anxious to conceive, bravely endured a wide range of uncomfortable procedures.[65]

In 1989 Cuban research showed that one in ten couples was experiencing difficulty in conceiving. The most common causes proved to be low sperm count, abortion-related obstructions, and pelvic inflammation due to IUDs. Each of the patients treated for infertility cost the Cuban state some two hundred pesos, primarily for medicines to stimulate ovulation.[66] Fertility counseling was available to patients aged twenty to forty. To be accepted for treatment, a couple had to have been having a stable sexual relationship for two to three years. Sometimes exercises, special diets, and vitamin supplements were prescribed to help with conception, and fertility drugs were also used.[67]

In December 1986 Baby Luis, Cuba's first test-tube baby, was born in Havana. The mother, an office worker, had had an abortion at age fourteen which left her fallopian tubes permanently blocked. By June 1989 four babies had been born in Cuba as a result of in vitro fertilization, and there there were currently four more in vitro pregnancies in progress; 260 women between the ages of twenty and thirty-five were enrolled in the program.

The expansion, modernization, and democratization of the Cuban health care system which occurred after 1959 was a boon for Cuban women.

By 1992 virtually all Cuban women had access to regular, free, and relatively high-quality medical care. Life expectancy had been greatly extended. Infectious and communicable diseases (except certain sexually transmitted diseases) had been significantly reduced. Pregnancy, birth, and infancy were now rarely life-threatening events.

The benefits offered by the Cuban health system were an important source of support for the regime, consistently cited by the Cuban public as one of the greatest achievements of the revolution. Women, in turn, were reminded that the revolution had women's best interests in mind and that the socialist system could best ensure that their needs were met. To underscore this message, government authorities often informed women of the inadequacies and high costs of health care in capitalist countries.

The revolution made a major effort to modernize the entire process of maternity and childbirth through substantial investments in education, research, and technology. It took enormous pride in its low maternal and infant mortality rates, successes that may well be undone by the economic crisis of the 1990s.

While the overall achievements of revolutionary health are undeniable, certain aspects of Cuban health policy were inconsistent with Cuba's egalitarian goals. For example, in the 1960s Cuban policy makers displayed a fundamental lack of understanding of the importance of abortion as a birth control option. Only when illegal abortions threatened maternal health statistics, and thus international prestige, did policy makers decide to improve and extend the service. Twenty years passed before abortion was formally legalized.

A number of other dilemmas hampered women's reproductive choices in Cuba. Periodic shortages of birth control devices occurred throughout the years, not only because of the U.S. economic embargo and the recent dissolution of the Soviet bloc, but also from inadequate planning by health administrators. There was a lack of clarity regarding the process for diagnosing sexually transmitted diseases in women. Even worse was the apparent misinformation among gynecologists regarding which birth control devices were appropriate for women at different times in their reproductive life. This lack of knowledge was particularly perplexing given the large number of women practitioners in the medical field.

From the collectivist perspective of the Cuban revolution it was the rightful business of the community to monitor the activities of pregnant women. This concern for collective good was also behind Cuba's AIDS policy of compulsory quarantine.

Health education played an important role in the new Cuban system. Many traditional notions, particularly regarding the mysteries of women's reproductive cycle, were challenged. At the same time, some traditional cultural assumptions about women's sexuality were reinforced by the revolutionary "scientific" information machine (see chapter 14). The manipulation of information reflected the paternalistic mold of the

Cuban system. For example, in its eagerness to promote the use of birth control devices, the health education machine for years remained mum regarding the potential risks of certain contraceptive methods.

The Cuban experience has shown, in fact, that simply providing birth control materials and information does not automatically change traditional patterns of behavior. Cuban women continued to shun routine contraceptive use. The proliferation of abortion seemed to facilitate its abuse as a means of birth control. And ironically the best-educated Cubans, the youngest, appeared the least aware in their reproductive choices—or lack of them. Further research is needed into why this is so.

The health system came to rival the military as the most prestigious institution in Cuban society. Unlike the military, it was largely staffed by women—doctors, nurses, researchers, practitioners, and volunteers. Although women were underrepresented in leadership posts, this trend was less pronounced in health care than in other sectors. For women, the new health system was arguably the most successful innovation of the Cuban revolution.

7

Women and the Revolution in Education

The revolution signifies study for all . . . the right to improve oneself, to become a useful citizen, to be able to fully develop one's intelligence.

The Federation of Cuban Women (1970)[1]

Thanks to the revolution, we are now teachers! Viva Cuba! Viva Fidel! Long live socialism!

Women literacy workers (1962)[2]

If we made our selection on the basis of academic record alone, two out of every three medical school students would be women.

Fidel Castro (1988)[3]

We must move beyond the paternalistic concepts that are so deeply imbedded in our schools and in our society.

Yolanda Marrero, Cuban schoolteacher (1989)[4]

The school year in revolutionary Cuba typically began with a celebration: student performances, sports events, balloons, and speeches. These ceremonies honored one of the revolution's proudest achievements, the creation of a modern, free, and universal education system. It was an education system designed to be an engine for social change, to achieve what the educational guru Paulo Freire called the "reinvention of Cuban society."[5]

Education in revolutionary Cuba meant social mobility. A washerwoman's daughter could attend university and become a white-collar professional. Education expanded women's horizons, opportunities, and options. The educational revolution also created hundreds of thousands of new positions for teachers and administrators, many filled by women. By the early 1990s Cuba had ten times as many teachers as in 1959.[6]

When Castro first broached his ideas about education in "History Will Absolve Me" (1953), more than half a million Cuban women were illiterate and most had no more than a few years of schooling. Thirty years later a ninth-grade education was the norm, and women constituted nearly half of all students attending high schools, 44 percent of those enrolled in technical schools, and more than half of the university students.[7]

First Steps

Cuba's educational system grew rapidly following Castro's victory in 1959. Thousands of new teachers were hired, mostly women. In the countryside 671 primary schools with 1,700 rooms, many simply peasant huts, were opened from 1959 to 1961. In the cities 339 new primary schools with 3,400 rooms were opened. The number of students rose from 700,000 in 1959 to over a million in 1960 and 1.2 million in 1961.[8] Abandoned mansions and former army barracks were transformed into schools. Cuba's largest military base, Camp Columbia, became *Ciudad Libertad,* an educational complex which by 1961 had 14,000 students.[9]

A training program was developed to prepare new teachers. At first they spent nine months at a former guerrilla camp high in the Sierra Maestra, where, in the purifying mountain air, they learned to associate education with austerity and military discipline. Later, students completed their program at a teachers' college in the seaside resort of Tarara. In addition, since there were not enough primary teachers for the enormous number of new students, thousands of volunteers or "people's teachers" were recruited. Many were high school girls of thirteen or fourteen. In some cases the volunteers attended school in the morning and then taught, mostly first graders, in the afternoon.

In September 1960 Castro launched Cuba's great literacy campaign. Declaring 1961 the "Year of Education," Castro asked the island's high school students, boys and girls alike, to become literacy volunteers. Over a hundred thousand volunteered, half of them young women. The students were organized in brigades, wore olive green uniforms, and talked about illiteracy as the enemy. Although some remained in the cities teaching the urban poor, most went into the countryside, armed with lanterns, blanket rolls and hammocks, a primer, a teacher's manual, and a book of poems by José Martí, the father of Cuban independence.

The literacy campaign was designed to make the poor literate and to make middle-class youths aware of the difficult lives of their poorer compatriots. Parents of young women were alarmed, however. They did not want to lose control of their daughters. In the 1950s proper young women had chaperones even for an afternoon at the movies; now they were to go off alone to the countryside. Racial prejudice also surfaced:

some people feared their daughters would be easy prey for unscrupulous blacks. "One goes out and two come back" was the refrain.[10]

Mónica Ramos, a Havana high school student, wanted to volunteer. Her aunts and uncles were horrified, but her mother was supportive, and Mónica joined the campaign. She spent a week in training at Varadero beach and then was dropped off at a small farm in Las Villas province. She became ill, was harassed, but nonetheless persisted. "By the end of my eight months I had taught almost all the illiterates in my section to read and write," she later said. "We hauled up our pink flag, declaring the area free of illiteracy."[11]

The peasants sometimes found the behavior of the literacy workers quite shocking. The young women wore pants! Some even smoked! Some *campesinas* saw no need to learn to read. Despite a thousand obstacles, the campaign pressed forward. On December 22, 1961, Fidel Castro declared Cuba a literate nation. Seven hundred thousand Cubans, more than half of them women, had learned to read and write. Castro offered scholarships to the literacy volunteers so that they could go on to become professional teachers.

A New Educational System

The literacy campaign was part of the first stage of a broader effort to transform Cuban education. The new system emphasized the development of scientific and technical skills. It stressed the legitimacy of the revolution and encouraged public trust in the primacy of the state. The racial prejudice and sexual inequities of the old Cuba were blamed on capitalism; socialism meant the end of such vices. Unity and obedience to directives from Havana were paramount.

Fidel Castro wanted to reduce the social distance between workers and students and to eliminate the national disdain for manual labor which was a legacy of the colonial era and slavery. In 1962 he announced that "work must be the chief teacher of the young."[12] Children at day care centers and primary schools planted vegetable gardens. Secondary students worked on agricultural projects or in light manufacturing in factories attached to their schools. High school students were asked to volunteer for agricultural work during their vacations. In the summer of 1962 forty thousand students went off for six weeks to harvest coffee beans and "fortify themselves physically and ideologically."[13] This agricultural program lasted until the 1990s. Many students didn't mind, even looking on it as a kind of holiday. Young women had their hair and nails done before heading for the fields.

If one face of the educational revolution reflected idealism and optimism, the other was marked by anger and resistance. Older career teachers, many of them women who had struggled for years to achieve their modest positions, felt threatened. They complained about being required to indoctrinate students with revolutionary ideas. Special seminars and group discussions were organized to help these older teachers adapt. One teacher noted: "We were all pressured into collaborating with the new regime . . . the school started to change radically. There was no way you could oppose any move because you would be considered counter-revolutionary."[14]

Teachers also feared that some of their students were spies, and grade inflation became a widespread phenomenon. Teachers who had struggled to earn university degrees were distressed too by the introduction of un-certified teachers and administrators, some of whom were barely literate.

Significant changes were made in the curriculum. New textbooks featuring revolutionary heroes—Fidel, Che, Camilo, all men—were introduced into the schools. Libraries were purged of politically "inappropriate" books. Prerevolutionary history books were eliminated, and compulsory classes in Marxist theory were introduced.

New demands were made on the teaching profession. Instructors were asked to "volunteer" to teach adults after regular hours, or to guard their schools, and those who refused risked losing their jobs. Older teachers were offered early retirement. Some accepted, others left the country. By 1961 more than ten thousand teachers had departed for Miami.

In June 1961 Castro announced the nationalization of all private schools. Most of Cuba's twenty-seven hundred nuns, many of whom had taught the young women of the upper and middle classes in schools such as the Sacred Heart Academy of Havana, left the island.

In the wake of the literacy crusade came the "Battle for the Sixth Grade," a campaign designed to bring the education of adults up to the sixth-grade level by 1980 through a two-year general curriculum of day and night classes. Housewives, a particular focus of the program, were recruited by the FMC in door-to-door sweeps. Thereafter the FMC shepherded the women along, periodically checking on their progress. By 1984 more than 300,000 housewives had completed the sixth grade.[15]

For rural poor women the new education system was a powerful engine of social mobility. One woman from Fe de Corralitos recalled that before the revolution the nearest school was nine miles away and one had to go there on horseback. Some of her eleven brothers and sisters went, but she didn't. Somehow the literacy campaign of 1961 passed her by. But in 1963 an adult education class began near her home, and by 1967 she had completed primary and secondary school and was taking night classes to prepare for the university. Some of her brothers and sisters went on to study in the Soviet Union and become professionals.[16]

In 1967 primary education was made compulsory. Between 1968 and 1975 the number of teachers in primary education, most of whom were women, rose by 62 percent.[17] Even so, the system was nearly overwhelmed by surging enrollments. By 1975 there were two million students in primary education, almost three times as many as before the revolution.

To accommodate this wave of students, double shifts were introduced. Students went to school in either the morning or the afternoon, but for the other half of the day they were on their own. Since working mothers worried about their unattended children, "day boarding" programs were begun. Children were given lunch and supervised activities when their classes were not in session. By 1990 more than 400,000 children were enrolled as "day boarders." [18]

Although many schools were built, the two-shift system remained. In 1987 the minister of education reported that all primary school students in the city of Havana attended only half a day. The government worried that footloose children would become juvenile delinquents, and teachers worried about the effect of the double shift on their students' academic progress. By 1989 all primary schools in Havana, Sancti Espiritus, and Camagüey provinces had full-day sessions, but the rest of the provinces did not. [19] In some cases children from areas with half-day sessions went to live with relatives in communities where the schools offered full-time instruction. [20]

While the educational revolution revamped curriculum and texts to reflect modern notions, old-fashioned sexual stereotypes were sometimes overlooked. For example, one sixth-grade reader of the 1980s portrayed men as doctors, warriors, farmers, heroes, revolutionaries, policemen, and poets, while women appeared as teachers, mothers, wives, grand-mothers, pioneer leaders, and lion tamers. [21] Nevertheless some efforts were made to teach new gender roles. The Family Code's (1975) insis-tence on equality within the home meant boys needed to learn about housework and child care. In some day care centers boys were encour-aged to prepare meals on play stoves. Some school books also reflected changing sex roles, such as the following poem for sixth graders:

> Mama Bear says that Papa bear is a good husband.
> He helps her wash the clothes.
> He helps her make soups.
> But when Papa bear smokes he dirties all the ashtrays.
> And when he's finished with his newspaper he throws it on the floor.
> Isn't it possible, Papa bear, to have a little more consideration and improve
>   these bad habits? [22]

Secondary Education

By the 1970s the great wave of students that had entered primary school in the 1960s was coursing on to junior high. A national system of rural boarding high schools was created: junior high schools called ESBECs (Escuelas Secundarias Básicas en el Campo, or basic secondary schools in the countryside), academic high schools, polytechnical and vocational schools. The boarding schools were coeducational to ensure the "normal" development of relations between the sexes. They were designed to break students away from the influence of families with their prerevolutionary values. Working women were particularly keen on boarding schools, since they provided full scholarships covering books, tuition, transportation, clothing, and food. Their children were given priority placement.

Construction of the ESBECs began in the late 1960s, and by 1990 there were nearly 450, sufficient to serve more than a third of Cuba's junior high students. In 1983–1984 boys outnumbered girls at the boarding schools 54 percent to 46 percent, a ratio that may have reflected the reluctance of some parents, particularly in rural sectors, to send their daughters away from home.[23]

At the ESBECs the students worked part-time on agricultural projects or in light manufacturing. Student labor generated income for the schools and labor for the state and was factored into national economic plans. In fact rural schools were often built in areas with labor shortages.[24]

In 1986 the "Battle of Jigüe" ESBEC near Havana had 636 students, half girls and half boys. In its dormitories, which had ranks of double bunks, no personal items such as posters or photographs or other manifestations of "individualism" were permitted. Students divided their day between classes and work in nearby strawberry fields, where they periodically rested on their hoes, chatted, flirted, and played tag. When the work period was over the young women rode back to the dormitories in a truck while the boys walked.[25]

The revolution's program of rural boarding schools had its critics. According to Manuel Sánchez Pérez, a former vice minister for planning who defected in 1985, boarding school students had too much freedom and too little supervision. This lack of restrictions, he alleged, led to juvenile delinquency and sexual promiscuity. Sánchez said that the ESBEC system had cost two billion dollars, too much for a poor nation like Cuba.[26]

Certain *rezagos*, or old habits, continued at the boarding schools. In the mid-1980s at the "Osvaldo Herrera" ESBEC it was customary for young women to do their boyfriends' laundry. Did the boys ever wash the girls clothes? No! This widespread practice was criticized by FMC officials as exploitative.[27]

The students were not always enthusiastic about living in the countryside. At the "October Revolution" ESBEC in 1988, young women spoke of boredom and regimentation: "We wake up at 5:30 A.M. and we are on the run until bedtime," one noted. Students complained about a lack of books in the library, and a lack of advice on their prospective careers. A shortage of gasoline prevented excursions in the school's buses. A professor at the University of Havana who defected in 1991 said students would do almost anything to avoid going to a rural school.[28]

In 1991 there were 35,000 vacancies in these schools. Cuban officials said they were due to a decline in the number of students of high school age. In 1992, empty boarding schools were being used to house agricultural workers as Cuba struggled to grow more food.[29]

In addition to the rural boarding schools, the revolution developed a range of technical and polytechical high schools to prepare technicians and skilled workers. A considerable effort was made to recruit women; by the mid-1980s they comprised almost half of the technical school students. Students could specialize in any of 140 careers ranging from sugar mill operations and sugar chemistry to motor vehicle mechanics and construction.[30]

In 1986, 288 (49 percent) of the 584 students at the prestigious "Martyrs of Humboldt Seven" polytechnical boarding high school were young women, including the top student. The director of Humboldt Seven commented that having young men and women live together had not been particularly problematical. He noted that while the school provided no birth control materials to the students, "We cannot prevent them from having sex!" The girls were aware, however, that if they got pregnant they had "lost their chance here."[31]

Coordination between Cuban education and the economy was less than ideal. In the late 1980s, even before the decline in Soviet aid began to take its toll, the baby boomers who entered the job market, women in particular, found slim pickings. In 1988 twenty thousand graduates of technical training programs were waiting for jobs in their field. A young woman who trained as a railroad technician waited three years for placement. She finally went to her community employment bureau, which offered her a job as a kitchen helper.[32]

The situation provoked widespread complaints among young people. One response was to reduce what Castro called excessive specialization in technical education. The regime shifted emphasis toward a broader based system in which workers were trained for a wider range of tasks.

Despite the massive effort to incorporate every student of school age in the system, some slipped through the cracks. In 1989, for example, 13 percent of children aged twelve to sixteen did not attend secondary school.[33] This question of *desvinculados,* or young people who neither studied nor worked, proved frustrating for the revolution. Castro wondered whether the *desvinculados* would become a permanent underclass likely to indulge in criminal activities.[34]

Another persistent frustration for the educational revolution was what Cuban officials called "ruralism." High school attendance were consistently lower and dropout rates higher among rural girls than among their urban counterparts. In Granma province in the late 1980s there were some twenty thousand young women who neither studied nor worked. Most had quit school because of marriage or pregnancy.[35]

The government adopted a variety of methods to deal with problem students. One approach was to create special "conduct" schools. As of 1987 there were 86 of these schools with sixty-five hundred problem students. Another answer was more vocational training centers such as the Clara Zetkin school in Havana, where teenage boys studied carpentry and mechanics while the girls learned to sew.[36]

The most problematic *desvinculados* were required to join brigades such as the Centennial Youth Column. These brigades, which in the 1970s, had about thirty thousand young people, boasted military organization with strict discipline and a spartan regimen. Column members worked in harvests and emergency projects.

Women in Higher Education

In 1959 Cuba had one major university, the University of Havana. There were also smaller state universities in Las Villas and Oriente provinces, and a few private institutions such as the Catholic University of Villanueva. Three decades later there were eight universities and more than thirty-five university-level institutes and research facilities. By 1990 there were about 280,000 university students, ten times the number in the late 1950s. More than half of Cuba's university students (57 percent) and graduates (55.3 percent) were women.[37]

The presence of women in higher education preceded the revolution. Their numbers had grown substantially in the 1930s. In 1953, women constituted 37 percent of university graduates. By 1956–1957, 45 percent of university students and 22 percent of professors were women. In the late 1950s, 622 women were studying in the school of pharmacy, 430 in law, and 388 in philosophy and letters; there were only 7 in agricultural engineering, 4 in civil engineering, and 3 in electrical engineering.[38]

After 1959 there was a great shake-up at the University of Havana. Prominent male Marxist professors won high positions while women professors of the left did not. Juan Marinello, a professor in the Institute of Modern Languages and also the head of the Cuban Communist party, became president of the university in 1962. Literary critic José Antonio Portuondo became president of the University of Oriente. Economics professor Carlos Rafael Rodríguez, a longtime Communist party leader, organized the university reform of 1962 and later became vice president of Cuba. Professor Raúl Roa was promoted to foreign minister. For distinguished women of the left, however, there were no such heady posts. Thus Mirta Aguirre, a Marxist literary critic, remained in the classroom, assigned to introducing Marxist studies in the educational system.

Professors who opposed the revolution or who were unhappy with changes in the university left for Miami. Ines Segura Bustamente, professor of logic and civics, left. Havana's medical school, once the jewel of the university, lost almost its entire faculty. The closing of the Catholic University by the reform law of 1962 drove additional women academics into exile. Mercedes García Tuduri left for Miami, as did anthropologist

Lydia Cabrera as well as Elena Mederos, the woman who had helped to create the University of Havana's social welfare department.

The government had introduced a fellowship program to help poor students pay for room, board, and other expenses, and by early 1962 this program was helping 120 women of modest resources to study medicine at the University of Havana. In that year five hundred of the twelve hundred students taking entrance exams for medical school were women.[39]

By the mid-1960s female students were moving into many new fields. In 1965 one young student, Hilda Amador, was impressed by a visiting female geologist from the Soviet Union. Five years later Hilda, along with three other women, was awarded a degree in geology. "Our male colleagues gave us flowers," she recalled.[40] Isabel Zamora was one of the first women to study at Cuba's new national institute of veterinary medicine, graduating in 1969. By 1974, women constituted 50 percent of Cuban veterinarians, and Dr. Zamora was in charge of the island's fifty-six veterinary laboratories.[41]

The new university women had their own views on changing sex roles. A student at the University of Havana told *Mujeres* magazine that she opposed women's liberation if that meant "a brainless and uncontrolled sexual liberation." Cuban women, she thought, "wanted to enjoy the same opportunities as men in both study and work."[42]

Despite all the changes, however, the pull of tradition remained powerful. In 1984 more than half of the university women were studying to be teachers—roughly the same percentage as prior to the revolution.[43] Furthermore, women who were good in math in high school still tended not to pursue math in college. The participants in Cuba's annual math Olympics were typically all men. Relatively few women received Ph.D.s in economics, an important career in a state-planned economy.[44]

Although many women became teachers, teaching was not necessarily their first choice. Indeed it was often a last resort for students with mediocre records. The best students wanted to be doctors. Between 1959 and 1991 Cuba had graduated more than forty-five thousand doctors, nearly half of them women.[45] Interestingly, the government came to view the large number of women in medicine as problematic. Fidel Castro explained in 1988 that more male doctors were needed, particularly for international service. He said asking women doctors with family responsibilities to go abroad was "unfair." To increase the number of male medical students, entrance requirements for men were lowered.[46]

After 1959 a significant number of young women studied abroad. Between 1961 and 1982 more than fifty-six thousand Cubans studied in the Soviet Union. The number rose from a thousand or so per year in the 1960s to almost nine thousand in 1981–1982. A much smaller number—549 in 1981–1982—studied in Eastern Europe. Study abroad was a privilege and an important indicator of one's future prospects. In the 1984–1985 university year 38 percent of Cuban students abroad were women.[47]

During the early years of the revolution the dropout rate at Cuban universities was very high. Even in the 1970s only about a quarter of the students were completing their degrees, thanks in part to other time-consuming demands of the revolution (such as the mass organizations and the militias) and to the relatively poor preparation the students received in Cuban high schools. This situation gradually improved. In 1981 the graduation rate was 48.5 percent; in 1987, 56.9 percent; and in 1989, 55.3 percent.[48]

The development of night school and home study programs was helpful to Cuban women. By 1984 half of the university students attended night classes. For example, Maggie de Llovio-Menéndez studied art history at night while her husband, José Luis, an official in the sugar ministry, studied law. They were the new Cuban couple, childless professionals, studying, moving up. It was an exhausting business: "Our time together was telescoped into a few hours on Sundays."[49]

By 1986, 145,000 women workers had college degrees, a third of them living in Havana province. About 10 percent of the female workforce in every province had a college degree. Working women with college degrees were most numerous in science and technology (31.3 percent of women workers), and least numerous in agriculture and farming (0.5 percent).[50]

Until the late 1980s Cuban universities did relatively little research on the changing status of women. A perusal of the card catalogue at the University of Havana in 1986 revealed a striking absence of such materials. The ten-thousand-volume library at the Cojimar Pedagogical School offered only thirteen entries under the subject "women," including ten books on Soviet and Eastern bloc women and a detective novel by Agatha Christie. Some Western literature on women was held in reserve collections at the national library but was accessible only by special permission. The FMC maintained its own small library, which included books—often not in Spanish—on Western feminism, left by foreign visitors.

More recently academic interest in women has increased, spurred in part by government concern over the state of the Cuban family. In the mid-1980s a number of professors at the University of Havana began researching women's role in society, and in 1991 a more formal interdisciplinary program on women and the family was begun at the University of Havana.

Rectifying Education

For many years Cuban officials shielded the inner workings of the educational system from outside view. This situation changed when Fidel Castro's "rectification" of 1986 encouraged educators to discuss their problems in public. A candid and at times painful assessment of Cuban education began. Some suggested that the system was too rigid and formalistic, that the quality of both students and teachers was often poor, and that cheating and corruption were widespread.[51]

In 1987 Castro announced that Cuba had too many teachers. The demographic wave was subsiding. This was not good news for the 165,000 women who constituted 65 percent of Cuba's teacher corps. Castro announced that a reserve corps of 17,000 teachers would be created. The "reservists" would receive sabbaticals to go back to college, with salary, "to increase their knowledge." Castro thought the number of academic "reservists" might increase to 40,000.[52]

In the late 1980s a ceiling was placed on the number of college students. Too many wanted to go to the university and become white-collar workers. *Granma*'s education writer Georgina Jiménez wondered, "Can we develop without manual laborers?" She noted that Cuba had over 380,000 university graduates, with 33,000 more graduating every year, and she concluded that the crux of the problem was that "concepts of social prestige are not in line with the profound changes that have taken place in the country."[53]

The government put much of the blame for the deficiencies of the educational system on parents. Parents were to blame for instilling their children's distorted values, for encouraging the materialism and careerism of the younger generation, for being too absorbed by their own careers and problems, for not reviewing their children's homework. Officials concluded that parents wanted the schools to raise their children. The regime tried to engage parents in their children's education, failing to recognize that its own contradictory policies about the role of the family were part of the problem.

"Rectification" led to the first public discussions of gender and education. Cuban researchers discovered that girls outperformed boys in elementary school, reached higher ranks in the Young Pioneers, an integrated, communist version of the Boy and Girl Scouts, and participated more in grade school activities. Indeed women received better grades than men in high school and in higher education.[54] But grades seemed to make little difference as boys continued to play a dominant role. Girls in school were often given the least rewarding tasks, such as serving others and cleaning up. Cuban psychologist Patricia Arés Muzio noted that boys' habitual dominance was also reinforced by behavior learned inside the family.[55]

There were some exceptions to this rule. For example, young women led the Federation of Secondary Students (Federación de Estudiantes de Enseñanza Media, or FEEM) for many years. Once they reached the university, however, they began to fade from public view, as men continued to dominate the Federation of University Students (Federación Estudantil Universitaria, or FEU). In 1991 only four of the fourteen members of the FEU national secretariat were women. Nevertheless, in that year Carmen Rosa Báez became the second woman ever elected to head the FEU. A twenty-four-year-old psychology student at Las Villas University, she had climbed up the organizational ladder from the Young Pioneers to the FEEM to the Young Communists.[56]

Carmen Rosa Báez's views offered an indication of the tenor of university life in the early 1990s. She told an interviewer that she was "fully identified with the revolution and with Fidel. . . . We cannot permit anyone to question our principles. Today more than ever the university is for revolutionaries." It was the business of the FEU, she said, to identify counterrevolutionary students.[57]

Three decades of revolutionary changes in education provided a boon to Cuban women, creating a vast, universal system which offered them an unprecedented opportunity to improve their lives and become full citizens. Cuba's educational system was designed to be a driving force in the modernization and development of the nation. By providing educational opportunities to all regardless of race or geographical region, the new system would help eliminate the divisions of the old society. Cuban education would engender the *conciencia* (consciousness) necessary for the construction of a new society by inculcating youth with new socialist values of earnestness, equality, austerity, communitarianism, and patriotism.

The educational revolution also helped to win support for Fidel Castro's political and economic revolution, particularly from lower-class women, who before 1959 had been hindered from getting an education by geographic isolation, poverty, ignorance, and racial discrimination.

While the new educational system was of great benefit to women, it was unable to change some old habits. In 1993 a powerful patriarchal ethos still dominated the system much as it did in the first half of the century. Children's school books were full of tributes to Fidel, Che, and Camilo as the heroic guerrilla fighters who had made everything possible. Teachers' offices were decorated with drawings and photographs of the heroic warrior. The study of "Cuban philosophy" amounted to the study of Fidel Castro's speeches. The schools themselves were named after male heroes. Children sang "I want to be like Che," the perpetual warrior who in 1967 set out to create "one, two, three, many Vietnams in Latin America."

In this patriarchal and militaristic milieu, science and technology offered women a new route to power and greater equality. In the early 1990s agricultural and pharmaceutical research was viewed as holding great promise for the Cuban economy. Women's role in these fields was substantial. The head of the Cuban Academy of Sciences, Rosa Elena Simeon, was a woman. Two of the new women in the Politburo were of the new generation of so-called "techies." In the early 1990s a new generation of women intellectuals in the social sciences, such as Patricia Arés Muzio, Marta Núñez Sarmiento, and Mónika Sorín Zocolsky, began publishing research relevant to the making of social policy. Their work received considerable attention in the national media.

The old notion that educational opportunity was a machine for the creation of loyal citizens seemed to be right. It advanced the lives of many women. But by 1990 this formula had run its course. The new generation of educated women was increasingly frustrated as the Cuban economy stumbled into ever greater difficulties. For most women the jobs and careers they dreamed of and trained for were no longer available. The educational triumphs of the past—the literacy campaign, the new schools, the countryside schools, the surge of universities—were no longer enough. Now a new generation, a generation educated by the revolution, awaited the opportunity to redefine Cuba's political, economic, and cultural system.

8

The Campaign for Women's Employment, 1959–1980

Many of the plans that the revolution is today . . . carrying out could not have been conceived until the great reservoir of human resources that our society possesses in its women was clearly recognized. These plans . . . could not have been conceived without the mass incorporation of women into the workforce.

Fidel Castro (1966)[1]

One of the central notions of Cuban socialism was that to achieve full equality, women must become engaged in paid labor outside the home. Through a variety of policies and specific employment campaigns, the Cuban revolution encouraged women to seek employment. By the early 1990s there were 1.2 million women workers in Cuba, nearly 40 percent of the total labor force.

The campaign to employ women would be affected by the dissonance between Marxism, the official ideology of the revolution, and Cuban culture. Marxist ideology maintains a clear dichotomy between the public realm of production and the private realm of the household. Public "production" is valued as socially useful and personally transforming, while domestic tasks are denigrated—when even acknowledged—as useless, wasteful, and numbing. Thus the home, the traditional source of women's public power, respect, and legitimacy in Cuban society, was dismissed in one bold stroke. Reproduction and child rearing were merely "burdens" that hindered women's participation in the redeeming male province of public production. This ideological view of domestic tasks shaped the revolution's efforts to resolve the dilemmas of women workers.

The campaign to put women to work, being but one component in the revolution's overall drive for economic and social development, had to deal with a number of dilemmas. Were the specific policies to promote

95

women's employment consistent with the revolution's goal of sexual equality? Did these policies treat women as a secondary labor force? Or did they in other various and perhaps unintended ways impede the progress of women workers?

First Steps

By 1940 Cuban laws regarding women workers were the most progressive in the Western hemisphere. The 1940 constitution prohibited sexual discrimination in employment and guaranteed equal pay for equal work. Occupational health and safety laws were enacted to protect working women and allow them certain rights, such as morning and afternoon breaks for nursing mothers. A generous maternity law gave women paid leaves for childbirth and guaranteed jobs upon their return. However, there was little effort to enforce these laws, and they were often ignored or evaded.[2]

According to the 1953 census, women constituted nearly 13 percent of the economically active population; one in seven women worked. More than one-quarter of working women (27 percent) were domestic servants who were not covered by much of Cuban labor legislation. Women represented 82 percent of the teachers (84 percent at primary, 90 percent at secondary, and 51 percent at the university level), 81 percent of Cuba's social workers, and 68 percent of its pharmacists. Interestingly, while women constituted 91 percent of the practical nurses and midwives, they comprised only 31 percent of the professional nurses.[3]

Women tended to be underrepresented in many professions, however. They were but 13 percent of the medical workers, 17 percent of lawyers, and 5 percent of administrators and managers. Furthermore, thousands of women were engaged in the informal sector of the economy as street vendors and prostitutes.

In rural areas women's labor was largely unrecognized. The sugar industry employed few women. Cuba had no handicraft tradition to provide a social, economic, and creative outlet to countrywomen. The 1953 census reported that women constituted only 1 percent of Cuba's agricultural workers, but this figure may be misleading given the strong cultural bias which inhibited male heads of household, particularly in the countryside, from admitting that "their" women worked. In fact, women frequently tended the small farm plots typical of the rural poor in Cuba and also participated in harvesting and processing cash crops.[4]

Beginning in 1959 the revolution began to change the profile of women's employment. Domestic service and prostitution were soon eliminated. Government programs to expand and democratize health care and education provided many new jobs for women. The first day care centers were opened. The agrarian reform of 1959 began a reorganization of Cuban agriculture that would bring new opportunities to thousands of rural women. Women were encouraged to enroll in the vocational training programs organized to provide needed technical workers. A modest handicraft industry was initiated and its products sold in female-staffed stores. In 1962 the FMC's *Mujeres* announced that henceforth "a woman can't be beautiful without economic independence and culture"[5] and began featuring articles celebrating women working in traditionally male fields.

Much of the labor performed by women in the early 1960s, however, was unremunerated and channeled in a way to avoid their competing with male workers. In fact, the widespread use of women's free labor would become characteristic of Cuban economic policy. As Vilma Espín, head of the FMC, later commented:

> Voluntary work opened new prospects for many women who wanted to contribute to the process. . . . Many of these women engaged in productive activity for the first time. Voluntary work was beginning to fulfill its purpose: opening new horizons for women, showing them it was possible to take part, creating a new consciousness.[6]

Women volunteers proved very useful during various national emergencies. When men were mobilized during the Bay of Pigs invasion in 1961 and the missile crisis in 1962, women took their places in factories and fields, working without pay. When Hurricane Flora buffeted the country in 1963, the FMC organized women to evacuate survivors, give aid, and operate emergency shelters. Afterwards women helped to replant fields and to harvest crops damaged by the storm.[7]

The supplemental labor of women volunteers was also important in agriculture, which by the early 1960s was plagued by labor shortages. In 1962 the Federation of Cuban Women organized four thousand units of women volunteers to cut cane and harvest peanuts, cotton, beans, and tomatoes. The FMC held production congresses to encourage women's participation in either salaried or volunteer work in agriculture and urged women's participation in nontraditional activities such as cattle breeding.[8]

In 1964 thousands of women volunteers were asked to help harvest coffee and other crops in Oriente province. To promote women's volunteer labor, the FMC declared 1965 the "Year of Agricultural Legions." Thousands of women left their homes and children for weeks or even months of volunteer labor in fruit, vegetable, and even fresh-water fish production. Urban women were also asked to work in farms near Havana and in the new craft shops in the city.[9]

In 1966 the Federation of Cuban Women–Small Farmer's Association (Asociación Nacional de Agricultores Pequeños, or ANAP) Mutual Aid brigades were established. The brigades consisted of FMC volunteers who assisted individual farmers. The government came to rely on these brigades to help solve seasonal agricultural labor shortages.[10]

Nonetheless, the government was enthusiastic about the economic potential of paid women workers. In 1965 Fidel Castro said Cuba would incorporate a million women into full-time paid labor by 1970. "One million women . . . signifies one billion pesos in created value." Women represented, he claimed, "a potential force . . . superior to anything that the most optimistic of us had ever dreamed of."[11] Cuba needed women workers. Since the mid-1960s "the expansion of the labor force was achieved fundamentally with the incorporation of women," which was necessary for national development."[12]

In 1966 a Secretariat of Production was created within the FMC leadership to help incorporate women into the workforce. One approach was contract labor. The government authorized the hiring of women as temporary workers according to the particular labor needs of a factory, farm, or other work enterprise. Contract work was viewed as an interim step to permanent employment for women. It gave women flexibility in doing their domestic tasks, and it benefited employers who could amplify their regular workforce when demand required.

The Impact of Policy

The government's insistence that women enter the labor force was resisted by many Cuban men, who wanted their wives to remain at home and under their control. Men were uneasy about the independence that came with women's incomes. They feared a loss of honor should their wives be seduced at the workplace, and they did not like patriarchal power being transferred to the state. Sociologist Geoffrey Fox found that the revolution's efforts to change women's roles created "extreme discomfort among working-class men" and was an important factor in the decision of some to leave Cuba.[13]

FMC president Vilma Espín stressed that the importance of women's participation in the revolution outweighed men's complaints:

> Our women had endured years of discrimination. We had to show them their own possibilities, their ability to do all kinds of work. We had to make them feel the urgent needs of our revolution in the construction of a new life. We had to change both women's image of herself and society's image of women.[14]

While government campaigns encouraged women's employment, however, a number of other government policies worked against it. For example, the government's wanting workers to work overtime without pay placed a substantial burden on working women with domestic responsibilities. "Socialist emulation," or the assigning of points according to the fulfillment of work quotas, punctuality, and participation in volunteer labor, also burdened working women. Workers with high scores were granted "vanguard worker" status and given medals, pennants, and other "moral rewards." Access to certain social benefits such as housing depended on positive marks in one's labor file.[15]

The introduction of moral incentives in the 1960s was complemented by the reduction or elimination of fees for many public services. The government hoped that if it reduced the need for money, the importance of wages would wane and enthusiasm for uncompensated work would grow. One young FMC member expressed her view that this was already the case among women:

> I think that women join the collective effort, in the majority of cases, because of their revolutionary consciousness. That is, they understand that their work is necessary for the country and, at the same time, that household activities dull their minds whereas work in society opens new horizons.[16]

But contrary to the hopes of the revolution, often women's motivation for seeking—or not seeking—employment was purely economic. In the early 1960s the onset of rationing (1962) and the lack of consumer goods meant there was little incentive for women to work. Between 1959 and 1964 only about eight thousand women per year joined the workforce. Minister of Labor Agosto Martínez Sánchez concluded that women's poor response was due not only to Cuba's "underdeveloped economy," but also to the revolution's inability to provide sufficient day care centers, school and workers' cafeterias, laundromats, and other needed services.[17]

Ironically, some working women found that the revolution's generous social policies made it possible for them to stop working outside the home. For example, in 1969 only one-quarter of the women in the Havana neighborhood of Buena Ventura were employed, whereas more than 90 percent had worked prior to the revolution.[18] Despite the revolution's best efforts, the home retained its powerful attraction for many women. In 1966 Fidel Castro admitted that his goal of one million women in production could not be reached by 1970, or perhaps even 1975.[19]

The Ten-Million-Ton Harvest

The significance of women's labor grew as Cuba geared up for the ten-million-ton harvest of 1970. The harvest's goal was to double Cuban sugar production, thereby enabling Cuba to pay its debts to the Soviet Union and have cash left over to purchase goods from the West. It was to be an "economic victory" of the same scale and audacity as the guerrilla victory against the Batista dictatorship.

A massive sugar harvest would require hundreds of thousands of workers, however, and male laborers were in short supply. Government stud-

ies showed that there were more than a million women of work age in
Cuba who were not employed.[20] The FMC pledged to persuade a hundred thousand women a year to join the workforce. Recruitment campaigns began in earnest, with FMC cadre visiting some four hundred
thousand women. Labor minister Jorge Risquet said these visits initiated
"an ideological dialogue between [women] and the revolution."[21]
Women were urged to take a variety of jobs that would free men to
participate in the sugar harvest. They also donated forty-one million
hours of volunteer labor.[22] A small number of women worked as cane
cutters while others took support jobs, washing clothes, cleaning dorms,
and organizing recreational activities.

Mujeres magazine claimed that the ten million harvest "began the massive incorporation of women into the first industry of the country."[23] In
fact, however, it was disappointing in terms of women's employment.
Although one out of four women visited by the FMC in 1969 agreed to
work, thousands of women already working left their jobs. The net gain
of the massive recruiting effort was only 27,000 women.[24]

The disappointing response was due in part to the lack of support
services and the continuing shortage of consumer goods. Why work if
there was nothing to buy? Many husbands continued to oppose their
wives' employment. Women workers complained of having to get up at
4:00 A.M. to prepare supper before going to work or face a furious husband in the evening.[25]

The ten-million-ton harvest did not succeed. Although a record 8.2
million tons of sugar were produced, the effort almost paralyzed the rest
of the economy. Thereafter the revolution veered onto a more conservative track of economic development, powerfully influenced and supported by the Soviet Union.

In the aftermath of the failure there was the inevitable search for scape-
goats. Why had so few women joined the great national effort? Why had
so many quit? Labor minister Jorge Risquet expressed scorn for Cuban
housewives, calling them a "dense layer of idle women" that was intolera-
ble in a country struggling for national development.[26] A Recovery
Commission was founded to "reclaim" all the women who had quit
work. A Permanence Commission was also established to study the problems of women in the workplace. The Commission called for amenities
such as lockers and separate bathrooms as well as greater attention to
hygiene and worker safety.[27]

At the end of 1969 there were 434,000 women in the workforce, less
than half of the million dreamed of by Castro. At the eighth Plenary of
the FMC in 1970 Labor Minister Risquet complained that much of the
revolution's effort in job creation and training had been undone by the
"tremendous turnover" among women workers.[28]

Some government officials blamed the FMC for women's failure to
join the harvest. Responsibility for overseeing the needs of women workers was transferred from the FMC to the newly established Feminine

Front of the Cuban trade unions (CTC). The Feminine Front was charged with keeping detailed records about a woman's work performance, absenteeism, and family life. It was also responsible for informing women of services such as openings in day care centers and children's boarding schools. When a woman was absent from work, a Feminine Front representative would visit her home to offer assistance and encourage her to return to work. The Feminine Front also worked with the FMC to make sure that unemployed women were informed of job openings.[29]

According to political scientist Jorge Domínguez, the FMC did not want to relinquish its role to the Feminine Front because it suspected that "the male-dominated trade unions would ignore women's concerns."[30] Time would show that the FMC's fears were well founded. In subsequent years there would be increasing tensions between the union and the FMC over the treatment of women workers.

In January 1971 a program was begun in Havana to "help guarantee permanence in the female workforce" by increasing the effectiveness of advocates for working women.[31] More than three hundred activists from the CTC, the Feminine Front, and the FMC were selected to attend classes in Havana in workplace hygiene, labor law, psychology, and social security.

In July 1971 Labor Minister Risquet renewed his complaints about women workers, saying that "there is still . . . a great difference between the number of working women and the total number of women of work age."[32] Thereafter the FMC initiated a number of changes. Women workers with child care problems were put on fixed shifts. Arrangements were made in factories so that women could send laundry directly from work to the cleaners. Some work centers established their own beauty parlors. Leaves of absence of up to one year without pay were made available to working women with children.[33]

Growth and Permanence

The failure of the ten-million-ton harvest led to dramatic changes in the Cuban economy. The moral incentives of the 1960s were put aside in favor of material incentives. Soviet advisors were added to every ministry. Then, in a serendipitous fillip, the price for sugar began to climb. The improving economy of the 1970s prompted a boom in women's employment. More than 350,000 new women workers entered the labor force, and most stayed. The percentage of women of work age in the labor force jumped from 24.9 in 1970 to 44.5 in 1979. At the end of the decade women represented 30 percent of Cuban workers.[34]

Women needed to work now because families had to pay for services, such as water and electricity, that had been free in the 1960s. The increased production and distribution of consumer goods also prompted women's employment. In 1972 a "parallel market" was inaugurated offering a range of goods at prices higher than under rationing. According to one estimate, women took 70 percent of the jobs created during the 1970s.[35] By 1974, women constituted 44 percent of the workers in light industry, where they produced consumer goods such as plastics, perfume, cosmetics, textiles, and furniture. Nearly 28 percent of the directors of the largest enterprises in this sector were women.[36]

In 1974 Fidel Castro urged the party and mass organizations to be particularly mindful of the needs of women workers because "First, it is a question of elemental justice; and second, it is an imperative necessity of the revolution . . . because at some point the male workforce will not be enough, it simply will not be enough."[37]

Although the government was becoming more sensitive to women's needs, many women were still gravitating to the least promising sectors of the labor force. Between 1974 and 1983, 43 percent of new women workers entered service or administrative jobs that had little potential for advancement.[38] The overwhelming majority of administrative workers in 1975 were women working primarily as receptionists and secretaries.[39] Many of the women's jobs in the service sector were duplicative, make-work positions. This systemic problem was evident in shops, hotels, restaurants, and ice cream parlors throughout Cuba, where two or more women were carrying out tasks that could easily be accomplished by one. Cuba's commitment to full employment often put efficiency on the back burner.

The concentration of women in certain "appropriate" fields continued and was now even codified by specific policy designed to "protect" women's reproductive capacity (see chapter 10). In 1974 the Ministries of Education and Health had more women workers than men.[40] The expansion in health and education helped to account for the tremendous growth in the number of women "technicians" and their relatively higher representation.[41] Counted as "technicians" were teachers and health workers, including paramedics, nurses, and doctors.

Women were also making progress in some agricultural sectors. They had long played a prominent role in tobacco. In 1953 they represented 52 percent of tobacco workers, and in 1974 they were more than half of the personnel in the tobacco ministry and 80 percent of the island's 15,000 tobacco workers.[42] Women's share of the total rural workforce grew to 11 percent by the mid-1970s.[43]

The introduction of a cooperative farm system in the 1970s had a significant impact on rural women. Previously agricultural production had occurred either on private family farms or on large state farms where workers were government employees. With cooperative farms, farmers pooled their land (donated it, in fact, to the government) and worked it collectively. Material and human assistance came from the government. The formation of co-ops was also encouraged by the building of new rural communities, which had apartments with running water, electricity, and appliances and offered services such as schools, social activities, and in some cases day care. By 1975, 282 new communities had been built throughout Cuba.[44]

The new rural communities were very attractive to women. They eased women's domestic burden and ended their isolation on the family farm, where, as Jean Stubbs and Mavis Alvarez have pointed out, women's work often "continued to go unrecorded and hence largely unheeded."[45] Women were more likely to be remunerated for their work in the co-ops. Such benefits prompted rural women to be "among the most ardent supporters of voluntary collectivization."[46] Economist Carmen Diana Deere similarly concluded that "women's enthusiasm for the new agricultural communities" was "a central factor" in the success of the cooperative movement.[47] By 1979 one-third of the cooperative members were women.[48]

Although the new rural towns improved women's living situation, as workers women continued to be treated as a reserve labor force while men continued to get first crack at paid permanent jobs.[49] Nonetheless, the modernization of Cuba's agriculture was gradually providing a new realm of work for women graduating from the new technical institutes as experts in animal husbandry, botany, engineering, and related fields.

Women's voluntary labor in the FMC–ANAP Mutual Aid brigades, Agricultural Contingents, and other bodies continued to be an important if little-recognized factor in the sugar, coffee, tobacco, and fruit harvests. In 1974 more than half the harvesters of these crops were women. Throughout Cuba 101,273 women were organized in nearly eight thousand FMC–ANAP brigades. By the mid-1970s some brigade members were paid, but most continued to work for free.[50]

Economic growth during the 1970s provided jobs for a growing number of single mothers like Sonia Hechevarria. In 1959, at age fifteen, Sonia was a wife, mother, and laundress. She became "incorporated" in the revolution, participating in volunteer work and joining the FMC. Her husband, alarmed by her new independence, told her to choose "either the revolution or me." She chose the revolution. In 1975 Sonia supported her seven children by working with 267 other women in a textile plant near Havana. Even without a husband she found that life had improved tremendously.[51]

While some husbands remained opposed to their wives' going off to work, others were intrigued by the idea of a second income. But there was a catch. With a working wife, the husband might have to help out at home. What to do? If men were ambivalent, the state was not. The state wanted to recoup its investment in women's education. As Fidel Castro observed:

> It costs a lot to train a nurse! It costs a lot of money to train a teacher! All those years . . . elementary school, high school. . . . And what a need we have for teachers! But if a young man made a good salary, and he married the teacher, he told her: "Don't go to work, we don't need the money. . . ." And the country lost a good teacher. Lost a good nurse.[52]

When young women didn't go to work after graduating from high school, parents were often the cause. A daughter at home meant extra help around the house. Furthermore, a daughter who worked violated tradition. In 1974 the FMC suggested that parents who refused to let their daughters work should reimburse the state for the cost of their daughters' educations.[53]

Meanwhile the FMC had concluded that managers were refusing to hire women because they were considered less reliable than men.[54] To combat this tendency, which the FMC held was erroneous, the media stressed women workers' professionalism and reliability. One article in 1977 profiled the forty-four workers at a baby clothes factory. The manager reported that no serious problems had resulted from having an all-female work force: "We have difficulties—the children, the home—but we also have strength and tenacity. We know how to accomplish our work and the tasks that the revolution has assigned us."[55]

New Laws and Policies

In the 1970s the Cuban government instituted a number of new policies to benefit working women. One of the first was Plan Jaba, or the shopping bag plan. It allowed working women to drop off shopping lists and grocery bags at local stores, where they would be filled while they were working. After work they would pick up their bags and pay for their groceries. Eligibility for the Plan Jaba required that all adults in the household work. By 1971 Plan Jaba was in place throughout Cuba.

A new maternity law in January 1974 granted all permanently employed mothers-to-be eighteen weeks paid leave. Pregnant women were given six full days or twelve half days off with pay for doctors' visits. For one year after the birth, working mothers could take one day off a month with pay for doctors' visits. Finally, a woman could choose to take an additional nine months' unpaid leave without losing her job, to be with her new child. In contrast to prerevolutionary maternity legislation, the new law would apply to virtually all women workers except those doing contract work. The FMC encouraged the hiring of extra workers to cover for women on maternity leave or doctors' visits. In day care centers and schools 10 percent more teachers and staff were hired.[56]

The most controversial social innovation of the mid-1970s was the Family Code, adopted on Valentine's Day 1975. It established the right of each spouse to get an education and pursue a profession. In effect the Family Code acknowledged that the government's intent to fully socialize household tasks was not feasible. Cuba could not afford all the day care centers, cafeterias, laundries, and other services that women needed, and so men would have to do their part. The Family Code required both husband and wife to share in household duties and child care, and couples would have to agree to these notions as part of their marriage contract. The Family Code also prescribed that, in case of a divorce, alimony be paid by a working spouse to a nonworking spouse for six months or a year depending on whether or not there were children.

Prior to its adoption, the Family Code was hotly debated by millions of Cubans at local meetings of the CDRs (block committees), the FMC, and the CTC (the labor organization), as well as in the streets. After years of championing changes in women's roles, the revolution was suggesting that men's roles should also change. Many men were appalled. One male People's Power representative told a foreign journalist that he hated the Family Code but had voted for it to avoid having his wife accuse him of being "a *machista* counterrevolutionary."[57] Following the Family Code's adoption some men grudgingly acknowledged that they "should help out" with domestic chores; the FMC reminded men that they were to "share," not "help out," an important distinction. The Family Code made it possible for women to legally divorce their husbands for not assuming domestic tasks, but this was not a useful threat since divorce typically left women worse off, with total responsibility for home and children.[58]

Not all labor policies introduced during the 1970s proved to be compatible with sexual equality in the workplace. In 1971 a Law Against Loafing was implemented which made it a crime for males of working age (17–60) to remain unemployed. The law encouraged women of working age (17–55) to get a job but did not require them to do so. Labor Minister Risquet explained that because women "have the job of reproducing as well as producing" it would be unreasonable to oblige them to work.[59]

Within three months the antiloafing law led more than a hundred thousand men to seek employment, half of whom had never held a job.[60] The FMC had wanted the law to require women to work as well. It was concerned that women's "disengagement" from the revolution was accepted while men's was not.[61]

The revolution's desire for equality and social justice in the workplace was severely tested by the new "rationalized" management system of 1975. This system emphasized efficiency by requiring that each enterprise be self-financing. As profits became important, labor costs came under closer scrutiny. Some administrators claimed that women workers, whose family responsibilities prompted frequent absences, hurt their plants' profitability. Ironically the new maternity law provided administrators with a rationale for not hiring women.[62]

In December 1975 the Communist party, with considerable input from the FMC, presented an analysis of the changing status of women entitled, "Thesis: On the Full Exercise of Women's Equality." The thesis concluded that working women's greatest problem was their exclusive responsibility for family matters. It acknowledged that this double responsibility meant fewer promotions, more turnover, and continued discrimination.[63] In acknowledging the tension between women's duties and the criteria for choosing exemplary workers, the party urged that special allowances be made for "working women with children." Thus the party was proposing a double standard to "help" women workers, thereby actually reinforcing the notion that domestic tasks remained women's exclusive responsibility. It suggested that, in the assessment of workers, women's domestic responsibilities should be taken into account while men's should not. The party thesis also called for more training for the "thousands of women [who were] willing to work" but who lacked the necessary skills.[64] It decried the concentration of women workers in menial jobs and called for further efforts to extend training programs to both the unemployed and those women who, with additional skills, could upgrade their position.

In 1979 a new social security law offered improved pensions and retirement benefits for women. Women who had worked twenty-five years would receive 40 percent of their pay at age fifty-five. Women workers who were incapacitated would receive pensions, provided they were over age forty-six and had worked for ten years.[65] The 1979 social security law also extended pension benefits to include cooperative farm members—an important first for rural workers. Female co-op workers became eligible for retirement at age sixty after fifteen years of work. Unlike urban workers, these rural women workers could "double dip," or continue to work at full pay and not lose their pensions.[66]

The criteria for widows' pensions were revised to end discrimination against working women. Under the new law a widow who worked, regardless of her age, would receive 25 percent of her widow's pension in addition to her salary. Widows who didn't work and who were younger than forty would receive a pension for two years to allow them to find a job.

New Fields

Despite the tendency to feminize certain ministries and occupations, women entered many new fields in the 1970s. Indeed hardly a week passed without a woman being celebrated in the media for going to work in a formerly male profession. Women started working in medical research, biotechnology, and computers, all fields that did not exist in the 1950s. This trend led one reporter to boast that those who think women ought to do things only at home "is on the way to extinction in Cuba."[67] Still, these women pioneers had to combat many stereotypical notions among both men and women. Occasionally it was even necessary to confront the state's restrictive laws and paternalistic attitudes (see chapter 10).

The Adalberto Gómez Núñez Electrical plant, begun in 1964, offers one example of how early training programs helped women move into nontraditional fields. The plant combined a factory with a hands-on technical school. By 1975, 65 of the factory's 116 workers were women. The director of the factory admitted that even though many of the women were mothers with small children, absenteeism was less than five percent.[68]

Men's response to women co-workers was mixed. In 1964 a woman mechanic found her male co-workers in a Havana automotive repair shop to be "very helpful." Although they were reserved at first, "once they saw I was ready to work, they made me feel right at home." A group of women shipbuilders at one Havana yard, however, complained that "some of the men were downright mean, trying to break us, to make us cry."[69] A former maid who joined the steel industry in 1962 was told by co-workers, "You'll never make it"; seventeen years later she was still on the job.[70]

When journalists wrote about women pioneers, they inevitably referred to their looks, their womanly delicacy, as if to allay fears that entering "male" trades would masculinize women. Thus Judith Pérez, a mining engineer, was described in 1977 as "soft and feminine but firm as nickel when concerned with . . . her work."[71] There was also Isis Galbán, a chemical engineer, who, "notwithstanding her youth and beauty," held an important post with the Cuban Institute of Sugar Research.[72]

Governmental encouragement of women's entrance into nontraditional fields was based on economic need as well as revolutionary egalitarianism. The great push for women's employment in the construction sector during the booming 1970s reflects the way the Cuban government directed female labor to fit development priorities. Thousands of buildings were needed—schools, polyclinics, hospitals, and multiple-unit housing. Where would the necessary workers be found? In 1974 Fidel Castro announced:

> If the construction sector doesn't develop, neither will the other sectors. This is one of the sectors that ought to grow the most in future years. Where are we going to find the workers? There is no doubt that we have no other recourse but to incorporate women into the construction sector. . . . We must make a special effort to bring women into the building trade.[73]

Fidel had spoken. The Federation of Cuban Women sprang into action. Recruitment began in earnest to convince housewives to take up hammer and trowel. Many responded, but there were problems. At the August 1975 meeting of the Union of Construction Workers women complained that they didn't have lockers or adequate toilet facilities at work and that work hours conflicted with their children's schedules. Many women were insufficiently trained, and training programs suffered from crowding and a lack of teachers. Women took construction jobs but soon quit.

Still women's response was gratifying. In October 1975 Vilma Espín told the First National Meeting of Women Construction Workers: "I remember how Fidel decided that we needed to incorporate women into construction. The response so far of fifteen thousand women who have gone right to work has exceeded all estimates."[74] Elida Valle, secretary of production for the FMC, praised women's "fervent desire to cooperate, to be useful." She noted that women brought more than just strong arms and a willing mind to work: "Now the work centers are more decorated, not just by the female presence, but by the order, adornments, and the cleanliness that women bring wherever they go."[75]

9

Progress and Problems in Women's Employment, 1980–1992

Cuban women are no longer satisfied with boring, dead-end jobs.

Digna Cires, Feminine Front (1986)[1]

Before, under capitalism, I earned my living making carbon in Matanzas when they paid 25 cents a sack. Now I am a winch operator in Old Havana, and when I get the opportunity I also participate in the agricultural brigades in the countryside.

Marta Delgado (1991)[2]

I don't like my work at all. It's monotonous and poorly paid.

Silvia, twenty-seven-year-old textile worker (1991)[3]

Always with a smile on their lips, they pass the hours singing in the hot summer sun.

Journalist describing twelve women members of an emergency plantain-planting brigade (1991)[4]

The surge of women's employment which began in the 1970s continued into the next decade. In 1984 a goal that was set twenty years before was achieved: one million Cuban women were at work. In 1990, women constituted 39.6 percent of the labor force.

The growth of the female workforce was propelled by an expanding economy. Sugar prices were good and significant aid was flowing in from the Soviet Union. Economic growth permitted the continued expansion of the service sector, health, and education, thus providing many jobs to women.[5] Women were graduating from the educational system trained to become workers at every level. A variety of material incentives enhanced the utility of women's employment. In addition, many of the growing numbers of single mothers had no choice but to work.

Women's employment had risen dramatically in the 1970s, yet in the 1980s there was a certain skepticism as to whether the economy could sustain this pace. Indeed as early as the mid-1970s the union, fearing a future labor glut, sought to scrap policies that gave women preferential treatment in employment in certain fields.[6] Fidel Castro warned in 1980 that further increases in women's employment might not be possible.[7]

During the 1980s three research projects on women workers—the first of their kind in revolutionary Cuba—provided new insight into working women's experience. One was a report on women workers in a brick and tile factory, published by sociologist Marta Núñez Sarmiento of the University of Havana. The other two were conducted by North Americans. Anthropologist Helen Safa carried out a study of women textile workers in conjunction with the FMC, and sociologist Marie Withers Osmond also studied women textile workers, but without official permission. The results of these inquiries into the situation of working women produced conclusions that called into question some of the most basic assumptions of Cuba's program for women's advancement.

Male Resistance

By the 1980s male resistance to the notion of women working outside the home was fading. Researchers found that while in the 1960s to have a wife who worked brought dishonor, in the 1980s the reverse was true. Now having a wife who didn't work was embarrassing and produced explanations such as these: "She isn't well." "She's having trouble with her nerves." "She has problems." "She's looking for something that would suit her."[8]

Throughout the 1980s the female labor force continued to grow at a steady rate despite a decline in government enthusiasm for women's employment. Between 1980 and 1990 more than half a million women workers joined the labor force, an increase of 64 percent. Nearly one out of two women of working age was now employed.[9] The profile of women's employment, however, changed more slowly.

Women's representation among service workers (restaurant personnel, shop clerks, etc.) grew from less than half a percent in 1975 to 62.5 percent in 1989. These low-skill, low-stress jobs were often attractive to women with heavy domestic responsibilities.[10] At the same time, women continued to make significant inroads in health and education. By 1990, women constituted 66 percent of the teachers, 48 percent of doctors, and 69 percent of dentists.[11] However, women's representation among manual workers remained low (18.9 percent in 1989), not only because of women's reluctance to take such jobs but also because Cuban labor laws prohibited them from work that could "damage" their reproductive capacity (see chapter 10). In fact between 1974 and 1983 the percentage of working women doing manual work decreased from 25 to 22 percent.[12] The FMC complained that while women entered more advanced technical programs in significant numbers—largely because of an affirmative action plan intended to guarantee that 50 percent of jobs in certain new industries went to women—they shied away from trades such as mechanics and assembly-line work, for which there was strong demand.[13]

The modernization, technification, and further collectivization of Cuban agriculture in the 1980s brought mixed results for women workers. Collectivization cut in half the number of private farms from the mid-1960s to the mid-1980s.[14] What became of the women on these farms? Some volunteered with the FMC–ANAP brigades while others became paid workers in cooperatives, on state farms, or in nonagricultural jobs. Moving to the new rural communities allowed more than a few women to quit farm work altogether to become housewives.[15] In 1989, women made up 26 percent of agricultural workers.[16] This figure may be misleading, however, because it includes part-time and short-term contract workers. Jean Stubbs and Mavis Alvarez reported in 1987: "Although agriculture is still today a major source of full-time paid employment for men, it only accounts for 10 percent of women in full-time occupations. A significant proportion of that 10 percent are in clerical and technical jobs."[17]

While the percentage of women workers on state farms crept up to 22 percent by 1991,[18] the number of women working in rural cooperatives declined. Between 1979 and 1991 the representation of women cooperative members dropped from one-third to 11 percent.[19] Economist Carmen Diana Deere concluded that women cooperative workers earned less money than men because "male" jobs were better paid and because women worked fewer hours than men. She also found that women were more likely to be temporary workers on both state farms and rural cooperatives.[20]

In 1990 the FMC reviewed the progress of women's employment and concluded that overall "women have not been incorporated with equal dynamism to the fundamental tasks in industry and the essential activities of the agricultural, forestry, and transport sectors."[21]

New Work at Home and Abroad

Despite certain disappointments in the pattern of female employment, women did make further inroads in new and nontraditional fields in the 1980s. In 1989 more than 30 percent of agricultural technicians and more than one-third of the fifteen hundred agricultural advisors assigned to cooperatives were women. At the same time, women constituted 41 percent of all agricultural engineers, 35 percent of forestry engineers, and up to 47 percent of engineers in a variety of fields.[22] In 1989 civil engineer Aleida Casas Morfe was in charge of building the highway between that Juragua nuclear plant and the city of Cienfuegos, and her workers were reportedly exceeding production plans. One male worker character-ized her as "very sweet, but very firm . . . an inspiration."[23]

However some female engineers had problems. Luz del Carmen Otero Arenal, the director of training in the petroleum industry, recalled in 1987 that male *petroleros* were shocked to see women on the job: "When a woman appeared in the area, they would give the shout of alarm . . . such language you have never heard . . . it was horrible."[24] Eventually things worked out, however. She noted also that the feminine penchant for neatness encouraged the men to dress better and keep their machin-ery cleaner.

Another female petroleum engineer was sent to a remote locale, where, to her surprise and displeasure, she was obliged to share a hut with her male boss. She argued that the state must ensure the existence of certain basic conditions "if they want women to move into this kind of labor."[25]

In the 1980s the progress of women in entirely new fields became more evident. In 1988 the first Cuban microchip was produced under the direction of Magaly Estrada, head of microelectronics at the Center for Digital Research. Indeed women represented more than 52 percent of the workers in the field of electronics and information.[26]

In the 1980s thousands of Cuban women worked abroad in various capacities as "internationalists" helping other developing countries. Half of the first contingent of twelve hundred teachers sent to Nicaragua to participate in the Sandinista literacy campaign in 1980 were women. Fi-del Castro proudly observed that "not one woman" had returned home because she "couldn't take the conditions."[27] Nor did difficult conditions keep 34 women from participating in a brigade of 366 Cubans sent to Siberia in 1987 to cut timber destined for Cuba's housing sector.[28]

Because international service brought prestige and often professional and political advancement, selection was competitive. In 1980 Fidel Cas-tro noted the problems involved when women go abroad: "When women must leave the family behind, the human sacrifice is greater than when a man leaves."[29] Nonetheless he vowed that mothers would not be excluded. Some women left their children behind with husbands and grandparents for stints of up to two years. Carmen García was one of these. A nurse, Communist party member, and mother of three, García went to Iraq on her first overseas mission in 1981. In 1987, when she was in Ethiopia on her second mission, this time at a children's clinic, President Mengistu Haile Mariam gave her his personal wristwatch as a token of appreciation.[30]

Policy Impact and Union Advocacy

As in the previous decade, more women in the 1980s went to work to pay the bills and also to take advantage of the increased availability of goods. A 1981 price hike for more than fifteen hundred consumer goods and services meant, according to economist Carmelo Mesa-Lago, a 50 percent increase in the cost of living.[31] The parallel market continued to expand, and farmers' markets offering good-quality fruits, vegetables, and meats at unregulated prices were opened.

Sometimes policies designed to "help" working women had contrary effects. As political scientist Elsa M. Chaney noted in 1979 in regard to all of Latin America:

> Maternity leaves, child care provisions, and protective legislation (such as prohibitions against overtime and night work for women) . . . ironically appear to work against the incorporation of women in developing econo- mies rather than in their favor. . . . such laws make women more expen- sive to hire than men, and more troublesome, since their jobs must be cov- ered somehow in their absence.[32]

The tension between the needs of working mothers and the economic efficiency of state enterprises was a major test for the idealistic notions of the revolution. For some managers the solution was not to hire women.[33] In 1980 Fidel Castro warned managers not to push the idea of profitability too far: "We can't go just by a strictly economic criterion without ever taking into account social justice. We're not capitalists, we're socialists, and we want to be communists."[34] The lack of a clear criterion, however, left managers torn between revolutionary idealism and the practical demands of running a factory. With little specific incen- tive to promote equality, efficiency often won the day. Women workers complained to the FMC, which routinely exposed such discrimination in its publications. FMC president Vilma Espín became an outspoken critic of sexist labor practices (see chapter 10).

In theory the Confederation of Cuban Workers (CTC) should have played an important role in negotiating a balance between profitability and social justice, but under the revolution the CTC had a dual role as defender of the workers and agent of the state. It functioned largely in the latter capacity. The CTC failed to defend women workers even though most full-time women workers belonged to the union and a sub- stantial number of women served as officials. Even so, in 1988 there was only one woman among the twenty-four members of the union's Executive Secretariat.[35]

In her 1989 study of the Ariguanabo textile mill, anthropologist Helen Safa found that 62 percent of the 168 women interviewed thought the union had benefited women workers, but they could not say how. They went on to say that "they were not listened to in union meetings."[36] When women were asked to whom they presented their work com- plaints, the "overwhelming response" was "management," not the union. The FMC was identified by the women workers as the organization that "had done the most for working women."

In a study of the Angel Guerra brick and tile factory in Marianao,

Cuban sociologist Marta Núñez Sarmiento found that two-thirds of its more than fifty women workers thought the union was indifferent to their concerns.[37] And in discussing working conditions in a Cuban textile factory, the sixty-one female textile workers interviewed by Marie Withers Osmond found the union so inconsequential that they did not even mention it.[38]

Economist Linda Fuller concluded that after 1970, Cuban unions "were not always willing or able to defend members whose rights were violated."[39] She cited several cases in which union support for or abandonment of women workers in conflicts with management seemed arbitrary, based more on personalities than on organizational mandate. In one case the union refused to assist a woman who had been fired for her forceful advocacy on behalf of her fellow workers. On another occasion the union did stand behind a woman complaining of sexual harassment by her supervisor, but in this case the union had party support, and it was the party that protected the complainant from reprisals.[40]

In 1990, thanks to pressure from the FMC, the CTC congress for the first time took notice of issues of special concern to women workers. The union agreed that workers who did not pay child support or attend to their children should be thrown out, and that the union should work toward promoting appropriate family values. The CTC also recognized the need to promote women into management and to give them fuller access to training programs, particularly in tourism, which was an increasingly important source of hard currency in the late 1980s.[41]

Women in Management

The presence of women in management grew significantly over time but still did not correspond to women's overall participation in the labor force. In 1974, women constituted 25.3 percent of the workforce and 15 percent of managers.[42] In 1989 those figures were 38.6 and 26.5, respectively. Even in female-dominated fields, such as education and health, men typically held most of the higher-level positions.[43] Research confirmed the existence of a glass ceiling; women managers were only rarely present beyond midlevel positions.[44]

A number of studies were carried out to determine public views regarding women in management. In 1988, 70 percent of the respondents to a *Mujeres* magazine survey indicated that workers' ability and not their sex should be the basis for promotion. Twelve percent of the women interviewed preferred to work for men, while 18 percent preferred women because they are "much more organized and polite."[45] The rest had no preference.

Cuban officials alleged that the scarcity of women managers was due to their lack of leadership qualities. Some women supported this notion. In a debate over the promotion of women at a textile plant in Pinar del

Río one woman commented: "[M]anagement requires authority, which comes naturally to men. Managers have to think of the plant above everything, and women are incapable of this."[46]

One might assume that achieving managerial positions would be an important goal for many Cuban women, but the double demands of work and home left many women with no desire to take on more responsibility (see also chapter 11). As Isabel Larguía and John Dumoulin concluded in 1986, "If women had to work twelve hours a day, between their place of work and the domestic sphere, they tended to prefer jobs that were easier than men's and with less responsibility so as to have energy left over for the second shift at home."[47] Yet this unwillingness to serve, what the revolution called "self-limitation" *(autolimitarse)*, may be overstated. While in a 1974 survey 54.3 percent of the women respondents said they would not want to assume leadership roles,[48] a 1988 survey indicated that 65 percent of women workers questioned would be willing to serve. Three-quarters of the women workers in the Núñez (1992) study indicated they would be willing to serve in supervisory positions, while only 26 percent of the men expressed interest.[49] Nevertheless, virtually all the supervisors at Núñez's brick factory were male.

Interestingly, job turnover in the late 1980s was significantly higher among *male* workers. Beginning in the 1980s women workers were in general better educated than their male counterparts and were more likely to hold a particular job longer than men. Job stability among women hovered at 95 percent for most of the decade.[50]

In the brick factory studied by Marta Núñez, male workers thought that the greatest barrier to women's advancement was their relative lack of education and qualifications; in truth, the women were better educated and more qualified than the men. Men also saw women's double day, management's preference for men, and women's aversion to leadership as barriers to their advancement. Women viewed these factors differently, however. For them the number one problem was management's preference for men, followed by the double day, women's disinclination to lead, and last, women's alleged lack of education and qualifications.[51]

The sexual division of labor, a widespread practice in Cuba, also contributed to the dearth of women managers. For example, supervisors at the Ariguanabo textile mill, one-third of whose workforce was female, were typically chosen from the ranks of the mechanics, but there were no women mechanics. The result was that only thirteen of ninety-four work brigades in the plant were headed by women.[52]

Still another impediment to women's progress was prejudice against older women. The different ages for male and female retirement—sixty for men and fifty-five for women—reinforced the idea that women age more quickly. Nonetheless, at its fourth congress the FMC requested a further reduction in the female retirement age from fifty-five to fifty, in part to guarantee job openings for young women.[53]

Even the National Bank of Cuba, widely considered a model for female employment and promotion, had its problems. In 1985, 43.8 percent of bank officials were women, but most held low or middle-range
positions. There was only one woman, revolutionary heroine Melba Hernández, among the twenty-nine bank presidents, vice presidents, and directors.[54] Still, women were pleased with their situation at the bank.
One female department head observed that "here there are no factors of
inequality, of undervaluing of women, or concepts of false paternalism
. . . which exist in other places." An older female official recalled the
frustration of the 1950s when the highest rung on the career ladder for
women at the bank was private secretary. Before 1959, women were not
even considered for cashier's positions.[55]

One reason given for women's success in the National Bank was the
support of husbands and parents. Others cited the National Bank's exten-
sive training program and its sensitivity to problems faced by women
with small children. Other factors that aided women bankers were their
generally high level of education, the location of the bank in Havana,
and the fact that women employees were more numerous than men in
the finance sector.

Problems of a New Generation

The 1980s witnessed a growing generational divide among women
workers. The young female brick workers studied by Marta Núñez, for
example, were mostly high school graduates, whereas their mothers had
only completed fourth grade. The young women were working in a nontraditional field newly opened to women; only 40 percent of their mothers were or had been workers, and they worked in fields, where traditionally large numbers of women were employed.[56]

Older women, particularly working-class women, who remembered
how difficult life had been before 1959, were often grateful for any
steady job. Hilda Reyes López, a fish packer who in 1987 earned the
title "National Vanguard Worker" by routinely producing nearly twice
the daily norm, was motivated by a profound sense of gratitude to the
revolution. One of ten children from a poor family from Bayamo, her
highest aspiration was that "my daughter will never have to experience
the suffering and sacrifices of my childhood."[57]

But while the older generation of Cuban workers appreciated the
changes brought by the revolution, younger women, with their advanced
educations and high aspirations, were frustrated by the limited possibilities offered by the Cuban economy. This situation presented a dilemma
for the regime. The educational system was creating hopes for upward
mobility that the island's economy could not satisfy.

Young women in the 1980s faced a paradoxical problem: as female
employment increased, so did female unemployment.[58] In 1981 the gov-

ernment responded to the problem of female unemployment by creating Women's Employment Commissions at the national, provincial, and municipal levels. The commissions, composed of representatives from the Ministry of Labor, the CTC, the FMC, and the Social Security and Employment Commission, were to keep tabs on the availability of jobs for women, with emphasis placed on securing employment for single mothers.

The FMC soon concluded that the Women's Employment Commissions were not doing their job, and they themselves wanted a larger role in the employment process. In 1985 the FMC urged the Women's Employment Commission to sanction managers who violated laws and norms in the hiring of women. Nothing happened. The FMC also called for forced retirement to ensure job openings for younger workers.[59]

The fumbling efforts to deal with female unemployment reflected the systemic dilemmas of bureaucratic overlap and lack of coordination. When a reader wrote to *Mujeres* magazine in 1983 that she could not find a job in her town, the magazine suggested that she contact potential employers directly or visit her municipality's job bank.[60] No mention was made of the Women's Employment Commissions. Several years later researchers at the Institute of Labor Research concluded that Cuba's job placement services, especially for beginning workers, were inadequate, that little effort was being made to meet the job interests and aptitudes of applicants. A leading labor official thought the work of the various commissions was mired in bureaucracy, "a cobweb of statistics and models."[61] In 1990 Vilma Espín complained that the Women's Employment Commissions "[didn't] have the authority it should have."[62]

Female unemployment in the 1980s was also a result of the educational system's output of narrowly trained specialists who found it difficult to adapt to new tasks. Still a greater dilemma was the reluctance of young women to do manual labor. Parents who were themselves manual laborers wanted their children to be university graduates and white-collar workers. After graduation their daughters would come home, where they were supported by their parents until an "appropriate" job came along. It was unfortunate, wrote one journalist, that white-collar professional jobs were still considered the most prestigious in Cuba. "But we must ask ourselves, who is going to produce the goods?"[63] The revolution itself had to share the blame, she admitted, for offering higher pay to professionals and too few incentives to manual workers.

Another challenge for young women workers was finding work near home. Such was the case with Lexa Espinosa and her husband. The Espinosas, both recent graduates of the same meat inspection program, moved to eastern Cuba, where the husband was hired. When he later left Cuba on an internationalist mission, Lexa filled his position, and upon his return, she was let go. For a while she worked as a secretary in a nearby fish plant, but eventually she abandoned the job and her marriage in favor of more satisfying work in Havana—in another field.[64]

Occasionally young women graduates were told there were no jobs in their field only to discover that the positions being applied for had been given to young men. Thus a young female graduate in electrical mechanics was advised that it was "very difficult for women" to find jobs in electrical mechanics. Time passed. She married, had a daughter, and was eventually offered a job sewing baseball gloves. She accepted. After six years in the sports factory she had given up all hope of finding work in her field.[65]

In 1988 the Young Communist League and the Federation of Middle Level Students announced that twenty thousand young middle-level technicians, both men and women, were unable to find jobs in their fields. Fidel Castro called for the creation of a "qualified reserve." The Ministry of Labor began offering the young people interim jobs in other fields such as construction and tourism.[66] In 1990 Vilma Espín announced that a retraining program designed by the state labor commission for unemployed middle-level technicians had been very helpful for many women.

Rectification and Beyond

In 1986 the rectification campaign presented a new series of challenges for Cuba's working women. While the campaign did allow greater public criticism—within limits—of certain policies and practices in the Cuban workplace, its emphasis on austerity and efficiency challenged some of the advances made by women workers.

One important element of the rectification campaign was the drive to reduce excess employment, or *empleomania*. Fidel Castro complained that administrators were employing two or three times more workers than necessary. In 1986 there was an estimated surplus of ten thousand public health workers in Havana alone. In November 1987 Castro indicated that "factories that once employed fourteen hundred are now producing more with six hundred workers."[67] The government provided benefits and pensions to "excess workers" to ease the transition.

The attack on excess employment ended one of the revolution's efforts to accommodate working mothers. Many women were part of a "buffer hiring" program—which reached 10 percent of staff in some ministries—designed to cover maternity-related absences. Ironically, as Castro was trying to cut excess workers, the FMC was calling for the extension of buffer hiring to other fields.[68]

Despite Fidel Castro's push to trim excess workers, *empleomania* was still very much in evidence in the tourist sector in the spring of 1992. Elevators in one hotel were attended by not one but two female operators each. Tourist shops the size of a double bed boasted three female clerks.

One of the key themes of rectification was to restore volunteer work to the eminence it had had during the 1960s. Workers were asked to donate part of their workday to help reduce production costs. Workers at a hardware factory in Guanabacoa, for example, worked two hours overtime every day—without pay.[69]

The cost cutting required by "rectification" also meant problems for women. In December 1987 a reporter visiting an industrial parts factory found that women workers could not arrange for child care during two of its three shifts because the plant hours had been extended beyond day care hours. The solution, according to the union representative, a woman, was to replace the female workers with men.[70]

To absorb surplus labor created by personnel cuts, Castro reactivated the microbrigade construction program to produce needed housing, day care, and tourist facilities that the Ministry of Construction seemed unable to provide. Some of the microbrigade workers were housewives and retirees, although most were workers on leave from their overstaffed factories. The microbrigades had been abandoned in the 1970s because of their excessive cost and poor workmanship, but in 1987 they were back in vogue, at least for a while. By summer 1989 approximately thirty-three thousand workers had been placed in microbrigades. Only 6 percent of those were women.[71]

Castro applauded the brigades for routinely putting in ten and twelve hour days. He praised a brigade of women tile installers in Havana who were working fourteen hours a day, including Saturday and sometimes Sunday.[72] Marta Levda, a trained chemist and mother of two children, had been reassigned to a tile-laying microbrigade in 1987 and was working twelve to fourteen hours daily. She lamented the fact that not only did she rarely see her young sons, she was unable to make adequate day care arrangements. "I know there are many women in my situation," she said.[73]

In the spring of 1990 Castro announced that Cuba's loss of trade and aid from the Eastern bloc meant that the Cuban economy would have to become more self-sufficient. Agricultural brigades were organized to grow foodstuffs. Workers were given leave from their jobs for periods of two weeks to two years to work in the brigades. Urban workers were transported to rural areas, where they were assigned to barracks with communal cooking and eating facilities, a first in socialist Cuba. Brigades were usually sex segregated, and, because they were organized according to factory and not family, husbands and wives and children were often separated, sometimes for extended periods of time.

In 1992 the women workers of the Colonel Juan Delgado agricultural brigade were working in vegetable production in Batabanó. The brigade included textile workers, students, and a professor; some of the workers were women with young children. One woman noted that she enjoyed working with the oxen that had replaced tractors in Cuban fields. Another, formerly an artist, felt she was repaying a debt, since she had been born in the countryside but had never worked on the land. "Now I have done everything, and I feel better than before," she said.[74] Talia Fung, a professor at the University of Havana, said she didn't mind the work; it kept her in good shape, even if stoop labor was a little difficult for a woman in her fifties.[75] The big lure of the agricultural brigades was food: the workers were well fed.

The FMC began to organize housewives to do voluntary labor in agriculture. By 1991 these groups were responsible for a significant portion of food crops. Housewives also contributed through a program of family gardens for public consumption. As of January 1991, ten thousand hectares had been converted to family garden plots.[76]

The emergency economy of the 1990s created new difficulties for women workers. To save fuel, bus services were sharply reduced, and so getting to work was a nightmare. For workers who lived in the outlying neighborhoods it could take three hours to get to downtown Havana. The bicycles that were imported from China and sold in workplaces were no solution for most women. An informal count in May 1992 showed that eight times more men than women were riding bicycles, despite the fact that the bikes were distributed through the workplace and that women constituted 40 percent of the workers.[77] How then were women getting to work? Or were they staying home?

The emergency economy of the early 1990s raised serious questions about future prospects for working women. Would women now be encouraged to stay home or be channeled into volunteer labor? A 1991 change in day care rules which increased the minimum age of day care eligibility from forty-five days to six months hinted in that direction.[78] Or would the growing number of highly trained working women prove to be essential in difficult times? The economic and political crises of the 1990s will demonstrate to what degree Cuba's working women constitute a reserve labor force.

10

Sexual Discrimination in the Workplace

Socialist society must eradicate every form of discrimination against women. . . . But women also have other functions in society. . . . They are the creators par excellence of the human being. And I say this because instead of being the object of discrimination and inequality, women deserve special consideration from society.

Fidel Castro (1974) [1]

To care for chickens may seem a trivial thing. Nevertheless, it requires special qualities of patience and care on the part of the worker. This is why women, with their innate faculties for lavishing care, represent the highest percentage of workers in poultry farms.

Male director of Camagüey chicken farm (1983) [2]

It is undeniable that we have made much progress in the struggle for equality, but it is also true that discriminatory practices still exist. Consequently it is essential that the leaders and militants of the Cuban Communist party energetically combat any unjust action . . . that they valiantly combat all remnants of bourgeois ideology that still prevail.

Vilma Espín (1986) [3]

Egalitarianism was a central value of the Cuban revolution. A key test of Cuban egalitarianism was the treatment accorded to women in the workplace. While the revolution was committed to sexual equality in theory and rhetoric, this commitment was often undercut by persistent traditional notions of women's role as well as by the pressing need for economic efficiency.

In the fields and on the shop floor women were often seen not as equals but rather as helpers, or as temporary substitutes for men in jobs

121

that did not require men's superior strength. The revolution also sought to "protect" women by legally restricting their access to jobs that supposedly endangered their reproductive capacity. These policies were a factor in the feminization of certain fields.

In adopting labor laws and policies that discriminated against women, Cuba's male policy makers were acting in accord with the traditional Latin American view that a woman's primary role is reproduction and that this role had to be privileged and protected. The revolution, according to one spokesman, was struggling to "correctly situate the objective possibilities of the feminine workforce."[4] It was also trying to avoid alienating male workers, many of whom were hostile to the idea of working with women.

Sex-Based Restrictions

Cuba's prerevolutionary "protective" labor legislation was derived from European laws, which, beginning in the late nineteenth century and influenced by the women's rights movement, were aimed at defending working women's maternal role. The intent of these laws was not to limit opportunities for women, but rather to support their employment while also guarding their socially valued role as mothers.[5]

In Cuba, where veneration of motherhood is a cornerstone of national culture, the revolutionary government expressed concern that the new emphasis on women's employment might prompt women to enter fields that were not "appropriate," because "the feminine organism has its limitations." These limitations were due not only to women's physique "and the development of her organs," but also to the fact that women suffer "profound changes during menstruation and maternity."[6] The labor union's (CTC) newspaper *Trabajo* concluded in 1964:

> In offices, teaching, and stores, women are better situated than men, who should be doing labor where there is a greater necessity of physical force. . . . Women are particularly apt for work that requires manual dexterity; also they are better at monotonous jobs which cause men to despair because of their more impatient nature.[7]

Trabajo insisted that women should not be required to stand for long periods, to use physical strength, or to do dangerous work.

In January 1965 Fidel Castro called for a study to determine which jobs were appropriate for women. The result was Resolutions 47 and 48. Resolution 47 allocated 437 kinds of jobs exclusively to women. All men doing "female" jobs were asked voluntarily to transfer to jobs more appropriate for their sex; they were not to suffer any reduction in salary. The FMC, seeing Resolution 47 as a boon to working women, tried to persuade men doing "women's work" to change jobs. Twenty-five thousand men agreed.[8]

While the FMC was enthusiastic about Resolution 47, it quietly opposed Resolution 48, which prohibited women from working in 498 jobs considered dangerous to their reproductive function, including subterranean work, work in quarries, work under water, work where physical force is required, work at heights, work with equipment that produces "large vibrations" (e.g., driving bulldozers), work at high and low temperatures, and work in "dangerous places." The resolution required the temporary transfer of pregnant women from jobs that could pose a potential health danger, and it guaranteed that women transferred from banned jobs would not suffer reduced pay.[9]

Resolution 48 proved difficult to enforce, and Resolution 47 proved to be unworkable. Too few women applied for the special jobs. Many of the 25,000 men who had agreed to transfer to more "masculine" work reneged, while others refused to consider any change. In 1973 the CTC requested that both resolutions be revoked. In a classic case of ambivalence, the union urged that women be trained for jobs in all fields while urging that their reproductive capacity be protected, even if that meant instituting gender-based job bans.[10] Resolution 47, which was favored by the FMC, was eventually revoked by the Ministry of Labor. Resolution 48 remained in force.

In 1976 the FMC helped draft Resolution 40, which reduced the number of jobs forbidden to women to 300. Still the FMC was uneasy about such restrictions. At its third congress in 1980 the FMC publicly called Resolution 40 "an obstacle to women's advancement."[11] The resolution was later revised, then abolished, only to be replaced by a similar Resolution 51. In 1986 Vilma Espín claimed that sex-based jobs were being reassessed on a "truly scientific basis."[12] Four years later the FMC was still complaining that Resolution 51 was discriminatory.[13]

Cuba's 1982 occupational safety and hygiene law affirmed that women should not be employed in positions "that can result in physical injury."[14] It obliged factories to create proper work conditions and provide "necessary installations for women workers," such as separate bathrooms, lockers, and changing facilities. Pregnant women and those with children under one year of age were exempted from overtime work, double shifts, and work outside the locality. Finally, pregnant women were not to work night shifts. A doctor could have a pregnant woman transferred to another less stressful position.

A reporter for *Mujeres* magazine alleged in 1982 that employers regularly violated the occupational safety law. She admonished women to keep their workplaces clean and well ordered, reminding them that "by caring for your health, you guarantee the future of our homeland."[15]

Concern over working women's reproductive capacity was so fundamental a part of Cuban labor policy that it was even included in the Cuban constitution of 1976. Article 43 stipulated that while women "have the same rights as men," the state must "ensure that women are given jobs in keeping with their physical makeup."[16] Sixteen years later the constitution of 1992 did not contain any sex-based labor restrictions.[17]

In 1980 a second series of sex-based policies, Resolutions 511 and 512, sought to promote women's employment in certain fields. Resolution 511 was an affirmative action initiative that identified a number of jobs considered "preferential" for women. Resolution 512 set aside one percent of factory jobs for "persons with diminished capacity or serious economic need," such as single mothers. In 1986 Vilma Espín pointed out that because of the increasing number of female-headed households in Cuba, more jobs needed to be reserved for "economically disadvantaged" applicants than the one percent stipulated in Resolution 512.[18]

The Impact of Policy

The revolution's sex-based employment policies contributed to a notable sexual division of labor in revolutionary Cuba. While men and women were educated side by side in the classroom, they were often kept apart on the job. The revolution established all-women factories, all-women work brigades, and all-women farm projects.

In 1966 Fidel Castro announced that projects involving large numbers of women ought to be run by women. During a visit to an agricultural project, most of whose workers were women, Castro decided:

. . . it would be reasonable and an excellent thing indeed to have a woman directing a plan involving thousands of women workers. [Applause] . . . Thus the workers, the brigade leaders, and the technicians—that is, the technical and administrative staff—is going to be made up almost entirely of women. Yes, women! [Applause][19]

The segregation of workers by sex was particularly evident in agriculture. Elena, a farm worker and cooperative member, told a visitor in 1980 that women were prohibited from performing the hardest chores and from spraying the crops. Spraying, despite precautions, might be "harmful to their [women's] reproductive systems." Men could choose whether or not to risk the work, which paid well because of the potential hazard. On the other hand, only women could pick peppers. But when there were no peppers to be picked, or other "suitable" jobs, the women were sent home.[20]

In addition to certain agricultural tasks, specific sections of Cuban production such as light industry became female strongholds. In 1980, for example, women constituted 80 percent of the workers in candy factories.[21] Women also continued to dominate traditional fields such as primary school teaching. The large percentage of women employed as clerks and secretaries increased over the years. Women were the majority of poultry workers and goose pluckers, and they came to bear primary responsibility for the development of Cuban goat herds. In the early 1970s a foreign visitor asked a woman worker at a fishing enterprise what would happen if a woman expressed a desire to do a "male" job. "We would argue with her and try to convince her that . . . women have fields of work proper for them," was the answer.[22] A construction worker at a housing project near Havana was more specific: "Usually we put the women in social work—work proper to women—because construction work is very hard. Women work in the schools, nurseries, and the dining room."[23]

The FMC publicized the role of women in "male" jobs such as auto repair, construction, and sugar cane cutting, but it had neither the will nor the power to challenge the male bureaucrats who ran the revolution. Thus for many years the FMC made no public statements against sex-based policies. Nevertheless *Mujeres* continued to publish articles about women doing "men's" work as cane cutters, electricians, and mechanics.

At its fourth congress, in 1984, the FMC explained that although it agreed with the need to "investigate" the effect of certain occupations on pregnancy, it viewed regulations that barred all women from a particular job as unscientific, discriminatory, and unrealistic.[24] Digna Cires, director of the CTC's Women's Affairs Department (formerly the Feminine Front), concurred.[25] The FMC's Vilma Espín pointed out what sex-based policies meant:

> We had to forbid some vanguard women cane cutters from doing their jobs because the resolution applied to them . . . [but we] have examples of female combine operators, construction workers, truck drivers, and so forth who have remained in perfect health and carry out their work efficiently.[26]

Ironically, the need for physical strength was increasingly irrelevant as Cuba substituted mechanical energy for human strength in field and factory. In 1975 Education Minister José Ramón Fernández said that there were "fewer and fewer jobs that require substantial physical force, and more and more that require specific knowledge."[27] Mechanization opened new jobs for women as it eliminated manual jobs for men. Thus before the revolution stevedores had carried 325-pound sacks of sugar onto ships at Cienfuegos. By 1978 the sugar was flowing into ships' holds on a conveyor belt operated by a woman.

The sex-based restrictions in Cuban labor law have not proven to be absolute. In some cases women have won the right to hold "men's jobs." In October 1986 Nora Torres García was hired to cut henequen, a cactus useful for its fiber. Four months later she lost her job because someone discovered that Resolution 40 prohibited women from cutting henequen. She contacted a lawyer, and the local FMC office complained to the Cuban Employment Commission. Torres García was advised to get a medical certificate indicating she was capable of cutting henequen, but her enterprise still refused to rehire her. Eventually reinstated in her work, Torres García observed:

> I have worked in the countryside since I was a little girl. My mother was left alone with a large family to maintain. I was the oldest and so I had to help her cutting cane and making carbon. Let me tell you from experience that both of these are much more difficult than cutting henequen.[28]

Torres García's fellow workers, many of whom were retirees, confirmed that women had cut henequen for generations. Ironically, many henequen-cutting jobs went unfilled because men did not want them.

Wage Differentials and Contract Work

The wage differential between male and female labor was widened by legislation such as Resolution 48. As laws were modified over the years, however, the discrepancy between male and female wages was somewhat diminished.

Women's double day also prompted differences in take-home pay, because women often worked fewer hours than men. Thus sociologist Marta Núñez discovered that women at the brick factory she studied had many more absences from work, justified and unjustified, than did men. Núñez found that the women earned fifty-four cents for every peso earned by male workers. The administration pointed out that men held the higher-paying jobs that were prohibited to women by Resolution 40. Managers apparently were unaware that Resolution 40 had been abolished some years before.[29]

Women also earned less than men as contract laborers. Contract work was introduced in Cuba in the 1960s as a means of allowing managers to supplement their workforce as the workload demanded. It offered women more flexible work hours, but without such benefits as pensions, paid maternity leave, vacations, access to day care, or access to the household appliances distributed through work centers.

As contract laborers, primarily in agriculture, thousands of women workers served as a cheap, semipermanent, auxiliary labor force. At one sugar mill in Las Tunas more than a hundred women workers had been working for as long as ten years on three-week contracts while male workers were hired for permanent positions. The women claimed they didn't know where to turn for help until the FMC, which had focused most of its attention in the region on housewives, held a meeting of women workers. The Women's Employment Commission and the director of the sugar mill denied the women's claim, stating that surely these women were working only from time to time. Finally the sugar mill's chief of personnel admitted that female agricultural workers had been discriminated against for years. He attributed this discrimination to male resentment. The FMC protest resulted in the mill's giving the women permanent jobs with retroactive benefits.[30]

The abuse of female contract labor was widespread. At Marta Núñez's brick factory twenty-six women were doing contract labor. Núñez raised the issue of their treatment at a workers assembly in 1989, and thereafter these women were granted access to day care and appliances, but they were still denied paid vacations.[31]

Other Discrimination

In addition to sex-based restrictions, wage differentials, and the misuse of contract labor, women workers in revolutionary Cuba had to face other kinds of discrimination. One of the most common had to do with male managers trying to reduce the impact of women's maternity leaves. For example, the Institute of Advanced Pedagogy refused to hire a professor because she was pregnant. A money collector in Santiago de Cuba was fired after becoming pregnant; management argued that carrying the money bags would be a strain on her.[32]

Managers were also anxious to avoid the absenteeism caused by women workers' domestic responsibilities. In 1986 Vilma Espín acknowledged that certain policies, such as requiring working women to take ill children home from the day care center (which the FMC had earlier supported), reinforced the double role of working women. She decried the fact that the number of children in the family was never taken into consideration in the hiring of a male, while it was often the first question asked of women applicants. Espín then offered a revolutionary suggestion: Why not include an evaluation of a worker's performance at home as part of the overall promotion procedure?[33] This suggestion went nowhere.

In order to ease the domestic burden on women, the FMC in 1985 urged that men be given the right to take unpaid leaves to attend to family matters, an option guaranteed to women by the 1974 maternity law. The FMC argued that the family should decide which spouse should take the leave.[34] By 1990 paternal leaves were available, but Espín commented that Cuban men were not taking advantage of this new opportunity.[35]

Usually the women in greatest need of employment, such as single mothers, were those least desired by managers anxious to avoid "problems." In 1984 the FMC magazine *Mujeres* investigated a confrontation between single mothers and management at a Havana taxi stand. Fifteen women drivers had been ordered to work on Sundays, a day on which day care centers and schools were closed, so the women began driving with their children on board. Management forbade them to continue. One mother of two girls, aged eleven and thirteen, explained:

I am divorced and my family lives in Oriente. The commission decided that my girls are old enough and can remain alone on Sundays. They don't realize that when the girls get home [during the week], I am not in the house either. When they were younger, I paid someone to care for them. During that time I received help from their father, but he left the country. We depend on my salary.[36]

The women also complained about sexual harassment and illegal pay practices. Finally the administration yielded to the pressure of publicity: they reassigned some of the women to taxi stands closer to their homes and offered others office assignments that did not require Sunday work.

In 1987 the municipality of Mella in Santiago de Cuba had a substantial number of female-headed households and a high rate of female unemployment. The major employer in the area was the Mella sugar mill, which employed 5,000, of whom 150 were women. On one occasion when more than a hundred jobs became available, not a single woman was hired. The plant's personnel director admitted that more than twenty women had applied for every job opening. Many were single mothers. Workers at the mill claimed that the administration did not want to hire women. The sugar mill's subdirector responded: "The great problem is that the majority don't have the training required. I don't deny that women can do many things. . . . But next year we are going to study this more seriously. I don't doubt that 30 percent of our jobs could be carried out by women."[37]

Even female job quotas do little to increase women's employment when there are no institutionalized means of enforcing these quotas. In one case the directors of an electrical engineering plant reduced the number of jobs set aside for women, claiming that there were no qualified women available. When confronted by the CTC's Feminine Front, the personnel director admitted that he preferred to hire men.[38]

The widespread and routine use of women as volunteer laborers, which in itself some might condemn as exploitative, has led to abuse. In one instance the FMC organized a crew of women volunteers to build a bakery, with the understanding that when it opened, the women would be hired as full-time paid workers. After the women finished the building, the administrators hired men.[39]

Vilma Espín complained that the "promotion logic" to determine advancement in some work centers emphasized different qualities for men and for women. Many male administrators, she said, considered physical appearance and marital status when hiring or promoting women.[40] Women's sexual behavior was also a source of discrimination. Women were sometimes fired for "improper" behavior in their private lives. One unmarried worker from Las Tunas province lost her job when she became pregnant. A Matanzas cafeteria worker was fired for having been unfaithful to her husband, while her lover, also married and a party militant, did not suffer any penalty.[41]

The Communist party addressed this double standard in its 1975 "Thesis on the Full Exercise of Women's Equality," which declared that "there cannot be one morality for women and another for men."[42] Still the double standard persisted. Thus in the early 1980s the government published a notice of a job training program which invited applications from men but indicated that only "women of certifiable moral character" need apply. Vilma Espín called this "an extreme violation of socialist legality" and wondered "what organism has the power to authorize such a document?"[43]

Cuban officials complained that women continued to limit themselves by choosing to remain in traditional—and more poorly paid—"female" jobs rather than opting for "male" jobs such as carpentry or mechanics. Espín blamed parents who discouraged their daughters from pursuing nontraditional careers. To combat this tendency to self-limitation, the FMC and other mass organizations developed a plan to encourage young women's entrance into technical schools. In 1986 thirty thousand Cuban women were enrolled in such programs, although some would discover upon graduation that no jobs were available for women.[44]

In revolutionary Cuba, as elsewhere, there was a tendency to devalue work done by women. Relatively little was done to add prestige to "women's work." Men generally avoided seeking work in "female fields." Thus in the early 1990s, just as in the 1950s, the great majority of primary school teachers were women. And while men comprised the majority of trained nurses before 1959, by 1990 their representation had fallen to 12.5 percent.[45]

In Cuba men were hired or promoted over qualified women, even when women had applied first. Some administrators claimed that male workers "won't understand it" if women were placed in positions of authority.[46] When a local party leader was asked in 1987 why there were only male bosses in the all-women workshops in his jurisdiction, he replied that it had never occurred to him that this was a problem: "The FMC periodically appears before the party and they don't say anything. I don't mean to imply that it's not our problem . . . but the *compañeras* have to insist on it. . . . The party here has not felt the pressure of the FMC."[47]

Clearly the FMC's power to advance women's position in the workplace was limited. Employment discrimination in Cuba was not simply a matter of a few factory managers. In case after case officials from the CTC, the Feminine Front, the Ministry of Labor, and the Communist party failed to guard women's rights. In 1986 FMC chief Vilma Espín admitted that discrimination was systemwide and systematic, and she blasted the Communist party for leaving it to the FMC to combat it and promote women to positions of greater authority. "The party cannot passively observe those who commit injustices," she wrote.[48]

The FMC insisted that women be fully informed about their rights in order to help them avoid or redress incidents of discrimination. Nonetheless, despite the existence of the CTC's Office of Women's Affairs (formerly the Feminine Front) and various other interested organizations, no clear grievance procedure was established. Research showed that Cuban women continued to be generally ignorant of their labor rights.[49]

11

Day Care and Other Services

There will not be true liberation [for women] until there is a network of cafeterias, laundromats, day care centers and, schools that help to alleviate . . . domestic tasks.

Cuban journalist (1962) [1]

It is impossible to construct the required thousands of children's day nurseries, school dining halls, laundries, workers' dining halls, and boarding schools in four years. In fact, merely to meet present needs, great effort is necessary on all fronts.

Fidel Castro (1966) [2]

If you asked the Ministry of Construction to build one day care center in Guanabacoa, one single day care center, why they practically fainted!

Fidel Castro (1987) [3]

A fundamental problem with male-directed social movements is that their leaders rarely think about who is going to do the dishes. That is, they typically ignore the economic value of domestic labor, of "women's work." Marxist theory shares this tendency by focusing on public "production" while the home, the realm of women, remains invisible. When domestic work is viewed as having no economic value, there is little incentive to alleviate women's double shift.

Although the Cuban revolution displayed an early willingness to provide certain services such as day care, government planners had little understanding of the scope or relevance of the work women do in the home. They viewed housewives as idlers and dreamed of putting their "unutilized" labor to good use in real jobs. But as women went to work, they had less time for cooking, cleaning, shopping, and caring for children. It soon became clear that if the state wanted women to work outside the home, then it would have to institutionalize what Marxists called the "idiotic" business of housework. This process proved to be far more problematic and expensive than revolutionary theorists had imagined. In 1966, seven years after the triumph of the revolution, an incredulous Fidel Castro wondered aloud before an audience of FMC members: "Who is going to care for unweaned infants, or babies of two, three, and four years of age? Who is going to prepare dinner for the man when he comes home from work? Who is going to wash, clean all those things?"[4] These were questions that Cuban women had been asking for some time and would continue to ask for years to come. Yet year after year the revolution's goals for the provision of services to working women went unmet while other initiatives of greater interest to male elites, such as foreign military adventures, took priority.

Day Care

Child care was perhaps the greatest single dilemma confronted by Cuba's working mothers. Prior to the revolution older children, grandmothers and other members of the extended family, and even neighbors often took care of the children of working mothers. For the middle class there were maids and nannies. After 1959 a host of new activities—work, school, mass organizations, volunteer activities—came to engage many family and community members while at the same time revolutionary policies virtually abolished domestic services such as maids and nannies.

Although the government encouraged the FMC to pursue day care, it did not provide much funding. At the first congress of the FMC in 1962 Fidel Castro explained that day care was expensive and that it was really women's concern:

> I said to them [FMC leaders], "You are the ones with the problems with the children . . . if you don't fight for these things [day care, school cafeterias, laundromats], it is possible that the rest of the organizations will not do it either. You must promote and oversee services that can help liberate women from these enslaving tasks that rob them of an enormous amount of time that could go to production.[5]

In 1962 the FMC vowed to raise more money so that the government could "reduce its economic support considerably."[6]

Some of the first day care centers created by the revolution were at workplaces such as the Ministry of Foreign Relations (MINREX). The lack of child care prompted many of MINREX's female employees to take leaves of absence, quit, or even bring their children to work. In response the FMC helped MINREX establish its own day care center.[7] But day care in the workplace was a logistical nightmare. In Havana women had to commute on crowded buses with children in tow. Neighborhood centers soon came to be preferred.

Eligibility for day care was limited to the children of full-time working women. The centers provided meals, snacks, baths, and periodic medical checkups to children from age forty-five days to five years. The fee was based on parental income, but in 1967, as part of the Guevarist experiment in "building communism now," fees for day care were eliminated. At that time Cuba had 332 day care centers serving 38,702 children, seven thousand more than the centers' capacity.[8] Since there were approximately 390,000 women in the workforce at the time, there was only one day care slot available for every ten working women.

In 1971 the Ministry of Education took control of the day care system from the FMC to ensure that the children received an appropriate curriculum. Funding for new centers, however, remained scant, even after fees based on parental income were reinstituted in the 1970s. The maximum charge was forty pesos a month, but the actual cost to the state, according to the Ministry of Education in 1989, was seventy-eight pesos a month per child.[9] Parents could obtain a discount for children absent more than three days.

The construction of day care centers was not linked to the growth in women's employment. Only 196 were built between 1975 and 1986, a period of rapid growth in the female workforce.[10] By 1986 there were a hundred thousand day care slots available to more than a million women workers. The ratio of roughly one slot per ten working women held into the 1990s.

The new day care centers were handsome two-story buildings with ample playrooms, baths, kitchens, and offices. The ratio of child care workers to children was high. Although the educational requirements for day care workers rose over the years, salaries remained low. Almost all day care employees were women, and day care training was exclusively for girls. As one day care official observed, "Men don't like to work with children."[11] Men were assumed to lack the qualities of patience and care giving that small children require. Visitors to one Havana day care center in 1985 were told by the director that only women who were themselves mothers could work with infants under a year old.[12]

Day care centers offered the Cuban state an opportunity to mold the new citizen. According to Fidel Castro, these centers were likely more important than universities because "there they [the children] learn to integrate into society, to collaborate with others."[13]

In a firsthand study of Cuban day care in the early 1980s, anthropologist Sandra Malmquist found the centers to be clean, the children well supervised, and the workers affectionate and professional. She noted as well the rigidity and inflexibility of the daily schedule—created in Havana—which governed every center. Any impulse to individualism or indulgences in personal comfort, such as the use of favorite blankets or pacifiers, was disallowed. Even the nipples on milk bottles were sliced to minimize suckling and quicken feedings in order to conform to the schedule. It was a system, she thought, designed to create dependency at every level.[14]

Child Care Problems and Solutions

Cuba's day care system was impressive and invaluable, but not without its problems. First of all, the hours of care, 7:00 A.M. to 7:00 P.M., did not mesh with the schedules of factories that had weekend or rotating shifts. As a result, some women had to arrange for private care for at least part of their shift. Often a grandmother or a neighbor was asked to help. Some neighborhoods created their own private day care networks, an action that was technically illegal but one the government chose to overlook. In the late 1980s one day care center in Encrucijada experimented with night hours. Children whose mothers worked the evening or night shifts at the local factory slept at the center. The experiment was halted in 1990 for being too disruptive of the children's schedules.[15]

The maintenance of day care centers was sometimes inadequate. The interruption of water and electricity, a perennial problem in Havana, obliged centers to call mothers to take the children home.[16] In June 1988, 14 of Havana's 399 day care centers were closed for various reasons, including leaking roofs and faulty plumbing.[17] The closings wreaked havoc with working women's schedules. The FMC commented that no one in the Cuban bureaucracy seemed to care.

Women's complaints about day care problems were so intense in the mid-1980s that the FMC suggested that it once again take control of the entire program:[18]

> We cannot accept attitudes of indolence or resignation. The day care centers are particularly loved by the members of the FMC, many of whom helped to build them and start their functioning. Therefore, we cannot allow carelessness that harms this service, which is so highly esteemed and cherished by our people.[19]

There were also complaints about day care policies. Children who became ill at day care centers were routinely sent home. In 1975, the year of the Family Code, the government ruled that only mothers, not fathers, could be called at work to take their sick children home. FMC president Vilma Espín accepted this decision, saying it reflected "the special bond that exists between a mother and her child."[20]

But mothers who left work to attend to ill children were viewed as delinquent by their employers. In Holguín a female sugar worker was frequently summoned to the day care center because of her three-year-old daughter's illnesses. Management claimed her absences were unjustified, and the provincial union found in favor of management. She sued, but a provincial tribunal agreed with the union. She appealed. The Supreme Tribunal threw the case out for lack of evidence of discrimination.[21]

In 1985 Minister of Education José Ramón Fernández said he had no objection to fathers participating in day care activities, or to their picking up sick children at day care centers, but the minister of work and social security was worried that men might use such license to avoid work.[22]

Interestingly, many delegates at the 1985 FMC congress—in contrast to the FMC leadership—concurred. They particularly worried that men would use the extra time for womanizing.[23] Fidel Castro sided with Fernández, saying that there were ways of combatting absenteeism other than a policy that discriminated against men and impeded women's advancement.

In 1985 the FMC persuaded the government to provide infirmaries at day care centers so that children who were not seriously ill did not have to be sent home. The FMC was also successful in arranging partial fee reimbursement to parents of children absent for extended periods because of illness. There was no response, however, to FMC requests that women who missed work to attend a sick child be paid a portion of their salary.[24]

Another problematic day care policy was the requirement that mothers of newly enrolled children remain at the day care center during an "adjustment period" of up to a month. Factory administrators complained that day care directors, "without a thought in their head about production," were encouraging women's absences.[25] In 1985 the FMC called for a reduction of the "adjustment period" and requested new legislation to address this dilemma.[26]

In 1986 Fidel Castro made the construction of day care facilities in Havana—where nearly half of the workforce was female—a primary goal of the renewed microbrigades program. Castro said that the needs of women workers had been ignored and that it was "tragic" that working women had to pay as much as eighty pesos plus meals for private child care. He ridiculed "technocrats" who "failed to understand that day care was indispensable to national production."[27]

Pushed by Castro, within a few years the microbrigades had built 110 new day care centers, thereby increasing the island's day care capacity to 140,000. Since there were approximately 1.4 million women workers in 1990, day care continued in its ratio of one opening for every ten working women. Still there was greater availability in urban areas. The shortage of rural day care led to a call for a renewal of *círculos guerrilleros,* informal child care networks organized by the residents of cooperative communities.[28]

In 1990 there were hints that private day care might be legalized. One FMC study showed that in the municipality of Matanzas 156 women were caring for about two thousand children in their homes. The FMC acknowledged that "these women resolved a problem that had no other solution." The women even looked after sick children so their mothers didn't have to leave work. Said the FMC: If these women, who have no educational preparation, can do these things, then we can do them too. The Ministry of Education is in a position to analyze this situation and respond to the needs of women workers.[29] Fidel Castro agreed, saying that Cuba must seek "open and flexible" solutions that would benefit working women.

Taking care of school-age children posed another dilemma for working women. In 1974 the FMC requested that children of working mothers be given priority access to boarding schools. It also "insisted" that the program to offer children meals in schools be improved.[30] Summer camps and special programs and excursions were organized to address the disjunction between school and work vacation schedules.

In the 1970s Cubans were asked to work two Saturdays a month to increase national production. Day care centers were opened on "working Saturdays," but schools were not. The FMC requested that women be exempted from Saturday work, but Castro refused, explaining that the country could not afford the lost hours. The CTC rejected a proposal to eliminate Saturday work in order to help women. The CTC's secretary general observed that working women's problems "cannot be resolved by working less . . . [but] only by working more."[31]

Appliances and Other Services

The revolution made a considerable effort to provide Cuban families with appliances such as refrigerators, washing machines, pressure cookers, and other labor-saving devices. Between 1975 and 1985 the number of refrigerators increased from fifteen to fifty per one hundred homes and washing machines from six to fifty-nine per hundred households.[32] These appliances required electrical networks to carry energy, generators to provide it, and petroleum or other energy sources to drive the generators. Thus the employment of women was linked to Cuba's dependence on the Soviet Union. The giant oil fields in Siberia would drive electric mixers in the kitchens of Camagüey.

Electrical appliances were distributed through the workplace to employees on the basis of their performance and political activism. This system led to complaints by women workers who claimed they needed appliances in order to speed the very domestic tasks that kept them from achieving the production quotas that would make them eligible to receive the appliances. In 1985 the FMC requested that working women, especially single mothers, be given priority. The union refused, announcing that "in no case will sex be considered in assigning priority" and that "men and women have the same right [to appliances]."[33]

The number and variety of services slowly improved over time. By 1985 there were nearly six hundred dry cleaners and laundries in Cuba.[34] By 1980, cafeterias were present in 51 percent of Cuban workplaces.[35] Fast food stalls began to dot the urban landscape. But if some services improved, others did not. For example, Cuba's rationing system, while guaranteeing each family the basic foods and clothing it required, involved waiting in long lines for poor-quality products. The availability of foodstuffs and consumer goods was unpredictable. In the early 1980s free peasant markets helped the situation by providing abundant supplies of fresh vegetables—albeit at higher prices than in the state markets.

But even in the best of times shopping was a frustrating affair. Inconvenient hours and long lines obliged many working women to leave their jobs early in order to do the shopping. Administrators took umbrage, claiming that women displayed inadequate "discipline." Women said they had no choice. Children, grandparents, husbands, and neighbors were pressed into service to do the shopping for working women. A new occupation, *colero,* or professional line waiter, appeared.[36]

In the late 1970s, after years of complaints from women, store hours in Havana were expanded on a trial basis. To the dismay of the FMC, the program was suspended after a few months despite its clear success. Over the next few years it was slowly reintroduced in various locations in Cuba, although the FMC at its 1980 and 1985 congresses announced that extended hours remained insufficient.[37]

The reluctance to change shopping hours reflected the system's inflexibility and indifference to popular demand. Stores, bakeries, butchers, and day care centers were unable to respond to local needs. A frustrated FMC had to lobby *for years* before butchers and dairies were added to the Plan Jaba. The FMC spent *more than twenty years* trying to establish night hours in beauty salons. These dilemmas were supposed to be resolved by the local branch of the People's Power, but the People's Power didn't seem to take much interest in the problem of store hours. This inattention may be related to the fact that only 16 percent of People's Power representatives at the municipal level were women.

In response to the needs of working families, domestic service reemerged in a number of unofficial and official guises. Although the revolution abolished maid service, a widespread informal network of women who cleaned house, cooked, and washed clothes professionally soon emerged. Young women continued to move from the countryside to become maids for urban families. A woman who worked in a Havana radio station commented to a foreign visitor that she had a neighbor come in once a week to wash the floors.[38] There were also a significant number of "service personnel," mostly women, who cleaned up and looked after the homes of the elites. Vilma Espín herself admitted that she could not have managed her own career without maids and nannies to help out with her children.[39]

In 1980 an officially sanctioned maid service, United Family Services, was implemented through the People's Power with assistance from the FMC. It offered house cleaning, care for children and for the sick and infirm, landscaping, in-home laundry service, and sewing to families in which all adults worked. The FMC heralded the program not only as a boon to working women but also as a source of employment for "women who cannot aspire to other work."[40] United Family Services was said to be different from the domestic service of the past, since its workers would be employees of the state and thus guaranteed proper wages and benefits.[41]

The rectification program of 1986 brought new demands for economic efficiency. Workers' dining facilities and school meals were cut back, and charges for workers meals were increased. The free peasant markets were accused of excessive profits and shut down. Ironically, a year earlier the FMC had expressed its satisfaction with free peasant markets and urged that they be expanded.[42]

Under the rectification program public criticism of the service sector was encouraged. The press was flooded with stories of incompetence and indifferent service. Why did it take months to make simple repairs to an electrical appliance? Repair shops responded by extending their hours. Some urban supermarkets were reorganized into a series of local corner stores, which helped to diminish the long lines of shoppers. A grocery in San Francisco de Paula initiated home delivery service. It was a hit and spread to other neighborhoods.

Working at Home

One solution to the dilemma of paid employment versus domestic responsibilities was for women to work at home. For more than twenty years the FMC administered home work programs for seamstresses, tobacco rollers, and craftswomen. A government official periodically visited the women's homes to assess their work.

One such project was begun in Camajuaní in Villa Clara province in 1982. Thirty women sold homemade clothing to a local buyer, who paid according to quality level. The clothing was then offered to the public in the parallel market. The number of participants in the project soon swelled to more than 260 housewives, who earned between 100 and 140 pesos monthly.[43] A similar program was introduced in 1983 in the town of Union de Reyes, where three hundred housewives assembled and embroidered precut clothing for a local factory.[44]

The home-work program represented a pragmatic if essentially traditional solution: let women do it all, work and home. Women in this program might have lost the sociability of working with others outside the home, but their stress was often greatly reduced. Furthermore, their children had a parent nearby, and they did not have to arrange child care or wonder what was occurring at home while they were at work. Government concern over juvenile delinquency may also have been a factor in the development of the home-work plan. The number of women working at home increased from 15,000 in 1967 to 62,428 in 1989. Despite a request by the FMC, home workers did not receive social security benefits, nor were they represented in the CTC.[45] It is likely that the number of women engaged in home work will increase during the economic difficulties of the 1990s, with women being paid only according to what they produce and requiring fewer services and benefits.

Women's Employment: Theory and Observation

The central notion of the revolution's program for women's liberation was the Marxist belief that women's entry into the paid labor force would bring gender equality. Toward that end, women were encouraged to enter the labor force and some effort was made to accommodate their particular needs.

Unfortunately the revolution failed to engage in any debate over this central notion. Nor did it acknowledge that Marxist analyses of gender were at best fragmentary and incomplete.[46] Thus the irony articulated by Sheila Rowbotham that "not to work" for the women of the middle classes "became the mark of class superiority at the very moment when their men were establishing work as the criterion of dignity and worth."[47] Indeed, Marxist theorists and long-time Cuban residents Isabel Larguía and John Dumoulin were appalled to discover that many poor Cuban women wanted finally to be free to quit their jobs and become housewives in a consumer society.[48]

A key weakness of Marxist theory was its failure to come to grips with the significance of housework, the mundane and infinitely important tasks from child care to food preparation. Similarly, Cuban leaders simply could not accept that domestic work was a critical aspect of national production. In this sense the Cuban revolution, for all of its inventiveness, broke no new ground.

From the beginning the Cuban government, in addition to seeking liberation for women through work, foresaw the need for an expanded female labor force in order to supplement male labor for the attainment of national development goals. Opinions differ as to the degree to which idealism and pragmatism were complementary or in conflict in the program for women's advancement in revolutionary Cuba. Socialist feminist Margaret Randall concluded after more than a decade in Cuba that the revolution had laid the "material and ideological bases . . . for women to pursue their full capacities as human beings."[49] While Randall acknowledged certain obstacles for women en route to their full participation in production, she perceived the state and party as supportive of women "in their struggle." The fundamental question, according to Randall, was whether having been encouraged by the revolution to go to work Cuban women had adequate influence on "what the state . . . intends to do with her as a working person."[50] Randall would amplify this concern a decade later in a more critical reassessment of socialism and its unresponsiveness to feminist ideas.[51]

Susan Kaufman Purcell argued that the Cuban government's real interest was overall development and that the "substantial modernization of women" (through education and employment) was a necessary part of the process. The advancement of women, while a "serious" goal, was "not one of the highest priority goals of the Castro regime."[52] She suggested that this position was evidenced by the policy choices made by the government in the allocation of limited resources. Political scientist Max Azicri similarly concluded that the Cuban government manipulated the female labor force to achieve development goals.[53]

Jorge Domínguez suggested that the growth in women's employment in Cuba was a function of modernization that was duplicated or even bettered in other Latin American countries.[54] In contrast, Carollee Bengelsdorf argued that the specifics of the Cuban case made it unique. She found the growth of the female labor force "notable" in light of three developments which could have worked against increasing women's employment: the elimination of domestic service and the retraining of maids and prostitutes; the establishment of an open and free educational system that drained potential woman workers from the labor market; and economic policies that made it easier for families to live on one income.[55]

Bengelsdorf saw the continuing sexual division of labor evident throughout the Cuban economy, codified in labor policy based essentially on women's reproductive role as the most significant structural barrier to equality in Cuba. She noted that the basic assumptions that legitimized this sexual division of labor were left unchallenged, "above all the notions surrounding the female as mother and the absolute primacy of biological functions."[56] Many Cuban women, however, perceived their role as mother as a source not of servitude but of power in the family, community, and nation.

Isabel Larguía and John Dumoulin recognized that although women's domestic role had economic value, "as workers, housewives are abysmally unproductive."[57] They argued in favor of a genderless society oriented to current "male" characteristics, one in which women were not trained in "feminine traits" of nurturing and caretaking, which they claimed amounted to "a permanent cultural lobotomy" that justified discrimination based on biology. They concluded: "The extinction of a feminine social psychology is necessary for the development of the economy and the socialist conscience."[58]

Larguía and Dumoulin and others criticized revolutionary policies such as shortening the workday for married women workers, because such policies reinforced women's traditional gender roles. In their view, the ideal long-term resolution to the domestic task dilemma would be the collectivization of household work in which "men can share."[59]

The costs of providing day care and other services led to the 1975 Cuban Family Code, which did require men to share. Cuban law experts boasted that through the Family Code, domestic tasks were "valued in an economic sense" for the first time in Cuban law by a further requirement that a working spouse financially support the stay-at-home partner.[60] The Family Code also generated favorable reactions among many foreign observers. Economist Carmen Diana Deere called it "a most innovative" step, for although it was an admission that in an underdeveloped economy the collectivization of domestic tasks was impossible, it was at least a recognition that paid employment alone could not possibly free women as long as their reproductive function in society was not addressed.[61] Legal expert Debra Evenson viewed the Family Code as "an ideal against which progress could be measured."[62] Carollee Bengelsdorf noted that the Family Code was "commonly understood as a radical challenge to the inherited family structure."[63] Muriel Nazzari, however, perceived the Family Code as an illusory solution to "women's problems" by a government unable to provide women with more support.[64]

The overall consensus among analysts, both foreign and Cuban, was that the Family Code had been an important educative tool whose impact on male behavior remained to be seen. Indeed studies showed that while Cuban men expressed appropriate opinions about their shared responsibility at home, even years later they still didn't seem to be doing much.[65]

Sociologist Marie Withers Osmond discovered in her interviews with women textile workers in Cuba that the Family Code was not universally celebrated among the very women it was designed to support. Osmond cited the code as an example of "an empty beneficial policy" with no practical mechanisms for implementation.[66] The women workers she interviewed noted that even if a woman did divorce her husband for lack of help around the house, she would ultimately be left with total responsibility for domestic tasks. And while Osmond suggested that the code appeared to be a "a sharp reversal of official communist policy" by specifically making the family and not the state responsible for children, the women textile workers fretted that the code might have instead removed too much responsibility from the shoulders of husbands, who were, after all, men and thus essentially lazy and unreliable. These women found the law's notion of women's right to "financial independence" from marriage disturbing precisely because it raised the possibility of their having to carry the family alone. Might the Family Code require a woman to support a lower-earning or unemployed ex-husband? Wouldn't more than a few husbands be tempted never to get a job?[67]

The results of the Osmond study make clear the inadequacy of standard theoretical approaches and point out the importance of the critical missing factor in the debate over sexual equality in Cuba: women's own perception of employment and its impact on their lives. Wouldn't a government sincere in its effort to achieve sexual equality through employment take at least as much interest in assessing women's experience of work as in determining how best to use women workers?

A number of other important themes emerged in the two studies of women textile workers in Cuba conducted by Marie Withers Osmond and Helen Safa in the 1980s. First was that the concept of "work" for these women did not mean only paid employment but included family responsibilities. Of these two aspects of "women's work," family work was primary, and paid employment was viewed as benefiting the family as a whole. Thus when there was a conflict between job and care for husband and children, the home won. Job demands created considerable stress because of working women's strong sense that "they should be able to respond as family needs arise."[68] No wonder then that even thirty years after the triumph of the Cuban revolution many of the women workers viewed "liberation" as the freedom to abandon paid employment in order more adequately to carry out their domestic work. They were thus very interested in seeing *their husbands* advance to better jobs with higher pay and were suspicious of policies to promote women's employment, which they perceived as creating competition for their husbands' jobs.

Another theme hinted at in these studies was the importance that class differences made in the perception of women workers. In socialist Cuba, as elsewhere, education and economic status greatly affected women's outlook. Factory workers viewed employment more as a means of providing for their families than as a means of personal mobility and independence. In fact, factory women expressed more of a sense of sisterhood with men of the working class than with professional women. They preferred increasing men's responsibility to the family over fostering their own independence from it.[69]

Nevertheless this primary research did affirm that employment boosted Cuban women's self-image and confidence. Three-quarters of the women textile workers questioned in the Safa study thought women should work even if they have small children. At the same time, nearly 70 percent did not want their children to do factory work.[70] The growing disdain for manual labor by an increasingly educated labor force became a significant problem for the Cuban regime.

The insights offered by this primary research affirmed that while working-class women may derive personal satisfaction from work, their primary motivation is family betterment because, ultimately and still, their identity and main affirmation comes from the home. Thus, at least in the short term, it is economic and not moral incentives that are most effective in stimulating women's employment.

All working women, from the factory to the professions, wanted more services such as day care and more flexibility in dealing with daily details such as store hours, which had led to absenteeism and underemployment. The intransigence of the Cuban government in responding to these demands was perplexing. If the FMC could make hundreds of thousands of home visits to encourage women to work, why couldn't the means be found for the corner store to stay open until 8:00 P.M.?

The revolution's program for "equality" through employment brought women greater professional opportunity, social mobility, and the possibility of increased personal independence. It also legitimized the widespread use of women's volunteer labor and the channeling of men and women into different areas according to sex-based, scientifically suspect concerns over female reproductive capacity. Once working, women were left without adequate support in their struggle to juggle employment and domestic responsibilities and to counter systematic discrimination on the job. At times the government devised policies to "help" working women that in effect guaranteed their double shift, and then it marveled that women "worked" fewer hours than men.

Although the revolution's banner was "equality," the revolution clearly used women as a reserve labor force. Women were encouraged to enter educational programs that prepared them for a range of new roles in the economy, but they were left with nowhere to turn for help in overcoming the inevitable obstacles that arose. By not giving organizations such as the union or any of the other employment-related bureaucracies institutional independence and clear powers, these groups nestled into disinterest and unresponsiveness. The Federation of Cuban Women expressed an increasingly vocal frustration with formal and informal bias against women until the hour of crisis provoked by the collapse of the Soviet Union, when ranks closed, loyalty to the chief was reasserted, and the only powerful advocative tool available to the FMC, its magazines *Mujeres* and *Muchacha,* ceased publication in the paper drought of the early 1990s. In the end the serious systemic flaws of Cuba's male-dominated state impeded efforts to understand better the circumstance of women workers, and they rendered unlikely the possibility of resources being allocated to better address their needs.

12

Family and Revolution

The family is the only institution in Cuban society which remains some-what unprepared. . . . Each family acts in an individual way, at times headed by patriarchs who encourage customs and traditions from the past.

María Isabel Domínguez, Cuban Academy of Sciences (1987)[1]

The family isn't in crisis or on the road to extinction, but it is changing and evolving, although slowly and with difficulty.

Cuban psychologist (1988)[2]

Prior to 1959 the blood web of family loyalty dominated the political, economic, and social life of the nation. Castro's revolution worked profound changes in this scheme, reducing the family's public aspect by transferring its property and power to the state, and modifying its private aspect with a host of reforms which often had the most contradictory and unanticipated effects. After three decades of reform the "new Cuban family" was smaller, more democratic, better educated, less stable. In the economic crisis of the 1990s the balance between family and state was once again shifting. As the state floundered, the family seemed destined to recoup its dominant role in society.

Theory and Power

Paradoxically, while Castro's revolution affected profound changes in the Cuban family, Cuba did not have a specific family policy until 1975, when the Family Code became law. There were no great national debates on the family in the 1960s as had occurred after the Bolsheviks seized power in Russia in 1917. While the feminist and sexual revolutions were challenging the family in the West, Cuba's attention, as Che Guevara noted, was focused elsewhere.[3]

144

Although Simone de Beauvoir visited Cuba in the early 1960s, there were still no copies of her path-breaking *Second Sex* in Cuban libraries or bookstores in the mid-1980s. By the time Betty Friedan had published her famous attack on the traditional family in *The Feminine Mystique* (1962), Cuba's own social policies were being implemented.

If the idea of transforming the Cuban family was not discussed by Cubans, foreigners, particularly socialist feminists from the United States and Western Europe, gave it considerable attention. In *La mujer cubana ahora (Cuban Women Now)*, published in Havana in 1972, Margaret Randall rehearsed Friedrich Engels's arguments that the patriarchal family was *passé*. Socialism, Randall believed, would bring an equality which would make property ownership, inheritance, families, and patriarchs irrelevant.[4] Spaniard Verena Martínez-Alier, who, like Randall, lived in Cuba for a number of years, believed that "in an egalitarian society marriage as an institution regulating inheritance of status and property should be obsolete."[5] Swedish writers Gunnel Granlid and Goran Palm argued at the Cultural Congress of Havana in 1968 that "the more men and women of the working class dedicate themselves to family life, the more they get mutilated and corrupted."[6] Granlid and Palm argued that women's liberation could be achieved only through the melding of family and collective life. Perhaps, they said, Cuba would realize the new kind of family that Engels dreamed of, a socialist family united not by blood, but by affection, friendship, and convenience.

The Argentine Isabel Larguía and her American husband, John Dumoulin, both residents of Cuba for many years, complained that the Cuban revolution had not advanced the theoretical analysis of the family that classic Marxist works had only begun to address.[7] They saw the family as an "archaic institution . . . in conflict with the social economy transformed by the revolution." Collectivization of all family tasks was the remedy, but alas, the revolution's "theoretical inertia" allowed "the resurgence of . . . a glowing concept of the traditional family as a positive element in the construction of socialism," a notion that Larguía and Dumoulin found patently absurd.[8]

Indeed Cuban leaders, particularly the old communists, were deeply conservative in their views on the family. In 1960 Blas Roca and Carlos Rafael Rodríguez, both long-time leaders of the Popular Socialist party (Cuba's prerevolutionary Communist party), reissued their 1940s essay *Fundamentos de socialismo en Cuba,* in which they observed that "it is well-known that the Popular Socialist party struggles for the preservation of the family."[9] Thus while foreign visitors awaited the communal kitchens of the revolution, Cuba's first housing projects turned out to be single-family units with their own kitchens. In 1959 and 1960 the government organized marriage ceremonies to legalize the unions of common-law couples.

Yet even as the revolution sought to preserve the family, it was transferring the family's economic and political power to the state. After all, families owned many of Cuba's sugar plantations, banks, and industries; families played together at the country clubs in Havana and Santiago and intermarried to protect and enhance their estates. Family influence had been a key feature of government, as bureaucrats sought jobs and privileges for family members. Cuba's mercantile sector was dominated by family enterprises. The old man ran the store while wives, sons, daughters, nephews, nieces, and cousins were the clerks. Who else could one trust?

In the slums of Havana extended families lived together, and their livelihoods were often based on family labor. In the countryside the unremunerated labor of wives, children, and other family members was a key feature of the small farm. Furthermore, the island's social life was organized around the family. In the 1950s sociologist George Stabler found that people in small towns socialized most frequently with members of their extended family.[10]

This situation began to change with the onset of the revolutionary reforms. In 1960 and 1961 agrarian, banking, and property reforms authorized the seizure of property owned by the island's bourgeois families. Another wave of reforms in 1968 transferred to the state all the island's small businesses, from beauty parlors to sandwich carts. Only the smallest family farms were spared, and the government made it clear that they too would eventually be absorbed into cooperatives or state farms.

The revolutionary government concluded that the only permissible family property was the home. Families could not own businesses or land. A family's capacity to save would be limited by low salaries and very low interest rates at banks. Indeed, there was no reason for families to have large savings, since the government intended to provide all the social services they needed, free of charge. Thus by 1970 the family's role as an economic unit had been sharply reduced.

Invasion of the Private Sphere

The state also attempted to transform the internal life of the family. A key concern was the shaping of young minds. The government was suspicious of parental influence and abilities. It wanted to be "the primary, if not the only, agency of socialization."[11] The new educational system began to challenge parental authority.

In the late 1970s Cuban officials began to declare publicly that the only way to instill new values, to create the new man and woman, was to distance children from parents, grandmothers, uncles, and other retrograde influences. In a 1985 interview Education Minister José Ramón Fernández told a *Wall Street Journal* reporter that Cuban families were "overprotective" and "very united." The reporter concluded that "a major goal of Cuban education is to weaken the power of the Cuban family."[12]

The social changes brought on by the revolution were particularly significant for young women. New educational opportunities and the lure of work and social activities outside the home were challenging fathers' control of daughters. The newly created mass organizations invaded the family's private sphere. The Committees for the Defense of the Revolution (CDRs), the FMC, and the militias all demanded the time and attention of family members. Access to employment, housing, and education was influenced by an individual's participation in them. The CDRs, located on every block in urban Cuba, monitored the comings and goings of family members and visitors in order to sniff out counterrevolution. In its social role, the CDR might knock on the door to inquire why a housewife hadn't joined the workforce, or whether her children were going to school. The state was becoming a member of the family.

The revolution's policy of promoting women's employment shifted the internal balance of power in many families. A woman with her own income could be more assertive and independent. She could "marry for love" instead of economic security. She could risk divorce. Women's income, in combination with state services such as free education and health care, maternity payments, and social security for disabled and retired persons, diminished the classic role of the family as safety net.

The importance of the family was also reduced among those with access to various state-provided services such as day care, although the high cost of these services limited their availability. Those without state services relied even more heavily on the extended family for child care and other help. Some husbands began to take up family tasks, particularly after the Family Code of 1975 obliged men to share housework. But many men were uneasy with this new responsibility and feared being ridiculed by their male peers. Cubans joked that a man might do the laundry but he would not hang it out to dry, where he might be seen by his pals.

A television soap opera, "La Delegada" (1985), reflected the tensions created within families as women took on new roles. The protagonist of the series was a mother and textile worker who was elected to her town's municipal assembly. Her busy life was complicated by a husband who expected to be pampered at home and by a meddlesome mother-in-law who fought to influence the family. At one point divorce was in the air, but eventually the crisis was resolved when *la delegada*'s husband and children agreed to share the housework.[13]

Family Separation

Policies that encouraged overseas service had a significant impact on family life. Since the mid-1960s thousands of Cuban internationalists—doctors, engineers, construction workers, and more—had been going abroad to work. Service as an internationalist helped to advance one's career. From the early 1960s to the late 1980s thousands of Cubans also traveled to countries of the former Soviet bloc to study and work. These ventures meant lengthy separations for husbands, wives and children.

In addition, from 1975 until 1990 almost 400,000 Cuban troops and technicians served in Angola; 2,016 died there. The bodies of the dead soldiers were not returned to their families in Cuba until the war ended in 1989, a striking statement of the primacy of the state over the family.[14]

The Cuban family was also literally torn apart by emigration. Since 1959 more than a million Cubans have left the island. In many cases men fled, leaving their families behind. Seventy percent of the 125,000 who fled Cuba in the Mariel exodus of 1980 were men. Some were single; many were not. Husbands who went hoped to bring their families afterward.[15] In one extraordinary example, Captain Orestes Lorenzo, an air force pilot who defected in 1991, returned to Cuba from Miami in 1992 to collect his wife and two sons. He landed a small plane on a highway near the beach resort of Varadero, picked up his family, and flew back to Florida.

During the early 1960s thousands of middle-class families, frightened by rumors that the revolution planned to send their children to Russia for indoctrination, put them on planes to Miami. The Castro regime insisted that it had no intention of separating parents and children.[16] Nevertheless, fourteen thousand children eventually left Cuba.[17] Those children who did not have relatives in the United States were sent to live with foster families throughout the country.

In the late 1970s, during a brief era of improved relations with the United States, the Cuban government authorized a family reunification program which permitted the visit of Miami exiles to Havana. Several hundred thousand visited the island, their suitcases bulging with gifts for their relatives. These visits, which earned considerable cash for the Castro regime, ended in 1980. Traffic then slowed, consisting often of older women visiting relatives in hospitals or attending their funerals. In the late 1980s Radio Martí broadcast a telephone call-in program, "Puente Familiar," in which exiles sent messages to their relatives in Cuba. In 1991 Cuba dropped the age limit for family visits to twenty, and tens of thousands of Cubans flew to Miami, their trips paid for in hard currency by family members in Florida.

The tenacity of the family was also evidenced in the insistence of the exile community that, despite the U.S. embargo, it had the right to send food, clothing, medicine, eyeglasses, and even money to Cuba as a humanitarian gesture. This practice led to the growth of a substantial industry in Miami through which tens of millions of dollars worth of goods were forwarded to Cuba each year.

While some families retained their tenuous links with Havana, others were deeply split on ideological and political grounds. Fidel Castro's own family came asunder. Two of his sisters went into exile, while his brothers remained on the island. In 1994 Castro's daughter, the model Alina

Revuelta, who had long been forbidden to leave Cuba, put on a wig and sunglasses and, with false passport, escaped from the island. Shortly thereafter Revuelta, backed by a formidable international press campaign, was able to persuade Cuban authorities to let her daughter, Castro's granddaughter, emigrate to the United States.

The Family Home

In 1959 and 1960 the home became a focal point for relations between the revolutionary government and the Cuban family. In *History Will Absolve Me* (1954) Fidel Castro had taken note of the wretched housing of the poor: "four hundred thousand families . . . cramped into barracks and tenements."[18] He decried exorbitant rents, cruel evictions, and lack of toilets and electricity. Castro said that a revolutionary government "would solve the housing problem by cutting all rents in half . . . by tearing down hovels and replacing them with modern multiple-dwelling buildings, and by financing housing all over the island."[19] Once in power, Castro did cut rents, lower electric rates, and end evictions. The state became the nation's landlord; rents did not exceed 10 percent of a family's income, and over time renters became owners—measures that were enormously popular with the poor. The homes of the fleeing bourgeoisie were seized and transformed into schools and offices. In the early 1960s the government undertook large housing projects in urban areas and poured concrete floors in many *bohíos* (peasant huts) in the countryside. Plans for latrines were widely disseminated.

In Havana the dusty slum of Las Yaguas was flattened by bulldozers and its residents were moved to Buenaventura, a brand-new complex of modern row houses on the outskirts of Havana. But Buenaventura was not a panacea. By the late 1960s, 40 percent of its houses were overcrowded. In some cases four generations were living in one small house. Also repairs were scanted. One resident claimed in 1969 that "when it rains, it rains more on the inside than the outside."[20]

Crowding and dilapidation became the norm for Cuban housing. In 1967, maintenance crews in Havana were able to respond to only a third of the nine thousand requests a month for housing repairs. In 1980 a government study concluded that 30,625 dwellings in Havana (5.8 percent) were propped up with scaffolding to prevent them from collapsing.[21] The numbers increased as the years passed, and from time to time a building would fall. When four people died in such an incident in July 1987, Fidel Castro himself appeared on the scene. "Apparently the recent rains caused cracks which brought the house down," he concluded.[22]

Year after year the government set goals for housing construction, which it then failed to meet. From 1959 to 1988 it built about half a million units, some sixteen thousand a year, but to end the deficit it needed to build a hundred thousand a year.[23] During the same time

Cuba was building thousands of housing units in Africa and Nicaragua, but housing for the Cuban family had a very low priority.

In the 1970s bad housing conditions were repeatedly cited as the cause for divorce. Newlyweds could not find apartments and were obliged to live with their in-laws. Ingenious Cubans added *barbacoas,* or sleeping lofts, inside their apartments, sometimes with materials stolen from the state. Others built extra rooms on roofs, on terraces, in garages, in driveways, and in abandoned shops. Divorced couples, unable to find new housing, divided their apartments with sheets for privacy. Some young women, hopeful of escaping their parents' crowded quarters, opted for early marriage. In 1987 a Cuban union official observed that the main desire of workers was for housing.[24] Crowded housing stimulated the use of *posadas,* or love hotels, which rented rooms by the hour to couples who sought a bit of privacy. Not only furtive lovers but also married couples lined up at these *posadas* (see chapter 15).[25]

A newer innovation in housing was the "new town" in the countryside. These were designed to encourage small farmers to surrender their lands and join state farms or co-ops. Housing in the new towns typically consisted of a series of four- or five-story concrete block apartment complexes. Critics called them *gallineros* (chicken coops), but many rural women found the new communities attractive. They offered sociability instead of rural isolation, electricity for home appliances, and education for children. For men, however, the move from the family farm, the fiefdom of masculine power, signaled a loss of control over family members. By 1978, 347 new rural communities had been built, sufficient to house about 5 percent of the Cuban population.[26]

While the new towns were well publicized, self-built family housing was not. For two decades the Cuban media studiously ignored the fact that many families were building their own houses. Indeed, from 1959 to 1988, families built roughly a million units, twice the number constructed by the government.[27] In the 1980s the government, yielding to reality, began to encourage family-built housing. It made construction materials available and permitted individuals to borrow cement mixers and other machines from state agencies on weekends. Between 1981 and 1983 almost four times as many houses were constructed by private families as by the government.[28] Even so, the president of the National Housing Institute concluded in 1987 that Cuba was falling so far behind in housing construction that it would need a million new houses in the year 2000.[29]

Cuban women who stayed home to raise families were depreciated, just as were their peers in the Western world. Housewives were applauded only when they emerged from the home to participate in some collective task: factory or agricultural labor, volunteer work or service in the mass organizations, the CDRs, the FMC and its various brigades. This emphasis on the "public" role of women had important ramifications for Cuban demography. As women spent less time at home, they also had fewer children. In the 1920s Cuban mothers were having an average of six children, but by 1953 they were having fewer than four, a decline linked to gradually improving levels of health and education and to the steady pace of urbanization.[30] In the 1960s Cuba experienced a baby boom stimulated by the redistribution of wealth, a ban on abortions, and a dearth of contraceptive materials. After peaking in 1964, fertility gradually declined because of the growing availability of contraceptive devices and abortion and also women's increasing participation in public life. By 1978 total fertility rates had dipped to 1.8 children per couple—below replacement level for the first time in Cuban history.[31] Cuba became the first country in Latin America to achieve zero population growth, and in the 1990s economic difficulties would drive the birth rate even lower.

The revolution also changed the nature of housework. Middle-class housewives had to cope without maids. For poor housewives, the revolution brought the benisons of running water and electricity, refrigerators and washing machines, which, at least in theory, made life easier. At the same time the revolution brought difficulties and frustrations which complicated housewives' work. There were periodic electric outages and shortages of water and various household items such as soap, toothpaste, and toilet paper. Housewives complained that laundry soap imported from the USSR was so caustic that it burned their hands. Shopping meant standing in line, and it was usually women who waited, wasting millions of hours, hours often taken off from jobs, lost hours which also hurt their work records.

While the foodstuffs provided by the revolution left much to be desired in terms of freshness and variety, the amount of food available was ample during the 1970s and 1980s. Indeed obesity became an important health issue (see chapter 5). Food was equitably distributed, thanks to the ration card system. Ration cards helped to bind families together since they were issued to family units rather than to individuals, and, for example, even after a divorce a husband who had not gone through the bureaucratic process of getting a new card might return to his old family for meals.

Food preparation remained a time-consuming affair. Few convenience foods were available. One solution was dining out. By 1982 a fifth of the population had at least one hot meal a day in government cafeterias at work or school. The cities had fast-food restaurants. Restaurants often had a better selection of food than government shops.

Prior to 1959 the family was the dominant social institution in Cuba. After 1959 it was the state. The walls of social behavior and organization which once isolated individual families from the larger community were hammered down by the revolution. Through a range of economic and social policies, the Cuban government literally and figuratively entered the home and became, for good or ill, part of the family.

But the state and the family were antagonists. The state did not want the family to be autonomous. The family's greatest expression of autonomy—its search for food and goods in the black market—was essentially subversive. On the other hand, a family without a substantial measure of autonomy and power could be a parasite, unable to contribute productively to the development of the nation.

The revolution had argued that in the old Cuba the family was too powerful for the good of the nation. By the 1980s the revolution was increasingly concerned that it had become too weak. Although early policies sought to limit the family's public power, the Cuban government came to take new interest in strengthening the family's internal structure so it might better serve the revolution. This is the subject of the next chapter.

13

Family Dynamics

The revolutionary process has insisted on a shared responsibility between parents, but we still have a long way to go in this respect

Mónica Sorín Zocolsky, psychologist (1990)[1]

The idea that the Cuban family is the fundamental cell of society looks nice on paper but in practice no one pays much attention to it.

Cuban divorcee (1988)[2]

Who doesn't have on their block a teenage girl, almost always without a stable partner, whose expectations of the future were nipped in the bud . . . by maternity; whose parents complain of having "to return to square one" in order to care for grandchildren or the young single mother with no resources?

Mirta Rodríguez Calderón, journalist (1989)[3]

The problem of paternal dysfunction and absence is a phenomenon with very deep roots, determined by sociocultural and psychological conditions that propagate the inequality between men and women.

Patricia Arés Muzio, sociologist (1990)[4]

Although the Cuban revolution did not have a clear and comprehensive family policy in its early years, it did have a central controlling notion that the state ought to assume many of the traditional functions of the family. By 1975 it was clear that this goal was too ambitious, that it entailed costs that the state simply could not afford. Moreover the state was alarmed by the meteoric rise in divorce, teenage pregnancy, single motherhood, and other apparent symptoms of family instability. Some began to talk of a crisis in the Cuban family. As a result, the Cuban

153

government began to reassess the family's role in society and to take new interest in the family's internal dynamics.

The 1975 Family Code

In 1974 Cuban lawyer Daniel A. Peral Collado wrote that the island's prerevolutionary family legislation reflected a "patriarchal and monogamous family based on private property" which ensured a "humiliating inferiority" for women, the absolute power of the patriarch, and discrimination against illegitimate children.[5] In 1975 Cuba adopted a new Family Code, which was hailed as "the first body of authentically Cuban legislation" on the family.[6]

The 1975 Family Code recognized the family as "the essential cell of society."[7] The revolutionary couple was to be monogamous and heterosexual, a merger of two equal partners. That given, the code sought to help bring about the following:

- the strengthening of the family and of the ties of affection, aid, and reciprocal respect between its members
- the strengthening of legally formalized or judicially recognized marriage, based on absolute equality of rights between men and women
- the . . . fulfillment of parental obligations for the protection, moral upbringing, and education of their children . . . as worthy citizens of a socialist society
- the absolute fulfillment of the principle of equality of all children.[8]

The Family Code prohibited discrimination against children born out of wedlock. Furthermore, it held consensual unions to be "just as binding as legally formalized marriages" in terms of property and parental responsibilities for their children.[9] To guarantee paternal support, Cuban birth certificates required a father's name. If a man denied paternity, a woman could begin a process which might eventually include genetic testing. Some hoped this would discourage men from initiating casual affairs.

In keeping with the Family Code's emphasis on equality, all income obtained by the couple during the marriage became joint property, with the exception of inheritances. In the event of the dissolution of a marriage, joint property was to be divided in half. Article 26 required both partners to contribute to the care, guidance, and education of their children and to cooperate in the smooth running of the home. Article 27 suggested that even if one parent was not working outside the home, the other must still share domestic responsibilities. Article 28 afforded both spouses the right to work and to further their education, as long as doing so did not disrupt family life.[10]

Marriage and Divorce

Even before the adoption of the Family Code the revolutionary government had tried to encourage Cubans to marry. State-operated "marriage palaces" were opened throughout Cuba. At one such place, Havana's elegant Casino Español, forty couples might marry on a given Saturday. The state also set aside rooms for honeymooners at hotels and vacation resorts. Marrying couples were permitted to purchase scarce items such as sheets, nail polish, and a "baby doll" nightgown for the bride-to-be.[11]

These incentives were not a sufficient lure for many Cuban couples. A 1989 study concluded that there was a decrease in the number and duration of marriages in Cuba, while consensual unions were becoming more common.[12] In 1981 more men than women reported themselves to be single (1,281,600 men, compared with 764,600 women).[13] Evidently men in cohabitating relationships tended to view themselves as unattached.

At the same time that the government was encouraging marriage, it was also making divorce easier. In 1958 there was one divorce for every eleven marriages. After 1959 the divorce rate surged, peaking in 1971 and again in 1989. In 1991 one out of every 2.3 marriages ended in divorce, one of the highest rates in the world.[14]

The familial instability of the larger society was reflected in the behavior of revolutionary elites. Fidel Castro divorced his first wife but never married Celia Sánchez, his companion of many years. He once observed that their relationship was not a "bourgeois" marriage.[15] In 1988 an intelligence officer who defected from Cuba said that Castro had at least four children[16]; a more recent biography claimed he had at least seven.[17] Another source said that for many years Castro had had a mistress, with whom he had five sons.[18] Castro himself told a reporter in 1994 that, as far as he knew, he had fewer than a dozen children: "Well, I don't have a tribe," he said.[19] First Vice President Raúl Castro also separated from his wife, FMC chief Vilma Espín, and in the 1980s it was widely rumored that he was living with a younger woman.[20] Second Vice President Carlos Rafael Rodríguez was enmeshed in a scandalous divorce in the early 1960s. Revolutionary heroine Haydée Santamaría's suicide in 1980 was reportedly prompted in part by an affair between her husband, Culture Minister Armando Hart, and a younger woman.[21] Indeed, sources at the FMC claimed that so many leading officials were having affairs with young women in the 1980s that the government was said to be in the grips of *"titimania."*

Viewed from the other side of the Florida Straits, the flurry of divorces and the tendency to consensual relationships were perceived as a sign of social decay. "What kind of society is being created by Castrismo?" asked exile journalist Agustín Tamargo:

Cuba is a passionate country where even the stones seem to be sexed. But Cuba's tropical sensuality . . . was, in the past, always contained by certain

limits, a certain natural modesty. Religion and the old Spanish customs and
. . . decorum imposed certain reserves even on the most defiant. The Cuban home was stable, even in the midst of poverty. Paternal authority was
never questioned. . . . Even the most humble father, white or black, on
discovering that his daughter had been deflowered sought out the perpetrator of the crime and said: Marry her or I will kill you![22]

Tamargo said the revolution had destroyed patriarchal authority on the
one hand and deprived Cuba's youth of all distractions on the other, a
situation that left the island's youth with "free love" as their only means
of diversion.

But Tamargo was challenged by fellow exile and journalist Nilda
Cepero-Llevada, who found his values old-fashioned. Why get excited
about consensual unions? There was nothing new about them. The important thing, she said, was not a marriage contract but rather choosing
the right partner. She saw no necessary nexus between matrimony, responsibility, and love. Nor did marriage guarantee child support. Indeed,
she argued, "thanks to artificial insemination there is really no need for
a permanent male companion in order to realize our maternal
function."[23]

Divorce and Cuban Law

The first divorce law in Cuba, passed in 1918, provided for no-fault
divorce, prescribed the terms of property settlement, accorded alimony
and child support payments, and allowed women authority over children.[24] Changes to the law in 1930 and 1934 made both partners responsible for family subsistence and stability—a theme adopted by the
revolution's Family Code—and decreased from five years to six months
the period of abandonment necessary as grounds for divorce. The award-
ing of custody emphasized the income of the parent and was thus problematical for women.[25]

The 1975 Family Code provided a simple no-fault divorce procedure.
A marriage could be ended by either party when it lost meaning "for the
couple and for the children and, thus, for society as a whole."[26] Both
parents remained responsible for the care and well-being of the children.
All other factors being equal, custody of children would be given to the
mother. Spouses without jobs were to receive alimony for six to twelve
months, depending on whether or not they had children. Long-term alimony would be awarded only in cases of illness, disability, age, or other
impediment to employment. This meant that a divorced woman was expected either to remarry or to get a job, regardless of whether she had
small children.[27] In the 1960s a divorce cost as little as forty pesos and
took but a few weeks; in the 1970s the government, alarmed by the
surge of divorces, raised the rate to one hundred pesos.

A number of studies were launched to try to find the reasons for the rising frequency of divorce. Prior to the revolution couples often stayed together to protect their children, but after 1959 state assistance for children and the availability of jobs for women made divorce more feasible. Two-thirds of the couples who divorced in 1968 had children—something Cuban researchers considered to be a "notable change" in attitudes.[28] In a 1971 survey 88 percent of divorcing couples cited "incompatibility of character" as the cause.[29] The housing shortage was also a likely factor. A 1973 study found that three-quarters of the couples under age twenty-four lived with either their relatives or someone else, with the resultant lack of privacy and possibly parental interference in their marriages.[30]

At the public's insistence the Family Code authorized the marriage of boys as young as sixteen and girls as young as fourteen, although in the 1980s the government came to perceive early marriage as an impediment to personal, educational, and professional development, especially for young women.[31] In 1987 thirty-two percent of marriages and more than one-third of the divorces occurred among adolescents.[32] In 1992 *Bohemia* reported that the majority of marriages occurred between partners younger than thirty and that half did not survive more than two years.[33]

Family separation was also an important problem. A young college graduate noted that after her marriage she and her husband were separated for two years in order to complete their obligatory service to the state. They rarely saw one another. When they did meet, they could not find a place to make love. Divorce resulted.[34]

In 1981, 59 percent of women over age fourteen lived with a husband or partner, while 12 percent were divorced or separated and 7 percent were widowed. At the same time, 8.9 percent of the total adult population were classified as divorced or separated, double the 1970 figure. Women in Havana, the ones most likely to hold a job, were also the most likely to be divorced (19 percent).[35]

Men were more likely than women to remarry after divorce. In 1970 census figures showed that there were more than twice as many divorced women as men, 126,036 versus 56,287. Cuban authorities opined that men remarried because they were "less able than women" to confront domestic tasks.[36] Men also tended to remarry women younger than their ex-wives. Some women, for their part, came to appreciate their independence after a failed marriage. Children, friends, family, work, and even an occasional lover provided satisfaction, and they were free from "always having to think of my husband."[37] Indeed, Cuban journalist Mirta Rodríguez Calderón wondered why unattached women were so often advised to "put your life together and leave your solitude behind" when, in general, these women were "neither lonely nor distraught."[38] In the 1980s when Cuban magazines ran "success" stories about women in the higher ranks of the Communist party or the bureaucracy, there was often no husband in sight. The women were typically reported to be living with their parents or grandparents.

Changing Sex Roles

One of the most intriguing issues about family life in Cuba is the impact of the revolution on sex roles. The revolution placed a great deal of emphasis on changing women's role but gave little attention to changing men's. This disparity became a major source of family tension. A 1973 study of seventy-seven divorced couples found a "lack of adjustment" between the revolutionary change in public life and the deep conservativism of family culture. Many couples were separating because they could not come to terms with new ideas about women in society.[39]

This tension between tradition and change was evident in the lives of Domingo and Rebeca, both engineers at a nickel mining complex in eastern Cuba. After ten years of marriage Domingo still found it a "spiritual struggle" to accept his wife's independence. When Rebeca drove Domingo to work in the family car, he was chided by his male friends: in Cuba men drove and women were passengers. Rebeca wanted a second child but was concerned that this would hurt her career.[40]

Women who embraced new public opportunities offered by the revolution chafed under the weight of traditional family arrangements. In the early 1970s almost half of the divorces in Cuba were occurring in Havana, where women were more likely to work and to participate in activities outside the home.[41] Even in the countryside fewer women were willing to spend a lifetime with an intractable *machista*. At the Celso Maragoto cooperative in Pinar del Río a woman farm worker advised a visitor to "ask around. You'll see that its almost always the woman who asks for a divorce, especially among the new generation."[42]

But while some women resisted, many others adapted to the new public demands on women while still continuing to fulfill the traditional role in the home. Researchers soon documented the resilience of tradition in two main areas of home life: decision making and the carrying out of domestic work.

As early as 1973, researchers at the University of Havana found that while some 60 percent of the men and women interviewed continued to believe that the husband should retain authority in the family, the remainder thought that power should be shared.[43] The study showed, however, that there was considerable disagreement as to who actually resolved family problems and made decisions. Wives thought they were much more influential than their husbands imagined or admitted.

A generation later traditional power relationships in the family were continuing. In one survey of one hundred young working couples in the late 1980s, the majority of women indicated they would yield to their husbands' advice regarding their own professional advancement. The majority of the men said they would urge their wives not to seek promotions.[44]

A 1990 study of 64 Havana families also revealed the persistence of traditional attitudes. Fifty-three percent of the men versus 33 percent of the women supported the traditional sexual division of labor. Similarly, more men (83 percent) than women (70 percent) were satisfied with the current distribution of domestic tasks.[45] Children queried in the survey indicated that eight of the seventeen basic household and caretaking activities were carried out by the mother alone and the other nine by both parents, but the fathers did not perform any of these activities alone. In a related study, when children drew pictures of their parents, 90 percent of the mothers were doing domestic tasks compared with 30 percent of the fathers. Eighty percent of the girls portrayed themselves as doing domestic work, compared with only 10 percent of the boys. Cuban sociologist Patricia Arés Muzio concluded that in 90 percent of the cases there was a "tendency by the children to reproduce traditional archetypes of the family with rigid sex roles."[46]

Such a conclusion would come as no surprise to Cuban journalist Cino Colina, who wrote this of men's "effort" to "help out" at home:

> A common scene is for the father to tell the mother that he is going to undertake some domestic chore, only to pass it off to his eldest son . . . who in turn hands it over to his younger sister or even asks his mother to do it for him because he's got an important meeting, or his friends or girlfriend are waiting for him. . . . In such cases it's incorrect to say that the father is not educating the children about domestic responsibilities.[47]

Arés Muzio's research offered a powerful confirmation of women's double day, for although a majority of the women she studied were also employed, they nevertheless continued to "care for and prepare children for life, take care of the home, and give their husbands the idea that he is the head of the family." These obligations, thought Arés Muzio, required women to demonstrate "a difficult and irreconcilable versatility, especially if attention to the home is not shared with her spouse or other family members."[48]

Many Cuban women were able to share the burden of domestic tasks with other family members, however. Living with the extended family was not simply a result of the housing crisis, it was a Cuban tradition that continued after 1959. For example, 43 percent of the children in one 1990 study lived in a household with one or more grandparents, 25 percent lived with one or more aunts or uncles, and 12 percent lived with at least one cousin.[49] The presence of grandparents in particular helped men to avoid housework. Anthropologist Helen Safa discovered in her interviews with women textile workers that the husbands most likely to participate in domestic tasks were younger men in nuclear family households where no members of the extended family were present. She concluded:

> Multi-generational cohabitation works to men's benefit by absolving them of home responsibilities, to older women's benefit by giving them great matriarchal power in family life, to younger women's benefit financially, and to the state's benefit by reducing demand for services.[50]

Ironically, while women in the Arés Muzio study cited conflicts as the cause of family difficulties, men blamed their own lack of time.[51] Yet available statistics showed that political and professional activities did not absorb substantially more of men's than working women's time.[52] What were men doing?

Arés Muzio's research showed fathers to be remote figures in family life. It was mothers who helped children with their homework (74.8 percent) and attended parent–teacher meetings (90.4 percent). When children were asked with whom they spent the most time, the over-whelming majority indicated their mother (86.1 percent) followed by their grandmother (25 percent). Fathers tied with other siblings at 20 percent.[53]

The activities in which fathers were most involved included showing their children off to the community through the customary neighbor-hood stroll, offering guidance, providing basic necessities, and main-taining discipline. When children were bad, women were most likely to discuss and sermonize (73.5 percent versus 25 percent of the fathers), while fathers tended to impose punishments (73 percent versus 30 per-cent of the mothers).[54] This remote authoritarian role of the Cuban fa-ther was viewed by Arés Muzio as being in conflict with long-term revo-lutionary goals of family stability and egalitarianism. Men's roles had to change. Policies such as Women Worker Days at local supermarkets, which put the onus of domestic tasks on women, had to be reevaluated, and more attention had to be given to Fathers' Day in order to encour-age male participation in the home.[55]

Single Motherhood

One important reason for growing government concern about the role of fathers was the increasing dilemma of single motherhood. From 1973 through 1988 fully 39 percent of all children born in Cuba were born to unmarried women. By 1989 the percentage had risen to 61.2, a figure that Mirta Rodríguez Calderón considered "extraordinary."[56] Clearly there was an erosion in the social importance of marriage. What re-mained unknown, however, was how many of these women were en-gaged in long-term relationships with the fathers of their children or, indeed, with someone else.

In 1987 FMC president Vilma Espín was unable to determine just how many single mothers there were in Cuba.[57] She found the lack of data remarkable. One foreign analyst estimated that "at least 10 per-cent—and more likely between 15 and 20 percent—of households with children are headed by women alone."[58] A nationwide survey of single mothers conducted in 1987 by the Center for Psychological and Socio-logical Research found that 27 percent of the women studied were not engaged in an ongoing relationship with the father of their child.[59]

The Cuban government was particularly concerned about teens becoming single mothers. In addition to being a health risk, teenage pregnancy limited young women's educational, social, and work options. Day care in Cuba was not available to high school students. Many young mothers declined to marry, and those who did tended separate and divorce. In the 1987 study 72 percent of the single mothers surveyed were under age twenty-five, and 38 percent were under age twenty.[60]

Despite the availability of contraception and abortion, many single mothers were, in fact, reluctant mothers. One study of two hundred single mothers of children with disciplinary problems revealed that 48 percent had wanted an abortion but, for reasons unknown, did not have one.[61] Single mothers tended to come from families with lower incomes and lower educational levels, and the majority were unemployed.[62]

Single motherhood has always been a feature of Cuban society. However, it was one that the revolution, with its insistence on the need for stable nuclear families, refused to accept as permanent and necessary. In a 1989 speech Vilma Espín stressed the importance of having a man in the family "to ensure its balanced social development." The "unfair and degrading concept of the father as a simple inseminator . . . should be replaced with the role of active educator and participant in all family activities."[63]

Cuban statistics showed that many Cuban fathers were failing their children. For example, while in 1989, 85.5 percent of the fathers of children born out of wedlock recognized their children, far fewer were helping to raise or support them.[64] A study of single mothers in the municipality of Cotorro showed that 59 percent of the fathers were not paying child support.[65] A University of Havana Law School study of 108 single mothers in the late 1980s showed that 85 percent of the fathers were completely or partially estranged from their children. Again, 59 percent of the men did not provide any child support while 31 percent paid only sporadically. The mothers in the study knew surprisingly little about these men. More than half (56 percent) did not know their address, 30 percent did not know if they had other children, and 66 percent did not know where they worked.[66] This lack of knowledge complicated efforts to gain child support.

The Cuban Family Code had no provision for ensuring the payment of child support. The best efforts of the Employment and Social Security Commission, the Civil Registry, and the police often failed. Some factory administrators even helped delinquent fathers avoid paying child support.[67] In 1990 Fidel Castro observed: "Women struggle very hard to resolve cases which unfortunately involve fathers who neglect their children, fathers who, although the law compels them to pay alimony, refuse to do so and who often change jobs to dodge support payments."[68] Various proposals such as automatically deducting support payments from delinquent fathers' savings accounts or pay checks were, as of early 1993, not yet fully implemented.

The state offered single mothers stipends of twenty-five to forty pesos a month.[69] The number of women nationwide who received such stipends is not clear. One study of single mothers in Havana found that 20 percent were receiving stipends.[70]

Cuba's mass organizations, including the FMC, were remarkably inattentive to the plight of single mothers. A 1988 study found that only 2.38 percent of the women who were receiving government aid had also sought assistance from the FMC.[71] The researchers, dismayed by their findings, called for the creation of Special Tribunals for Family Matters in order to provide speedy enforcement of child support payments.

Double Standards

Some Cubans were opposed to the notion of the state's assuming the responsibilities of delinquent fathers. Others believed that some limits should be set on a woman's ability to have children without a stable relationship.[72] Some commentators even argued that the rising tide of single mothers could be attributed to the Family Code's elimination of any stigma for illegitimate children.

Journalist Mirta Rodríguez Calderón defended single motherhood, arguing that it was women's "feminine right" to chart their own reproductive course. To have a child without work or housing, however, constituted, she said, "the worst irresponsibility, deserving of severe criticism as much for the mother as for the father with whom she made those children."[73] Olimpia Rosell, a specialist in the Social Security Administration, decried the double standard on parental responsibilities. She cited the case of a mother who had been given a nine-month prison sentence for abandoning her five children. "But what happens to the fathers of so many abandoned children?" she asked. The answer, of course, was nothing. She noted that so often after abandoning the offspring of a "thoughtless" impregnation, a man is free to "live the life that he wants, but if she [his ex-partner] tries to put together her life, if she begins a romance, then everyone condemns her for being a bad example." Rosell argued for the adoption of "very severe measures" to persuade fathers to pay child support.[74]

Ironically, Cubans tended to be much more sympathetic to the plight of single fathers, who constituted only a small fraction of single-parent households, than to single mothers. Single fathers experienced far fewer difficulties arranging for institutional assistance such as day care and full school shifts for their children.

Government unease over female-headed households was greatest regarding an issue of central importance to the revolution: the formation of new generations. Questions were raised about the capacity of single mothers to raise their children adequately. For example, a majority of single mothers who received welfare payments between 1985 and 1987 had only grade school educations. Moreover, 63 percent of their children were failing in school. From this limited sampling the researchers concluded that "single mothers tend to produce descendants who will be single mothers, and they submerge their families in unhappy circumstances."[75] Single mothers were even cited by the director of Cienfuego's Youth Orientation Center as the cause for Cuba's *roqueros*, rebellious youth who aped the alienation and long-haired mode of MTV's grunge rockers.[76]

Magda Cabrera, a municipal labor official, stated that the roots of the single motherhood "problem" lay not only in the home, where there was "a loss of family authority" and a lack of fathers to keep sons in step ("Truth is, the boys worry us most," she said), but also in "bad schools,"[77] where teachers often were only too anxious to see problem children drop out, because they required too much attention and their failures hurt teachers' promotion records.

In 1988 a Cuban sociologist observed that "in Cuba we place great emphasis on motherhood . . . but no one ever says anything about the pernicious influence of the absent father."[78] Subsequently Patricia Arés Muzio initiated a series of studies in order to understand the role of the father in the family and the impact of his absence. In one, the fathers of forty young children with psychological problems were categorized according to their emotional and physical participation in the home. The results showed that only 2.5 percent of those children with troubles had "active, present and affectionate" fathers, while 27.5 percent had "absent, passive and unaffectionate" fathers.[79] She concluded: "The stability and physical presence of the father figure is an important factor in the healthy and normal development of the children's personality."[80]

Yet in two studies of "normal" families Arés Muzio discovered that the mere physical presence of the father was no guarantee of familial stability nor of happy children. Indeed fathers' tendency to authoritarianism and their lack of participation in domestic work reinforced traditional patterns that worked against revolutionary goals.[81] Psychologist Mónica Sorín Zocolsky argued that one of the greatest threats to children's emotional health was the contrast between Cuban mothers' overprotectiveness and their fathers' authoritarianism.[82]

Distracted Parents and Problem Youth

Ironically, revolutionary policies have themselves been a major cause of family stress. The revolution demanded family participation in the public life of the revolution: militias, block committees, Young Pioneers, student organizations, unions, volunteer labor, overseas service, public demonstrations. Such participation was essential for winning promotions, access to education, and housing benefits, but they sharply reduced family time. Still the government did not perceive the resulting stress on the family. Parents were chided for a merely "pro forma" participation in public activities at the same time that they were being denounced as "neglectful" for putting their public life ahead of their families.

The revolution was concerned about parental guidance of children because of a worrisome rise in juvenile delinquency. In 1967, 41 percent of crimes were committed by juveniles; by 1971 it was 50 percent. In 1973 the age of criminal responsibility was lowered from eighteen to sixteen. In 1977 Castro called for a war on delinquency, a war that would last into the 1990s.[83] Parents were warned that they were responsible for the behavior of their children.

According to research by the Ministry of the Interior, in the 1970s the instability of Cuban families was a major factor in juvenile problems. Slightly more than half of the delinquents came from families in which one member, usually the father, was missing. About one-quarter came from families in which the children were living with stepparents.[84] More surprising was the discovery that a substantial number of youths who displayed "antisocial conduct" were the children of parents with "outstanding reputations in their field."[85] Local polyclinics began offering family counseling, and "Adolescence Clinics" were opened in various municipalities.[86]

By the late 1980s Cuba was experiencing a nationwide crisis in family time management. Children were being cared for by grandparents, relatives, neighbors, or no one at all. In one of a series of interviews with high school students in 1988 one young woman said she rarely saw her mother, who worked all day and attended classes in the evening. Another student said that when his parents arrived home they were "dead tired" and in no mood for family activities.[87] Some distracted parents pulled their sons out of school to put them to work, "because there they have a boss that directs them."[88]

Cuban leaders realized that the school system could not provide the affection, approval, and discipline that children needed. Social scientists warned:

> The day care center and the school are not warehouses in which to store our kids while we work. . . . We are parents twenty-four hours a day, including free Saturdays, Sundays, and vacations. We can have grandparents and neighbors who help—and thank goodness for them—but we are the parents, and the responsibility is (should be) ours.[89]

Cuban officials complained that busy parents, to assuage their guilt, were buying their children's affection with gifts.[90] They were also sheltering their children from careers that entailed monotonous physical work. Cuban parents, the government hinted, were guilty of producing a generation of lazy, materialistic, self-centered, and resentful youth.

Interestingly the model family as typically featured in state publications was a couple in their thirties with two, one, or even no children. Both worked, often as professionals, and both were active in mass organizations. One or both had served as an internationalist abroad. One or both were party members. They spoke serenely of their devotion to their children and their careers with barely a nod to the difficulties in managing both.

For years the FMC was the lone voice in urging the revolution toward a more holistic assessment of Cuban life, one that offered material and moral rewards not only for the overfulfillment of production quotas but also for energetic participation in the family. In the early 1990s other voices joined the chorus, calling for improved services, more productive use of time, and more parental guidance. Sociologist Patricia Arés Muzio agreed with the FMC that Cuba's "social requirements and evaluative mechanisms" were skewed toward "the delivery of unconditional time to work and political activities," while analysis of family problems and solutions were "left to the individual." She specifically criticized "internationalism, diplomatic missions, and social service" as often working against family stability.[91]

The Cuban revolution was deeply ambivalent about the family, particularly in terms of its role in raising the island's children, Cuba's future citizens. The family's role was welcome as long as it conformed to the revolutionary agenda of unswerving loyalty to the state, the promotion of more "equal" sex roles, significant parental involvement in children's lives, and parental willingness to let the state take the lead in determining the appropriate activities and destinies of Cuban children.

The state attempted to replace many of the functions of the family, but it gradually became evident that this approach was enormously expensive. As the years passed, the state increasingly blamed the family for social ills ranging from juvenile delinquency to the maintenance of traditional sex roles. Parents were criticized both for being indifferent to sexual promiscuity among their children and for forcing teenage lovers to marry when a pregnancy resulted.

The Cuban government's unwillingness to recognize the impact of its own policies on family life complicated efforts to identify and address specific family problems. The revolution could not accept that its achievements had a distinct downside. For example, families benefited from full employment and economic opportunity in the 1970s and 1980s, but these benisons caused parents to be away from the home for much of the day. Rural boarding schools had their virtues, but they were also specifically designed to enable the revolution—rather than the parents—to indoctrinate the children in social values. In a Cuba with few material goods to inherit and no stigma on illegitimacy, the social rationale for legal marriage became obscured. Divorce, single motherhood, and parenting without matrimony became increasingly common.

With the rectification campaign of 1986, journalists and social scientists, encouraged by the government's call for candor in discussing social issues, began to suggest that government policies might be responsible for family strain. Research on the family proliferated, but social scientists were most interested in the function of the family in society, in the social impact of family problems, rather than in their relation to individual happiness and personal fulfillment. Collectivism and cooperation rather than hierarchical authoritarianism were identified as the ideal expression of authority within the family.[92] Thus the state was asking something of the family that the state itself was not willing to provide: democratic decision making. This disharmony between social and political institutions—that the family should and to some extent did become more egalitarian and democratic while the state became more patriarchal and less democratic—constituted a glaring paradox in the life of the revolution.

Within the family men had lost power, although perhaps not as much as the state had hoped, and women's and children's legal rights were enhanced. Women's greater access to paid employment lessened their economic dependence on men. In addition, a variety of educational programs widened women's and children's world and increased their social mobility.

But patriarchy, if diminished, was not dead. Men continued to exercise the most authority within the home, and wives and daughters continued to shoulder virtually the entire burden of domestic work. In the old society motherhood had been venerated in theory at the same time that many women were forced to prostitute themselves, beg in the streets, or remain in unsatisfactory or even dangerous relationships in order to provide for their children. After 1959 the Cuban revolution brought mothers a considerable measure of security, from adequate prenatal care to education and jobs for their children.

But women, too, had lost some power. Before the revolution women's role as mothers afforded them a platform for political and social activism. In revolutionary Cuba, however, the Communist party usurped women's role as the guardian of public morality. While motherhood was still glorified after 1959, mothers were also expected to spend considerable time and energy in activities outside the home. The role of traditional housewife was denigrated. After a surge in the early 1960s the Cuban birth rate fell dramatically, even dipping below replacement level for a time. More mothers were single mothers, whom the government was hesitant to support. Indeed it often seemed that the goal of research on single mothers was less to assess their needs than to "prove" that women were largely incapable of raising children properly without a man in the house.

A common theme in family issues, from teenage pregnancy to single motherhood to women's continuing double day, was male irresponsibility. There was widespread agreement that men were self-centered, unreliable, lazy, and, when it came to domestic work, incompetent, and that trying to get them to share in the housework was more trouble for women than it was worth. Men sheepishly agreed that this was so. Women even argued against allowing men parental leave, suspecting they would use this new freedom to pursue other women. Issues as basic as adequate mechanisms to ensure child care payments by fathers remained unresolved. Cuba's authoritarian political culture forbade women to form autonomous organizations to press these issues.

Now the crisis of the 1990s has seen the withering away of the state's ability to provide basic necessities and social services. In this growing vacuum, the family is again emerging as the preeminent social institution in Cuban. Family networks will grow in importance as food and other resources become scarce. They are already serving as the fulcrum of nascent resistance to the Castro regime. In the long run they will be essential in the negotiation of any new, postsocialist state.

14

Sexuality and Revolution

Instead of raising barricades, issuing warnings, or threatening punishment . . . it is better to arm the young with knowledge. In doing so, their lives can be enriched and they can avoid danger.

Diana Martínez, journalist (1990)[1]

Despite good intentions, instead of imparting sexual information, the media often promotes sexual relations.

Professor Evelio Cabezas (1987)[2]

On average, a woman experiences her first orgasm two years after becoming sexually active.

Heidy González Cabrera, journalist (1989)[3]

I can't satisfy her . . . we just begin to make love and, bam, I'm finished. . . . I can tell that she is disillusioned.

Worried husband to sex therapist (1987)[4]

Over the past five or six years wives have been having more affairs. Now, however, men want to maintain their marriage. . . . This denotes a significant diminution of machismo, given that in the past such behavior would have provoked tragedies.

Professor Manuel Calvino (1990)[5]

Seductive rhythms undulate through the night air. The moon beams down through the palm trees. Waiters navigate the din of laughter and clinking glasses with bottles of rum held high on silver trays. In the sudden blaze of a spotlight a stage is revealed. Dancers in minimal costumes of sequins and plumage erupt from the shadows, a gyrating collage of flesh and color in an unabashed celebration of sexuality. The audi-

168

ence registers its appreciation with shouts and applause. The nightly show at Havana's world-renowned Tropicana nightclub has begun.

Exotic, sensual Cuba. Rumba. Mambo. The insistent beating of the drum. Cubans have long sought relief from life's burdens in dance and seduction. "We [Cubans]," noted one *habanera,* "have been able to elevate eroticism into national genius.[6] The Cuban revolution counted on this genius to lend its social experiment a unique flavor. It would be, said Che Guevara, "a revolution with *buchango* [pizazz]."[7]

Tropicana survived Cuba's socialist experiment, but other important elements of the nation's traditional sexual culture would eventually be challenged, directly or indirectly, by revolutionary reformers. Castro would attempt to mold sexuality to serve the revolution, but it would not be easy to "constructively" remodel this most personal of all activities.

Historical Roots

The roots of Cuba's contemporary sexual landscape lie in the nation's cultural heritage, which blends Spanish and African influences to form sexual "ideals" that continue to shape contemporary thought and behavior. The sexual mores of traditional Spanish society, deeply influenced by the Catholic church, emphasized the need to contain female sexuality while encouraging the expression of male sexuality. In colonial Cuba female virginity and chastity were important factors in social standing. A family's honor depended on the behavior of its women; an errant daughter could bring shame and ruin. Men's task was to guard family honor by defending the virtue of their wives and sisters. But at the same time they were pressed by their peers and the song of the heroic culture to make conquests, to raid the nests of others, seducing women as a proof of virility, as a natural expression of their irrepressible sexuality.

The church sought to differentiate between the spiritual (good) and the physical (bad) aspects of love. The burden of spirituality was to be shouldered by women. Anthropologist Mirta Mulhare explains this point of view of the church:

> For love to be sublime, it must exist in an unearthly, unselfish and totally pure form—devoid of the lust of the flesh, sexless. . . . To defile a virgin madonna wife with a macho's lust is akin to incest; she is the closest thing to a man's own mother and she is distant from all things sexual.[8]

According to Catholic tradition, then, men married women who rejected their advances. The more vehement a woman's rejection, the more respect she earned from her suitor. Even after marriage women were not allowed sensual pleasure. "Good" women were supposed to endure the base advances of their husbands in order to produce offspring, the true source of a woman's satisfaction.

Cuba's sexual panorama was complicated by race and class. The values of Spanish Catholicism—its sexual repressiveness and Moorish emphasis on containing women in the home—reigned among the middle and upper classes. Among the masses, however, Afro-Cuban religions had a powerful influence. These religions allowed men and women more equal status and recognized both male and female sexuality.

White society considered Afro-Cubans to be sexually supercharged. White men sought to protect "their" women from the perceived sexual danger posed by Cuba's men of color at the same time that they sexually exploited Afro-Cuban women whom they labeled promiscuous. A young woman who grew up in the Cuban countryside in the 1920s remembered her terror of black men: "At night I covered my head with the bedsheets in fear, and I often had bad dreams."[9]

Another important aspect of Cuba's traditional sexual culture was the perception that in sex there must be an active and a passive partner, and the active role of power and domination was reserved for males. Thus it is widely believed in Cuba that only the receptive partner in male-to-male sex is a homosexual. It was in choosing the female role that a man invited ridicule:

> Nothing is worse than to show signs of effeminacy. . . . I remember an obsessive awareness of my wrists; to let them hang limp was to be *maricón* [sissylike]. . . . I was in elementary school, way before I knew that the object of all this fear and loathing was homosexuality.[10]

Lesbianism attracted less attention because no male was involved. Because women have been traditionally thought of as childlike, and women's sexuality softer and more incidental, lesbianism was seen as an innocent perversion, one that could be corrected. In Cuba today there are some seven colloquial terms for lesbians while there are at least twenty-four for gay men.[11]

Boys, adored and indulged by doting mothers, were thought to experience their first erotic desires at age six or seven. By the onset of puberty this sexual drive was thought to be overpowering. Conventional wisdom held that masturbation could cause insanity, but no sexual release at all could be equally dangerous. If denied access to females, boys might engage in bestiality or, worse, homosexuality. In the interest of mental health, middle-class boys were encouraged to experiment with their maids' children. Others were taken by male relatives to be sexually initiated in a local bordello.

Early initiation, however, provided little relief from overwhelming sexuality. The "sexual imperative," as Mirta Mulhare has called it, created a sexually predatory society in which cunning young males sought to find young women for release as well as prestige among their male peers. The greatest triumph was to seduce a virgin. Though a man might perceive his attempt at seduction to be immoral, once aroused, a man was believed to be beyond self-control.

These notions of the imperiousness of male sexuality led to the need for the "fallen" woman, the mistress, the prostitute. Thus, while a wife might enjoy her husband's respect, it was his mistress who received his ardent attention. The number of mistresses and the manner in which they were kept were signs of male status. According to the masculine code, a husband must avoid embarrassing his wife by flaunting his liaisons, though he would certainly share news of his conquests with his male friends to enhance his masculinity. Any children born of such unions would be illegitimate, a distinct handicap in a family-oriented and lineage-conscious nation.

The social status of the fallen woman varied. Mistresses were allowed a certain amount of freedom unavailable to wives, and they could even attain high social standing. Prostitutes who consorted with upper-class men had a higher social position than those who sold themselves to field hands. And there were certain advantages to living outside of proper society. One former prostitute recalls choosing her trade over marriage during the 1950s because "my strongest desire was to be independent."[12] Prostitution afforded her a decent income and the freedom to spend it as she chose.

In the twentieth century, as more and more Cuban women entered the workforce, became educated, and were exposed to foreign mores, they began to question the roles assigned to them by society. The central ideal of femininity and motherhood lost some of its luster. Women now wanted smaller families, a notion reflected in the Cuban birth rate, which declined steadily after 1895. Modern *cubanas* came to view those women who were always "filled with children" to be "low class, or stupid, or very rich, or very extraordinary in some other way."[13]

Thus by the time of the revolution there was increasing conflict between social reality and the sexual ideal. In 1960 anthropologist Mirta Mulhare noted:

> Cuban women of the last thirty years before Castro, unlike their mothers and grandmothers, resent more and more their being cast either in the image of a virgin madonna or in the image of a whore. But the resistance of the male to change has been exceedingly strong.[14]

While these archetypal sexual ideals helped shape Cuban perceptions, sexual reality in Cuban society has been considerably more complex. There exists an open recognition of the mutual dependency and natural antagonism between the sexes. The fact that both women and men wield sexual power is celebrated in Cuba.

Cubans' notion of the ideal female body is more generous and realistic than the willowy women promoted by sexual merchandisers in Europe and North America. Women, and indeed mothers, of all shapes and sizes are considered sexually attractive. In fact, the more flesh the better. In Cuba, women who in the North would be counseled on how to hide bulges with yards of material and minimizing patterns sashay about in skimpy halters, miniskirts, and tight pants as if to announce, "Here I am and aren't I beautiful?" to which Cuban men respond, "Sí, sí!"

The constant flirtation or stimulation of the natural sexual tension between men and women is evident on any street corner through the *piropo,* or catcall. In the North the catcall often reflects sexual anger and aggression, but in Cuba the *piropo* is meant to initiate a dialogue. During her years in Cuba Margaret Randall found the *piropo* demeaning, but a Cuban woman upon returning from a visit to Chicago wondered, "Doesn't anybody in the States stare at anybody? My body was so lonely to be watched."[15]

Revolution and Tradition

The revolution which unfolded after 1959 had a powerful if unintended impact on the sexual sphere. First of all, as women were mobilized, swept up by domestic and international crises, certain traditional ideas of femininity were undermined. One volunteer in the 1961 literacy campaign recalled an experience the training camp for literacy workers at Varadero beach:

> We were strictly segregated from the boys. . . . One day there was an incident. We were all taken to the movies and a net was hung in the auditorium between the boys' side and the girls'! That created a lot of tension. . . . The boys tore down the net and rushed over to us. Immediately the supervisors gathered the girls together and made us file out, double-time.[16]

All their spare time at this camp was spent talking of boys. One of the girls, who "must have come from a lower-class family," told of her brother's amorous adventures with heifers. The volunteer, accustomed to hearing many dirty jokes at her convent school, was nonetheless "terribly shocked. . . . It hadn't occurred to me that a human being would do such a thing."[17]

A second challenge to Cuba's traditional sexual culture was the revolution's effort to end prostitution. After a brief bacchanal in which the triumphant revolutionaries and euphoric nation celebrated between the sheets, causing a boom in business for Cuban prostitutes, the government took a dramatic step. Nationalism came to the fore, and the Yankees were blamed for prostitution in Cuba. By closing down the brothels, Castro liberated Cuban women from the sexual control of foreigners and restored them to a position of respect in society. But for Cuban men, shutting down the bordellos created a problem: how were they to slake their sexuality?

If the revolution was cool to prostitution, it was aggressively hostile to homosexuality. The very notion of an effeminate man offended the heroic sensibilities of the revolutionary leadership. As the newspaper *Revolución* proclaimed: "No homosexual represents the Revolution, which is a matter for men, of fists and not feathers, of courage and not trembling, of certainty and not intrigue, of creative valor and not of sweet surprises."[18]

This abhorrence of homosexuality displayed early on by the regime raised serious questions about women's place in the revolution. If the revolution were "a matter for men," where did women fit in? That homosexuals, men who embraced the feminine realm, were perceived to be so threatening that the regime imprisoned them reflected the historical rigidity of Cuba's separate sexual spheres. Prostitutes, being women, could be rescued, but gay men, having rejected their masculinity, received no sympathy. While prostitutes attended school, living either at home or in government-provided dormitories, homosexual men were condemned to forced labor behind barbed wire.[19]

The worst homophobic excesses occurred during the first two decades of the revolution, yet in the mid-1980s the FMC still reportedly barred known lesbians from its ranks and provided a forum for neighbors to denounce others.[20] When a visitor in 1985 asked an FMC group in Cienfuegos about homosexuals and lesbians, the *federadas* laughed and replied: "Oh, we don't have problems with homosexuals. We make sure they are not in a position such as teaching school which will bring them in contact with children. There may not be laws against them, but we, the community, deal with the situation."[21]

International criticism of Cuban homophobia, particularly from friends of the revolution, plus lobbying by some Cuban health officials, helped to moderate the revolution's policies through the years. New sex education materials presented homosexuality as a "variation" instead of a "deviation." Finally in 1988 a revised criminal code decriminalized homosexual activity.[22]

By the end of the 1980s a new official tolerance of homosexuality had emerged in Cuba. Casual reference to homosexuality became routine in sex education materials. In conversations with Tomás Borge in 1992, Fidel Castro acknowledged the historical roots of Cuban homophobia and claimed not to support discriminatory policies against homosexuals.[23] Vilma Espín similarly called for an end to homophobia at the 1992 congress of the Young Communists Union. A new San Francisco-based solidarity organization called "Queers for Cuba" noted that recent public works of art and theater featured open and sympathetic portrayals of homosexuality.[24]

Nevertheless, hostility to homosexuals continued among the Cuban public. As of 1993 there were no officially sanctioned homosexual clubs, bars, or meeting places. One Cuban journalist concluded after interviewing more than sixty young people in 1991 that homosexuality remained a "taboo subject" that a majority "rejected unconditionally."[25] In 1994 a Cuban intellectual commented that the worst that could happen to one would be to be an Afro-Cuban lesbian, because "although officially this is not a problem, in daily life it most certainly is."[26]

Sex Education

Although national planning was a central feature of the Cuban revolution, the regime was hesitant to propose a comprehensive national policy regarding sex and reproduction. Birth control programs such as those supported in the developing world by the International Planned Parenthood Federation and similar institutions were regarded by Marxists as imperialist attempts to limit the size of the underclasses and thus avoid challenges to the status quo. Nonetheless, the government, desiring to engage Cuban women in the political and economic life of the nation, recognized the importance of birth control and family planning. The new notion that birth control might be a tool of liberation is reflected in a 1967 article in *Granma:*

> One can easily see that constant pregnancy, year in and year out, truly interferes with such activities [women's careers]. Contraceptives are therefore provided not so much as an economic measure, but rather as an effective means of freeing woman from the drudgery of household chores, releasing her for more productive service to society as a whole, and freeing her talents for the benefit of all.[27]

The sexual activities of the young became a topic of considerable interest at FMC meetings. *Mujeres* published a series of articles on the biology of sex. Menstruation and contraception were discussed at FMC meetings. At the FMC congress of 1974 women asked for sex education for their children. FMC researchers found that mothers themselves were often ignorant on sexual matters or hesitant to provide accurate information to their children. Soon basic sex education classes were introduced in primary and secondary school. In 1975 the Communist party's "Thesis on the Role of the Family in Socialism" addressed the reluctance of many parents to share sexual information with their children. It admonished parents for turning sex into something mysterious and perverse.

Sexual equality was to be a principal tenet of Cuba's new sex education program. The new Thesis stated that men and women should be "equally free and responsible in determining their relations in the area of their sexual lives."[28] Even so, the Communist party's ideas were quite conservative in many respects. In regard to sexual freedom, the party argued:

> [It] does not imply licentiousness, which degrades the beauty of relations between men and women. Relations within marriage under socialism flow from a different idea: they are established on the basis of equality, sincerity, and mutual respect and have to be based on clear and advanced ideas about the responsibility involved in sexual relations—the origin of life and the creator of the new generations.[29]

In 1977 The National Working Group on Sex Education (GNTES) was established to oversee a comprehensive national sex education effort. The GNTES began training teachers and health professionals and promoting print articles and television programs on topics related to sexuality. In the late 1970s a number of East German sex education primers were translated and published in Cuba. By 1986 more than a million were in circulation, and these would eventually be augmented by Cuban-authored works.[30] In 1989 the GNTES was renamed the National Center for Sex Education.

Cuba's sex educational materials challenged a number of traditional taboos and myths.[31] Whereas the original emphasis of Cuba's sex education program was to bring sexual and contraceptive information to young people, it now focused on the adult population, seeking to address the difficulties that impeded satisfactory conjugal life and thus contributed to social instability. To achieve a rewarding sex life, Cubans were advised to make sure that they were in love and to maintain open communication about each other's needs and desires. "When two people love each other any mutually satisfying sexual activity is morally correct."[32]

A key message conveyed in the education materials was that all women were sexual beings and their greatest sexual pleasure came from prolonged foreplay leading to a clitoral orgasm.[33] Women should expect their partners to accommodate this sexual reality. Furthermore, women have an orgasmic potential "that exceeds that of men in the second half of life." This "considerable difference" in the frequency of orgasm is called one of the "most aggravating" differences between male and female sexuality.[34] This message prompted one alarmed *machista* to denounce sex education officials for "making our women crazy. "We don't know how to fulfill all their expectations!" he complained.[35]

The average Cuban man could nevertheless take heart that there were still more than a few women who continued to submit docilely to their "matrimonial obligations" because they believed that men "need" sex more than women.[36] Sometimes this view was reinforced by sex education materials that were contradictory or confusing. For example, in 1989 one frequent writer on sexuality stated unequivocally that "the feminine libido is weaker than the masculine."[37]

These educational materials were neither particularly descriptive nor graphic. They were not the typical "how to" manuals of sexual mechanics common in the United States. There were few illustrations. were No one wrote testimonies for the media about what felt good to them. Indeed, revolutionary sex education materials in Cuba were almost prudish. Just how were men to learn to fulfill women's growing expectations?

One of the critical dilemmas that Cuban sex educators confronted in their effort to codify a socialist sexuality was that their message seemed to benefit women more than men. The new socialist code called for an elimination of the sexual double standard, the establishment of monogamy, and sincere attempts at mutual sexual satisfaction, all anathema to patriarchal traditionalism.

Cuban sex educators faced a daunting task. Few teachers were properly trained to teach the subject; high school classes on reproduction and sexuality were commonly conducted "amidst snickering and bad jokes."[38] Young Cubans continued to ask naive questions: Was it possible to get pregnant from only one sexual encounter? Could one contract venereal disease from a toilet seat?

Change and Tradition

In revolutionary Cuba certain sexual rituals of traditional society continued. Such was the case with the *quinceañera,* the fifteenth birthday party, which celebrates a young woman's coming of age. One might assume that the revolution, with its contempt for bourgeois values and its emphasis on sexual equality, would be particularly hostile to a puberty ritual celebrating extravagance, romanticism, and virginity. Instead of eliminating *quinceañeras,* however, revolutionary egalitarianism meant *quinceañeras* for all! The state even established bridal centers such as Havana's Palacio de las Novias de Galiano, where girls could rent dresses and book a photographer for the big event.

In a Cuba of material scarcities and ideological earnestness the *quinceañera* offered a rare opportunity for a festive family gathering. Christmas may have been eliminated, but the *quince* lived on. The costs of a *quince* need not exceed 150 to 200 pesos, or roughly one month's salary for a typical worker. Many families, however, would save money for many years for their daughters' *quince*. One family sold their refrigerator to help pay for an extravagant party; afterwards they had to beg ice and cold drinks from neighbors.[39]

The *quinceañera* is a curious holdover of a bygone era in which family dynasties could be forged and marriageable daughters were a critical asset in the accumulation of money, property, status, and influence. No longer were there prosperous suitors to lure with the glowing virgin. Indeed one could not even be sure that it was a virgin being presented.

In their daily life young women in revolutionary Cuba had to face a number of pressures, challenges, and decisions that were often nonexistent in the days of chaperons and limited career options. They had to decide for themselves how and when to explore sexuality, and Cuban society is full of contradictory signals regarding that decision. For example, girls were now routinely expected to have sex with their sweethearts. This expectation posed a difficult dilemma: "If they yield, they are giving in to *machismo;* if they don't, they lose their boyfriends."[40] Girls complained that boys still accrued status by sexual conquest; boys retorted that girls were adopting the same *modus operandi*. Students in Matanzas in 1987 told of girls who advertised their sexual activity as a "badge of feminine liberation."[41] Young women reluctant to have sexual relations with their boyfriends were sometimes ostracized by "in" groups.

Some Cuban observers lamented the lack of emotional commitment among young couples: Where were the romances written for young readers, one asked.[42] Young people were approaching sex like a game of accumulation, complained another, because "we forgot to teach them love."[43] A gynecologist lamented that sexual satisfaction and promiscuity had replaced the "beauty of love."[44] Some blamed the media for "promoting sexual relations" through racy soap operas and provocative films.[45]

A 1982 study conducted by the Young Communist League indicated that girls were better informed than boys on sexual matters. Fifty-six percent of those surveyed cited psychological and social maturity as a prerequisite for intercourse; 23 percent, a majority of whom were boys, thought physical attraction the most important factor. A study of university students in Matanzas province revealed that three-quarters of the young women rejected the idea that they should be virgin brides. Nonetheless, 44 percent of the male students said they wanted to marry virgins.[46]

Cuban sex education materials claimed that prior to 1959 women were, in effect, trained to desire sex less frequently than men.[47] This situation had changed. A 1985 sex education booklet suggested that women were more concerned with their own pleasure and were critical of male sexual performance. Also sexologists found that there was "almost no difference" between men and women in the frequency of extramarital affairs.[48]

This new female eroticism was not universally approved. Some sex education officials still wanted women to be the ones to apply the brakes in sexual liaisons.[49] One journalist admonished her fellow *cubanas* that they "are mistaken if they think that emancipation is to have sex whenever," and she urged them not to "learn too late" that for women "love can never be a simple acrobatic exercise or mere entertainment."[50]

Despite these changes in women's sexual activity, society continued to judge women according to traditional concepts of "appropriate" behavior. The FMC documented scores of cases in which women were penalized for sexual activity that violated the old Catholic code. FMC president Vilma Espín was an outspoken critic of this moral double standard. In 1983 she complained that the idea that men should have sexual experiences before marriage but women shouldn't presented a "mathematical problem" and was "totally absurd."[51]

Nonetheless, many young woman hesitated to reveal that they were sexually active because "the comments will be inevitable."[52] A survey of 226 young people in Guines and Melena revealed that many girls refused to ask for contraceptives at the local polyclinic to avoid being the object of gossip. This reluctance led officials to call for the sale of contraceptives in less obvious places, from video salons to barbershops.[53]

Sex and Dancing

In the moralistic fervor of the 1960s the revolution closed down not only the bordellos, sex shows, and gambling casinos but also most of the nation's nightclubs and dance halls—this in a country famous for its passion for rhythm and movement. A 1991 survey of 135 Havana residents showed that 98.5 percent of the respondents liked to dance.[54] Nevertheless, after 1959 the number of dance halls in Havana dropped from sixty (not including cabarets) to three.[55] Dance halls had not been a high priority for a government led by a *comandante* who didn't dance. Fidel Castro was, however, a great believer in sports. Thus the Liceo de Regla dance club in Havana, as well as many others throughout the island, was converted into a sports center in 1960. This, however, was not what people wanted. Seventeen years later local authorities reconverted the Liceo de Regla into a dance hall. As of August 1991 the Liceo de Regla had seven thousand members and a dance floor large enough to accommodate twelve hundred couples at a time.

Over the course of the revolution dance halls were also converted to houses of culture and workers' social clubs. Most young Cubans came to rely on private parties for opportunities to dance. But the lack of dance halls was decried as a cultural loss, because they promoted the use of live bands and thus helped to develop musicians and stimulate innovations in Cuban music. Private parties, on the other hand, relied on record players and foreign music.

The government was concerned that boredom among Cuban youth would lead to their alienation from the revolution. Such was the case with the resurgence of prostitution in Cuba. Increasing interest in "bourgeois" consumerism and the casual acceptance of sexual activity encouraged growing numbers of young women across the island to walk the streets in defiance of revolutionary values and expectations. The financial incentive was clear: it was possible to earn five to six thousand pesos each month, twenty times more than an engineer and fifteen times more than a government minister. Contemporary prostitution hovered around centers of foreign tourism; dollar-carrying tourists had access to consumer items in hard-currency stores that were off-limits to Cubans. A visitor to Varadero in 1994 found the beaches patrolled by young women looking for "companions" with dollars. Foreign bathers were even accosted by young women as they swam in the sea.[56] Although prostitutes could be sanctioned with up to two years' imprisonment (there was no penalty for their customers), law enforcement officials seemed largely indifferent.[57]

Another prerevolutionary institution to undergo a revival was the *posada*, or sex hotel, where couples could enjoy a few moments of privacy in housing-short Cuba. The love nests, often complete with room service, were rented for one or two pesos an hour to heterosexual couples, no questions asked. *Posadas* first appeared in Cuba in Spanish colonial times, differing from brothels in that they supplied only beds but not women. During the first years of the revolution a number of *posadas* were closed down and the buildings were employed for other functions. In 1969 there were only twelve *posadas* left in Havana; in 1987 there were more than fifty.[58]

The impact of the Cuban revolution on women's sexuality is captured in the life of the protagonist of the landmark 1979 film, *Portrait of Teresa.* Teresa is an intelligent working woman trying to chart a path through a society in flux. Her job has widened her social horizons and given her the confidence to question the traditional patterns evident in her private life. Her husband has an affair, which he considers unimportant, but he becomes incensed when he thinks she might have done the same. It is a double standard she cannot accept, and in the end she appears willing to sacrifice her marriage to avoid living under the male-biased rules of sexual tradition.

To a certain degree the development of sexual policy in revolutionary Cuba has not been based on a comprehensive or profoundly considered gender theory, but has been a reaction to specific social, demographic, and public health issues. The degree to which fundamental questions of power and sexuality have been left unexplored is evidenced in the many contradictory claims in revolutionary sex education materials and in the proliferation of simplistic statements such as "the cause of prostitution is the lack of work"[59] and "sexual stereotypes are based on economic dependency."[60] The role of sexuality in socialist society, according to the revolutionary program, is to provide a source of security and happiness for workers which will allow them smoothly and efficiently to perform their duties and ultimately—and perhaps most important—produce a new generation that conforms to revolutionary expectations.

The Castro regime, in encouraging changes in sexual life, risked considerable enmity among the population, particularly the men. The regime promoted birth control and made abortion legal. It questioned the moral double standard. But perhaps the most provocative venture of revolutionary sexual policy was the suggestion that women were sexual beings in their own right. Nothing could be more contrary to *machista* mores than the notion of an economically independent, sexually active, and informed woman who not only submits to sex but expects her partner to consider her pleasure as well as his!

The flip side to sexual policies in Cuba reflected the revolution's conservative underpinnings—thus the early efforts to eliminate prostitution and restrict abortion, and the ongoing refusal to discuss publicly rape, incest, and sexual abuse. Conservative notions were also evident in a sex education program that continued to portray the nuclear family—father, mother, and child—as the only proper formula.

A substantial gap continued to exist between contemporary sexual behavior in Cuba and the notions of the officials in charge of sexual policy.

A good part of the Cuban public rejected sex education as an encouragement to early sex and promiscuity; they continued to teach their sons
that only virgins make good brides. A gender division in sexual attitudes
emerged as women had greater incentive to change than did men. There
was also significant discord between the actual behavior of the men in
power and the views of the FMC. The latter's criticisms of sexual attitudes in the party, the media, and the office, factory, and field of Cuban
society still appeared to be cries in the wilderness as defectors disclosed
tales of orgies, prostitution, and promiscuity in the halls of government.[61]

The creation of Cuba's sex education program may prove to be one of
the most far-reaching and influential projects promoted by the FMC. Dr.
Monika Krause acknowledged that changing public views of women's
sexuality depended on society's ultimate willingness to redefine concepts
of appropriate male and female behavior. She admitted that compromises
were made, particularly early on, in the treatment of some sexual themes,
because of the strength of Cuba's traditional sexual culture. The reluctance of many educators and medical professionals to promote the revolution's sexual program suggested a long road ahead. It would take generations, said Krause, to achieve the revolution's goals in the realm of
sexuality.[62] Instead, time ran out.

Conclusion

Welcome to the theater of life, where men seek women who no longer exist, and women long for men who do not as yet exist.

Mirta Rodríguez Calderón, journalist (1992)[1]

Cuban society continues to be phallocentric, and we women are very far from real power.

Erena Hernández, historian and critic (1994)[2]

In Havana on August 23, 1994, in the shadow of the statue of Mariana Grajales, heroic mother of Cubans, the Federation of Cuban Women celebrated its thirty-fourth anniversary. Medals and certificates were presented to 244 women for distinguished service to the revolution. The FMC honored in particular those activists who had engaged in street fighting against "the enemy" eighteen days earlier when a massive street riot against the revolution had exploded in downtown Havana in plain daylight. The keynote speaker concluded that "when some wanted to kill all hope, we Cuban women feel more determined than ever in our faith in the revolution."[3]

In truth, however, this faith had been deeply shaken. A few blocks away from the FMC's celebration Cuban rafters were launching themselves into the sea in a second Mariel. By the time negotiations brought the flight to a halt in September, 35,000 Cubans had taken to the water, heading for Miami, and for the first time a significant number of the rafters were women and children. Time and time again mothers told reporters that they were risking their families' lives because there was no food and no hope in Cuba.

This tragic juncture raised profound questions about women and the revolution: had Cuban women benefited from three decades of socialism, or was it all a grand illusion?

As late as 1990 many women still thought well of the revolution. In that year *Bohemia* conducted a survey of one hundred women from different walks of life. When asked how much Cuban women had pro-

181

gressed in recent years, 63 percent said "quite a bit" *(bastante)* and 28 percent said "a lot" *(mucho)*. Only 9 percent said "little" *(poco)*.[4]

At its zenith in the mid-1980s the benefits of the revolution for women were substantial. State dominance of virtually the entire public realm guaranteed universal access to food and other basic necessities and also allowed the revolution to greatly expand and more equitably distribute critically important services such as health and education. State control of the economy and a policy of encouraging women's employment brought women greater economic independence and more diverse professional opportunities. Women's employment was transformed also with the elimination of domestic service and prostitution. In addition, no Cuban woman had to give birth without medical attention and then worry about providing her child with basics such as food, clothing, medical and dental care, and, later on, education and work opportunities. Socialism was providing social and economic security.

Because the revolution had crushed the Catholic church, the defender of the traditional social structure and mores, Cuban socialism could offer women universal access to divorce, abortion, and contraception, essential elements in women's advancement. New visions of women's sexuality emerged as patriarchal control of women's bodies was challenged.

While Cuban socialism was celebrated for its program of equality, for its eagerness to distribute, the one thing it was not able—or willing—to distribute was power. There were simply no routinely functioning mechanisms for ordinary citizens to influence the state. That is, there was no real democracy in Cuba.

At first this lack of democracy may have had certain benefits for Cuban women. The concentration of power at the top made possible the rapid implementation of a comprehensive program of sexual equality regardless of public opinion. In this sense the state truly became the vanguard of the people.

At the same time, however, centralism meant that national policies on issues of great interest to women would be made by men. This absence— even exclusion—of women from decision-making positions is reflected in rules that barred housewives from party membership for nearly thirty years. It is suggested also by the fact that abortion was disallowed for a number of years after the revolution, and that only recently was there public access to information on the potential side effects of certain birth control devices. It is evidenced by the militaristic and patriarchal bent of Cuban education. It is evidenced in the chronic underfunding of support services for working women while millions were spent to maintain tens of thousands of Cuban troops in Africa for more than ten years. It is suggested by the great official silence on domestic violence and rape.

Furthermore, the reins of power in revolutionary Cuba were not only male dominated, they were in the hands of one man, Fidel Castro. Without the establishment of autonomous institutions, socialism in Cuba became a camouflage to legitimize the lifelong reign of the *caudillo*. In such a system women remain effectively minors, beneficiaries of the goodwill and interest of the patriarch.

To a large degree women in Cuba were lucky in that women's advancement was of interest to the patriarch. Thus from the beginning women were encouraged to participate in a wide range of activities that established new, more independent, and more militant images of womanhood. Fidel Castro was an attentive participant in national gatherings on women's status. Consequently, Cuban laws and policies advanced beyond what might be called minimum ideological requirements. Sexual equality, unlike racial equality, was not simply declared a done deed and then forgotten by Cuban officialdom.

At the same time, from the earliest days of the insurrection Fidel Castro realized the tremendous utility of harnessing the energy and support of women. Thus, in addition to being beneficiaries of the Cuban system, women were also very much its subjects. This fact is evidenced in the constant mobilizations of women—mobilizations that often made use of women's voluntary, or unpaid, labor. From the workforce to the agricultural and health brigades to the organs of social vigilance to the militias, the Cuban government worked to ensure that women were engaged in active support of the regime and its predetermined policies.

An important tool in this effort was the Federation of Cuban Women. In the early days the FMC was an agent for change, getting women out of the house, organizing needed programs in health, education, work, and child care. The FMC also promoted the adoption of legislation such as the maternity law and the Family Code. But left without any formal power within the larger framework of the revolution, the FMC was incapable of acting predictably and forcefully in response to women's complaints against specific incidents and broader patterns of discrimination in the Cuban system. Instead it became the purveyor of socialist catechism for Cuban womanhood, seeking at the behest of the central government to convince all women above age fourteen that there were no alternatives to the revolution.

Yet Cuban women were isolated by the very ideology that purported to liberate them. All ideas that did not encourage women to march as commanded by the great patriarch, the *comandante*, were deemed "diversionary," enemy propaganda. The revolution presented women as a group united in purpose and belief, infinitely loyal to Castro, a group whose only necessary public manifestation was the FMC under the "socialism or death," "feminine not feminist" leadership of Castro's sister-in-law, Vilma Espín. This monolithic image of Cuban women was far from the case, however. Some fled the country. Others, like the internationally renowned ballerina Alicia Alonso, left quietly to take up residence abroad. Some women suffered a harder fate. Through the years significant numbers of women were imprisoned for opposing the revolution.

Perhaps the most notorious case was that of María Elena Cruz Varela,

a thirty-seven-year-old award-winning poet who had the temerity to challenge the patriarch. In an open letter to the commander-in-chief she protested the lack of democracy and respect for human rights in Cuba. In
response a "rapid reaction brigade" dragged her from her Havana apartment, beat her, and made her physically swallow some of her own writ-
ings. The woman who forced Cruz Varela literally to eat her own
words—and it was essential that the perpetrator be female, the revolution
being keenly mindful of symbol—commented that the attack was "a normal reaction of any revolutionary" in the face of a counterrevolutionary
provocation.[5] Cruz Varela was given a two-year prison sentence. She was
released in May 1993, after serving eighteen months, and was encouraged to emigrate to the United States.

In 1986, when the "rectification" program began, there were hopes
that this was the long-awaited second stage of the revolution in which
Cuba would move toward greater openness and democracy. Perhaps gender issues could now be more thoroughly analyzed. Instead Cuban periodicals, despite a more candid airing of problems, continued their three
decades of silence on central feminist debates. Cuban women remained
largely cut off from their peers in Latin America. Cuban women only
rarely appeared in *Mujer/Fempress,* the Chilean monthly which records
the activism of Latin American women.

The FMC was a latecomer to the feminist Encuentros, the periodic
diverse gatherings of women in Latin America. Indeed at an Encuentro
in Lima in 1983, Latin America feminists began to argue that "sexism
was not 'the outcome' of capitalism and imperialism but rather was
shaped by a relatively autonomous, patriarchal sex-gender system."[6] This
statement was a fundamental rejection of Cuba's long-maintained position of the primacy of the class struggle and the necessity of women's
obedience to central male authority.

Even if women in Cuba were unable to consider openly the phenomenon of patriarchy, it is an issue that is increasingly being addressed by
cubanas in exile. In 1994 Ileana Fuentes of Rutgers University argued
that patriarchy is the nemesis of Cuban history. In her view:

> [The revolution] enthroned machismo and all the demons that accompany
> it: intolerance, imperialist tendencies, war, lies, prison, political inquisition,
> the firing squad, torture, homophobia, censorship, dictatorship by force.[7]

Another exile, Uva de Aragón Calvijo, blamed *machismo* for blocking
negotiations between Miami and Havana because dialogue and compromise are perceived by *macho* leaders on both sides as a sign of weakness,
of being effeminate. Clavijo argued that the patriarchal demand that
mothers sacrifice their children to Mars was in fact uniting motherhood
with violence in the name of nationhood. The national symbol, the redeeming machete, thus became the national phallus, she asserted, symbol
of the patriarchal domination of Cuban culture?[8]

Nationalism, decried by some feminist theorists as a tool of patriarchy, was an important element in Cuba's hypersensitivity to criticism. But while the regime used nationalism to justify the squelching of debate, it was average Cubans themselves who, deeply proud of the achievements of Cuban socialism, were frequently hesitant to criticize, particularly to "outsiders," what they were taught to perceive as an embattled revolution in a hostile world.

It was Fidel Castro, Cuba's leading "feminist," who continually beat the militaristic drum. For more than thirty years Castro marched through the public arena dressed in the uniform of the perpetual warrior. In some respects Cuban militarism served women well. Because so many young men were in the military, there was more room in the universities and there were a wider than ever range of professions available to women. In addition, Cuba's foreign ventures enabled young women to visit socialist allies such as Vietnam, Angola, Grenada, Ethiopia, and Nicaragua.

But Cuban militarism had its downside as well. For three decades life in Cuba was a succession of military emergencies, sudden campaigns and heroic efforts which disrupted the civilian economy on which women depended. The home, private life, was depreciated. In the 1980s Cuba sent battalions of workers, machinery, and cement to build airports in Grenada and Nicaragua while Havana's housing crumbled for lack of paint, cement, and labor to make repairs.

While Cuban socialism offered ample evidence of the advantages for women of state domination, it also attested to the limits of state power to affect lasting social change. In fact, thirty-five years of revolution have proven the great tenacity of traditional culture, of *machismo*—or of *machismo-leninismo*, as some wags have termed it.

There were many disappointments in Cuban women's struggle for equality. A central dilemma was the failure of revolutionary ideologues and policy makers to consider adequately the cultural and economic implications of women's domestic responsibilities. The number of women workers increased but many were working at dead-end jobs, largely serving time to support their families. Women were widely present in the professions but rarely in policy-making positions. Increased demands on women's shrinking time brought frustration, discrimination, and exhaustion. Party officials expressed concern over the status of the Cuban family. Cuban women shunned contraception in favor of abortion. Meanwhile sexual double standards remained the rule of the day. The percentage of female-headed households was growing. Indeed, Cuban women had more than a little in common with the women of vastly different political systems. The lack of safe forums for public debate and the dearth of independently functioning institutions with clear powers complicated efforts to address and redress issues of particular interest to women in Cuba.

The economic crisis of the 1990s brought on by the collapse of the Soviet bloc challenged many of the gains made by women in Cuba. Many women, particularly members of the popular classes, had supported the revolution because it offered their children improved opportunities. Now the nation that had once looked forward to the future had come to dread it.

The reductions in Soviet aid in the late 1980s, combined with internal demographic changes and economic problems, threatened the service economy that provided both jobs and benefits for Cuban women. Could a Cuba cut adrift by the USSR afford a huge service sector? Was the service economy, and with it women's progress, a chimera sustained by Soviet largesse? Was the progress of Cuban women tied—ironically—to the Soviet Union's geopolitical ambitions?

When Soviet petroleum shipments to Cuba began to decline in 1990, it meant not only that the revolution would substitute bicycles for buses and oxen for tractors, but that women would lose one of the major gains of the revolution: the replacement of human by mechanical energy. At work it meant that physical strength would again become important. At home it meant that women could no longer count on electrical or gas appliances.

In 1992 journalist Mirta Rodríguez Calderón observed that the economic crisis was particularly devastating for Cuban women. The search for food was left largely to them. Women had to devise substitutes for soap, detergent, and other items no longer available in stores.[9] A visitor to Cuba in 1992 found sociologist Marta Núñez contemplating dinner with nothing more than a few avocados in her larder.[10] With whom could she trade? Women became routine scofflaws, negotiating the black market, which by 1993 had become the leading supplier of food in Cuba. Housewives were asked to volunteer in emergency food production programs in the countryside. Ironically, after more than thirty years of denigration, housewives were being celebrated in the media for their important role in daily life.

As Soviet aid diminished, Cuba rushed to develop tourism as an alternate source of income. The Cuban tourist board sponsored advertising campaigns featuring—despite the objections of the FMC—dark-skinned beauties in minimal bikinis to lure foreigners to Cuban beaches. In the spring of 1990 the government allowed *Playboy* to photograph topless *cubanas* romping on the beach at Varadero. The author of the article claimed that while the FMC had protested, authorization had come from men high in the government.[11] A top FMC official later reported that the leaders of her organization had been furious and dismayed; it was, she said, "a disaster."[12] By 1994 even foreign hoteliers were becoming worried that Cuba's growing image as a destination for sexual tourism would prejudice the possibilities for family vacationers.[13]

In the summer of 1991 the Castro regime was declaring that Cuban socialism would endure unchanged, despite the collapse of the USSR and Eastern Europe. We are not, Castro said, going to become a pale shadow of Miami.

But across the Florida Straits Cuban exiles were preparing to do precisely that: Miamize Cuba. The leading exile group, the Cuban American National Foundation—whose sixty-eight-member board in 1990 included only two women (3 percent) [14]—was calling for the overthrow of Castro and for a neo-conservative shock treatment which would demolish the basic elements of Cuban socialism. The interventionist state's emphasis on collectivity and equality were to be replaced by a stress on individualism, the family, and private and foreign capital. In this transformation, most of the social sector that had been such a boon to Cuban women would be undone.

In a post-Castro regime it is likely that the Catholic church would use its influence to attack laws that permit abortion on demand and easy divorce. Sex education could be eliminated and state support for contraception ended. Maternal death rates and the birth rate would thus simultaneously increase. Private maid service would reemerge and women would return to the informal sector.

Will it be possible for a post-Castro Cuba to balance the interests of the family and the state and preserve the most important social gains of the revolution? Or will the neo-conservative regime that many foresee forge policies to drive women back to the kitchen, back to their condition as dependents, seeking in effect to recreate women who, thanks in large part to the revolution, "no longer exist"? Ironically, the ultimate test of the achievements of the Cuban revolution for women will be women's ability to maneuver and progress in a postsocialist Cuba.

Notes

Introduction

1. Batya Weinbaum, *The Curious Courtship of Women's Liberation and Socialism* (Boston: South End Press, 1978).

2. Sandor Halebsky and John Kirk, eds., *Cuba: Twenty-five Years of Revolution, 1959–1984* (New York: Praeger, 1985), p. 5.

3. Mirta Aguirre, *Cuba y la revolución de octubre* (Havana: Editorial de Ciencias Sociales, 1987), p. 65. Unless otherwise noted, all translations from the Spanish are our own.

Chapter 1

1. Frederick Noa, "The Condition of Women in Cuba," *Outlook Magazine*, March 16, 1905, p. 647.

2. A. Soto Cobian, "Retrospectiva de la mujer cubana," *Mujeres*, March 1969, p. 4.

3. Gonzalo de Palacio, "La cubana es la reina de Edén," *Diario las Americas*, October 29, 1989, p. 6B.

4. Laurette Séjourné, *La mujer cubana en el quehacer de la historia* (Mexico City: Siglo Veintiuno, 1980), p. 37.

5. Luis de Posada, "Spotlight on Society," *The Diplomat* (Washington, D.C.), November 1958, p. 39.

6. Andrés Vargas Gómez, "La reverencia del hombre cubano por la mujer," *El Nuevo Herald*, November 16, 1991, p. 15A.

7. Lolo de la Torriente, "El mujer como factor de progreso en la vida cu-

bana," in *Libro de Cuba: Edición conmemorativa del cincuentenario de la independencia, 1902–1952* (Havana: n.p., 1954), p. 180.

8. Mirta Rodríguez Calderón, "Yo fui una prostituta: apuntes para la memoria necesaria." *Bohemia,* March 2, 1990, pp. 8–9.

9. Nelson Valdés with Nana Elsasser, "La Cachita y El Che: Patron Saints of Revolutionary Cuba," *Encounters* (Univ. of New Mexico) (Winter 1989), pp. 30–34.

10. Louis A. Pérez, *Cuba: Between Reform and Revolution* (New York: Oxford University Press, 1989), p. 46.

11. Manuel Moreno Fraginals, *El Ingenio,* vol. 2 (Havana: Editorial Ciencias Sociales, 1978), p. 53.

12. Pérez, *Cuba,* p. 87.

13. William Luis, "Cirilio Villaverde," in *Latin American Writers,* ed. Carlos A. Sole (New York: Scribners, 1989), p. 172.

14. Verena Martínez-Alier, *Marriage, Class and Colour in Nineteenth-Century Cuba* (London: Cambridge University Press, 1974), p. 113.

15. Esteban Montejo, *Diary of a Runaway Slave* (New York: Vintage, 1968), p. 88.

16. Benjamin de Céspedes, *La prostitución en la ciudad de la Habana* (Havana: O'Reilly, 1883), p. 66.

17. Ibid., p. 151.

18. Ibid., p. 299.

19. Ibid., pp. 228, 299.

20. Desi Arnaz, *A Book* (New York: William Morrow, 1976), p. 17.

21. Condesa de Merlin, *Viaje a la Habana* (Havana: Editorial de Arte y Literatura, 1974), p. 208.

22. Ibid., p. 108.

23. Hugh A. Harter, "Gertrudis Gómez de Avellaneda," in *Spanish American Women Writers,* ed. Diane E. Marting (Westport, Conn.: Greenwood Press, 1990), p. 217.

24. Kathryn Lynn Stoner, *From the House to the Streets: The Cuban Woman's Movement for Legal Reform, 1898–1940* (Durham, N.C.: Duke University Press, 1991), p. 22.

25. Marisel García Llanes and Marcia Alonso Martínez, "Algunas consideraciones martianas sobre la mujer," *Islas* (Univ. of Las Villas), no. 75 (May–August 1983): 165.

26. Ibid., p. 164.

27. Diego Vicente Tijera, *La Mujer Cubana* (Key West, Fla.: Club Cubano, 1898), p. 12.

28. Ibid., p. 12.

29. Graziella Méndez, "Domitila García, viuda de Coronado," *Mujeres,* March 1966, p. 45.

30. Robin Morgan, ed., *Sisterhood Is Global* (Garden City, N.Y.: Anchor Books, 1984), p. 168.

31. María Dolores Ortiz, *La mujer cubana en la educación superior* (Havana: Editorial Letras, 1985), p. 18.

32. Ibid., p. 16.

33. Rolando Alvarez Estévez, "Los clubs femeninos en la emigración," *Mujeres,* February 1970, pp. 44–45.

34. Armando O. Caballero, *La mujer en el 95* (Havana: Editorial Nueva Gente, 1982), pp. 24–31.

35. Pérez, *Cuba,* p. 190.

36. "The Condition of Women in Cuba," p. 643.

37. Ibid., p. 644.

38. Pérez, *Cuba,* p. 209.

39. Jean Stubbs, *Tobacco on the Periphery: A Case Study in Cuban Labor History* (London: Cambridge University Press, 1985), p. 71.

40. Francisco G. Mota, *Por primera vez en Cuba* (Havana: Editorial Gente Nueva, 1982), pp. 71–80.

41. Ibid., p. 88.

42. Ibid., pp. 104–8.

43. Pérez, *Cuba,* p. 206.

44. Mercedes García Tudurí, "Resumen de la historia de la educación en Cuba: su evaluación, problemas y soluciones del futuro," in *Temática cubana: primera reunión de estudios cubanos, Exilio 3* (Winter 1969–Spring 1970): 113.

45. Pérez, *Cuba,* p. 238.

46. Manuel Gongora Echenque, *Lo que he visto en Cuba* (Madrid: Imprenta Gongora, 1929), p. 123.

47. *Diario las Américas,* June 28, 1987, p. 4B.

48. Antonio Núñez Jiménez, *La abuela* (Lima, Peru: Campodonico-ediciones S. A., 1973), pp. 24–25, 36.

49. Heidy González Cabrera, "María Luisa o la tenacidad," *Mujeres,* July 1987, p. 18.

50. Peter Bourne, *Fidel: A Biography of Fidel Castro* (New York: Dodd, Mead, 1986), pp. 20–21.

51. Stoner, *From the House to the Streets,* pp. 40–46.

52. Ibid., pp. 46–53.

53. Ibid., p. 52.

54. Ibid., pp. 56–57.

55. Asunción Lavrin, "Female, Feminine and Feminist: Key Concepts in Understanding Women's History in Twentieth Century Latin America," *University of Bristol, Occasional Lecture Series,* no. 4 (November 1988): 1–17.

56. Mariblanca Sabás Alomá, *Feminismo: questiones sociales-crítica literaria* (Havana: Editorial Hermes, 1930), p. 134.

57. Kathryn Lynn Stoner, "Ofelia Domínguez Navarro: The Making of a Cuban Socialist Feminist," in *The Human Tradition in Latin America,* ed. William H. Beezley and Judith Ewell (Wilmington, Del.: Scholarly Resources, 1988), p. 121.

58. "Mirta Aguirre," *Bohemia,* August 15, 1980, p. 49.

59. Sabás Alomá, *Feminismo,* p. 31.

60. Ibid., p. 47.

61. Stoner, *From the House to the Streets,* p. 187.

62. FMC, *Mujeres Ejemplares* (Havana: Editorial Orbe, 1977), p. 164.

63. Ada Ortuzar-Young, "Lydia Cabrera," in *Spanish American Women Writers,* ed. Diane E. Marting (Westport, Conn.: Greenwood Press, 1990), pp. 105–14.

64. María Luisa Guerrero, *Elena Mederos: una mujer con perfil para la historia* (Miami: Ediciones Universal, 1991), p. 66.

65. María Begoñia Arostegui, "A cinquenta años de La Orquesta Femenina Ensueño," *Bohemia,* June 20, 1980, pp. 6–8.

66. Graziella Barinaga y Ponce de León, *El feminismo y el hogar* (pamphlet). Havana, 1930, pp. 7–9.

67. Stoner, *From the House to the Streets,* p. 173.

68. Concepción Duchesne, "La mujer trabajadora en la pseudo-república," *Bohemia,* May 2, 1975, pp. 88–93.

69. Inés Segura Bustamente, *Cuba Siglo XX y la generación de 1930* (Miami: Ediciones Universal, 1986), pp. 46–48.

70. Stoner, *From the House to the Streets,* pp. 177–78.

71. María Elena Capote, "Por ellas y para ellas," *Mujeres,* May 1973, pp. 52–55.

72. Mirta Aguirre, *Influencia de la mujer in Iberoamérica* (Havana: Imprenta P Fernández, 1947), p. 112.

73. Oficina Nacional de los Censos Demográfico y Electoral, *Censos de población, viviendas y electoral, 1953* (Havana), pp. 183, 204–5.

74. José A. Moreno, "From Traditional to Modern Values," in *Revolutionary Change in Cuba,* ed. Carmelo Mesa-Lago (Pittsburgh: University of Pittsburgh Press, 1971), p. 479.

75. *Censos de población, viviendas y electoral,* pp. 204–5.

76. María A. Martínez Guayanes, "La situación de la mujer en Cuba en 1953," *Santiago* (Univ. of Oriente), vol. 15 (September 1974): 206–7.

77. Alfred Padula, "Cuba: The Fall of the Bourgeoisie, 1959–1961" (Ph.D. diss., University of New Mexico, 1974), pp. 15–34.

78. Ibid., p. 30.

79. Mirta de la Torre Mulhare, "Sexual Ideology in Pre-Castro Cuba: A Cultural Analysis" (Ph.D. diss., University of Pittsburgh, 1969), p. 264.

Chapter 2

1. Haydée Santamaría, *Moncada* (Secaucus, N.J.: Lyle Stuart, 1980), p. 46.

2. Esther Mosak, "Natalia Bolivar," *Prisma,* April–May 1992, p. 47.

3. Dolores Nieves and Alina Feíjoo, eds., *Semillas de fuego,* 2 vols. (Havana: Editorial de Ciencias Sociales, 1989, 1990).

4. Sally Quinn, "Wilma *[sic]* Espín: The First Lady of the Revolution," *Washington Post,* March 26, 1977, p. B3.

5. Elsa M. Chaney, *Supermadre: Women in Politics in Latin America* (Austin: University of Texas Press, 1979), p. 51. This is less true in recent years as a new generation of high-level women has emerged on the Latin American political scene.

6. For example, with a postgraduate degree in chemical engineering and familiarity with the sugar industry, Vilma Espín was at least as qualified as Che Guevara to head the Ministry of Industry.

7. Sally Quinn, "To Die Is Much Easier," *The Washington Post,* March 21, 1977, p. B4.

8. Melba Hernández, "Sesenta y dos horas de mi vida desaparecieron," *Granma,* July 9, 1988, p. 4.

9. Quinn, "To Die Is Much Easier," p. B4.

10. Vilma Espín, "Deborah," *Santiago: Revista de la Universidad de Oriente* 17 (March 1975): 61.

11. Mirta Díaz-Balart, married to Fidel Castro in 1948, was only an occasional minor participant in early revolutionary activities. Castro divorced Mirta while in prison in the 1950s. They later fought a bitter battle over custody of their son, Fidelito, which Castro won.

12. Tad Szulc, *Fidel, A Critical Portrait* (New York: Avon Books, 1986), p. 343.

13. Delia Darias Pérez, "Gustavo decía que no se podía dar tregua a la tiranía," *Granma*, May 21, 1988, p. 3.

14. Szulc, *Fidel*, p. 345.

15. Melba Hernández, "A Gloria Cuadras mi gratitud y la de mis compañeros," *Granma*, August 27, 1987, p. 3.

16. Julio M. Llanes, *Celia nuestra y de las flores* (Havana: Editorial Gente Nueva, 1985).

17. Teresa Casuso, *Cuba and Castro* (New York: Random House, 1961).

18. Szulc, *Fidel*, p. 359.

19. Carmen Castro Porta et al., *La lección del maestro* (Havana: Editorial Ciencias Sociales, 1990), p. 74.

20. Fidel Castro, "De Fidel a Carmen," *Bohemia*, August 19, 1988, p. 62.

21. Ibid., p. 62.

22. Castro Porta, *La lección*, p. 101.

23. Mario Mencia, "Ahora sí se gana la revolución!" *Bohemia*, December 1, 1972, p. 64.

24. Espín, "Deborah," pp. 69–70.

25. Llanes, *Celia nuestra*, p. 30.

26. Herbert Matthews, *The Cuban Story* (New York: Braziller, 1961), p. 22.

27. Espín, "Deborah," p. 77.

28. Robert Pérez Betancourt, "Para hablar de Santiago, nuestro Santiago," *Bohemia*, January 6, 1984, p. 8.

29. Espín, "Deborah," p. 79.

30. "Vilma Espín: Firme combatiente y madre amorosa," *Mujeres*, August 15, 1962, p. 10.

31. Llanes, *Celia nuestra*, pp. 62, 46.

32. Szulc, *Fidel*, pp. 462–63.

33. Llanes, *Celia nuestra*, p. 53.

34. Ibid.

35. Szulc, *Fidel*, p. 463; Fidel Castro, "La fibra más íntima y querida de la revolución cubana," *Bohemia*, January 18, 1980, p. 43.

36. Carlos del Toro, "Lydia y Clodomira: estoicismo revolucionario," *Granma*, September 17, 1988, p. 2; Lázaro Torres Hernández, "Lidia y Clodomira," *Bohemia*, September 15, 1978, p. 41.

37. Mirta Rodríguez Calderón, "Combate tras las rejas," *Granma*, July 15, 1987, p. 3.

38. There has been some suggestion that Vilma Espín, a loyal *Fidelista*, may have played a role in the death of Frank País, a potential rival of Castro. See Ramón Bonachea and Marta San Martín, *The Cuban Insurrection* (New Brunswick, N.J.: Transaction Books, 1974), pp. 377–78; and Georgie Anne Geyer, *Guerrilla Prince: The Untold Story of Fidel Castro* (Boston: Little Brown, 1991), pp. 179–80.

39. Espín, "Deborah," p. 84.

40. Mirta Rodríguez Calderón, "Hilos para halar," *Granma,* April 21, 1988, p. 3.

41. Elena Alavez, "Dos jóvenes revolucionarias asasinadas por la tiranía batistiana," *Bohemia,* June 16, 1978, pp. 84–88; Carlos del Toro, "Las hermanas Giralt," *Granma,* June 15, 1988, p. 3.

42. Mirta Rodríguez Calderón, "De estrellas en las frentes," *Bohemia,* August 19, 1988, p. 61.

43. Mariano Rodríguez Herrera, "Cuban Women in the Rebel Army," *Granma Weekly Review,* November 6, 1988, p. 2.

44. Ernesto Che Guevara, *Obras, 1957–1967* (Paris: Documentos Latinoamericanos, 1970), vol. 1, p. 107.

45. Froylan Escobar and Félix Guerra, *El Che en la Sierra Maestra* (Mexico City: Editorial Diogenes, 1973), p. 36.

46. Bonachea and San Martín, "Cuban Insurrection," p. 183.

47. Rodríguez Herrera, "Cuban Women," p. 2.

48. Vilma Espín Guillois, *La mujer en Cuba: historia* (Havana: Editorial de la Mujer, 1990).

49. Rodríguez Herrera, "Cuban Women," p. 2.

50. Patricia Grogg, "Cara a cara con Isabel Rielo," *Cuba Internacional,* July 1989, p. 76.

51. Rodríguez Calderón, "De estrellas en las frentes," p. 61.

52. Fidel Castro, "Guisa: Preludio de la victoria," *Granma,* (special section), November 30, 1988, p. 12.

53. Fulgencio Batista y Zaldivar, *Cuba Betrayed* (New York: Vantage Press, 1962), pp. 125, 135.

54. Frank Hechavarría, "Oye, de dónde viene Mariana?" *Bohemia,* December 30, 1977, p. 47.

55. Ibid.

Chapter 3

1. *Work Plan of the Federation of Cuban Women* (Havana: Editorial Orbe, 1975).

2. *FMC Political Orientation Guide* (Havana, 1973), p. 6.

3. FMC, *Memories, Second Congress Cuban Women's Federation* (Havana: Editorial Orbe, 1975), p. 154.

4. Laurette Séjourné, *La mujer cubana en el quehacer de la historia* (Mexico City: Siglo Veintiuno, 1980), pp. 184–92.

5. Margaret Randall, *La mujer cubana ahora* (Havana: Editorial de Ciencias Sociales, 1972), pp. 298–99. See also Juan Antonio Blanco Gil, "Elena Gil: esencia y presencia," *Bohemia,* May 10, 1985, pp. 56–57.

6. Randall, *La mujer cubana,* p. 206.

7. Ilse Bulit, "Cómo se forjan los cuadros?" *Bohemia,* November 1, 1985, p. 56.

8. Teresa Casuso, *Cuba and Castro* (New York: Random House, 1961), p. 180; "Sin influencia comunista el congreso feminino de Chile," *Revolución,* November 4, 1959, p. 3.

9. "Regresan las delegadas al congreso feminino interamericano de Chile," *Revolución,* November 25, 1959, p. 16.

10. Séjourné, *La mujer cubana,* pp. 188–89.

11. Ibid., pp. 186, 191.
12. Victor Pino Yerovi, *De embajadora a prisionera política* (Miami: Ediciones Universal, 1991), p. 13.
13. Lourdes Meluza, "How Many Prisoners?" *The Miami Herald,* May 4, 1986, p. 4G.
14. Nestor Almendros and Orlando Jiménez-Leal, *Conducta impropia* (Madrid: Biblioteca Cubana Contemporánea), p. 160.
15. Carolina Aguilar and Nilda Navarrete, "Un recuento de luchas y de victoria," *Mujeres,* August 1985, p. 4.
16. Sally Quinn, "Wilma *[sic]* Espín: The First Lady of the Revolution," *The Washington Post,* March 26, 1977, pp. B1, B3.
17. FMC, *Memories, Second Congress,* p. 94.
18. FMC, *Memoria, Primer Congreso,* (Havana, 1962), p. 5.
19. Karen Wald, unpublished interview with Teté Puebla, Havana, March 1986, p. 3.
20. FMC, *Memoria, Primer Congreso,* pp. 13–14.
21. "Círculos infantiles: doce años de hermosa labor," *Mujeres,* April 1973, pp. 12–13.
22. Francisco Pita Rodríguez, "Flores de la vida," *Bohemia,* August 30, 1974, p. 66.
23. Carmen Alfonso, "Los primeros círculos infantiles," *Mujeres,* March 1985, pp. 44–47.
24. Ilse Bulit, "La otra revolución," *Bohemia,* August 23, 1985, p. 56.
25. Séjourné, *La mujer cubana,* p. 135.
26. Ibid., p. 134.
27. Ibid., p. 126.
28. Gladys Castaño, "Una forma de hacer justicia," *Mujeres,* August 1974, pp. 94–97.
29. Séjourné, *La mujer cubana,* p. 126.
30. Bulit, "La otra revolución," p. 56.
31. Ibid., p. 124.
32. Fidel Castro, "Un día grande para la educación cubana," *Bohemia,* July 12, 1985, pp. 60–67.
33. "Antes la batalla histórica de 10 millones," *Mujeres,* January 1969, pp. 12–20; FMC, p. 106.
34. Séjourné, *La mujer cubana,* p. 143.
35. Gladys Castaño, "Las doméstics: 'Qué eramos; qué somos?" *Mujeres,* August 1973, pp. 11–13.
36. Ibid., p. 11.
37. Oscar Lewis, Ruth M. Lewis, and Susan M. Rigdon, *Four Women* (Urbana: University of Illinois Press, 1977), p. 277.
38. "La eliminación de todas las formas de discriminación contra la mujer en Cuba," *Boletín FMC* (Havana, 1984), p. 12.
39. Lewis, Lewis, and Rigdon, *Four Women,* p. 279.
40. "Círculos de estudios FMC: Lección 2," *Mujeres,* February 1963, pp. 66–67.
41. "Círculos de estudios FMC: Lección 20: Período de transición del capitalismo a socialismo," *Mujeres,* September 1964, pp. 66–69; "Lenin y la emancipación de la mujer," *Mujeres,* January 1970, p. 4; Gladys Castaño, "Busca del lugar cimero," *Mujeres,* July 1983, p. 56.

42. "Círculos de estudios FMC: Lección 20," p. 67.

43. FMC, *Memorias del 3er Congreso* (Havana: Editorial de Ciencias Sociales, 1984), pp. 120–21.

44. FMC Boletín Especial (Havana, 1983), pp. 8, 13.

45. "Eliminación de todas las formas," p. 103.

46. Ibid., pp. 109–10.

47. Nancy Saporta Sternbach, Marysa Navarro-Aranguren, Patricia Chuchryk, and Sonia E. Alvarez, "Feminisms in Latin America: From Bogotá to San Bernardo," in *The Making of Social Movements in Latin America: Identity, Strategy and Democracy,* ed. Arturo Escobar and Sonia E. Alvarez (Boulder, Colo.: Westview Press, 1992), p. 234. The Encuentros, which have involved up to several thousand women of all classes and positions, provide clear proof that feminism can no longer be considered a merely bourgeois preserve but is indeed one of the most dynamic and diverse social movements in Latin America today.

48. *Tercer Boletín de la FMC* (Havana, 1982), p. 17.

49. "Eliminación de todas las formas," p. 129.

50. Janet Salvá and Isolina Triay, "Caso cerrado," *Bohemia,* August 21, 1981, pp. 48–49.

51. Ibid., p. 48.

52. Fidel Castro, "Marchamos hacia adelante . . . ," speech to the Fourth Congress of the FMC, *Granma,* March 11, 1985, pp. 1–5.

53. Vilma Espín, "Jamás seremos esclavas a una potencia extranjera o de un patrón capitalista," *Granma,* March 7, 1990, pp. 4–5.

54. Vilma Espín, interview, *Mujeres,* August 1970, pp. 8–11; FMC, *Memories, Second Congress,* p. 113; FMC, *Memorias del 3er Congreso,* p. 138.

55. Luisa Espinosa Hechevarría, "Así ayudamos," *Mujeres,* May 1975, p. 73.

56. "Las madres y educación," *Mujeres,* May 1971, pp. 58–60; Miriam Jiménez, "Una labora admirar," *Mujeres,* December 1979, pp. 56–57; *Tercer Boletín de la FMC,* p. 15; Castro, "Marchamos hacia adelante . . . ," p. 4.

57. *Tercer Boletín de la FMC,* p. 15.

58. *FMC IV Congreso: Draft Thesis, Cuban Women, 25 Years of Revolution* (Havana, 1985), p. 47.

Chapter 4

1. *FMC IV Congreso: Draft Thesis,* p. 72.

2. Fidel Castro, speech at the close of the Third FMC Congress, in *Women and the Cuban Revolution,* ed. Elizabeth Stone (New York: Pathfinder Press, 1981), p. 122.

3. *Constitución de la República de Cuba, 1976* (Havana: Editorial de Ciencias Sociales, 1985), p. 23.

4. *Constitución de la República de Cuba, Granma,* September 22, 1992, p. 6.

5. *Europa World Book,* vol. 1 (London: Europa Publications, 1984), p. 215.

6. Fidel Castro, Main report to the 3rd Congress of the Cuban Communist Party, *Granma Weekly Review,* February 16, 1986, pp. 2–22; quote on p. 15.

7. *Directory of Officials of the Cuban Republic* (Washington, D.C.: Directorate of Intelligence, CIA, 1989), pp. 3–7.

8. Mimi Whitefield, "Youthful Leaders Emerge in Cuba," *The Miami Herald,* October 27, 1991, p. 25A.

9. "Miembros del Comité Central," *Granma,* October 15, 1991, p. 3.

10. *Directory of Officials of the Cuban Republic,* 1989, pp. 29–33.

11. Communist Party of Cuba, "Thesis on the Full Exercise of Women's Equality," in *Women and the Cuban Revolution,* ed. Stone, p. 91; Magaly Pérez and Noemí Pascual, *Estadísticas sobre la mujer cubana* (Havana: Editorial Letras Cubanas, 1985), p. 18; Sarah Santana and Carmen Hernández, "El reto actual: sobre la mujer y el hombre en Cuba," *Areito,* no. 5 (November 1990): 15.

12. *Europa World Book,* vol. 1 (London: Europa Publications, 1990), pp. 803–4.

13. Juan M. del Aguila, *Cuba: Dilemmas of a Revolution* (Boulder, Colo.: Westview Press, 1985), p. 151.

14. *Cuba Update,* March–June 1984, p. 3; Susana Lee, "13,256 Delegates Elected to Municipal Assemblies of People's Power," *Granma Weekly Review,* November 16, 1986, p. 1.

15. Enrique Sans Fals, "Votó más del 92% de los electores que fueron a segunda vuelta," *Granma,* May 8, 1989, p. 1.

16. "Presidentes de las 169 asambleas municipales del Poder Popular," *Granma,* May 23, 1989, p. 4.

17. *FMC V Congreso: Proyecto de informe central* (Havana, 1990), p. 20.

18. Susana Lee, "Elegidos los 13,865 delegados a las asambleas municipales," *Granma,* December 29, 1992.

19. "Presidentes y vicepresidentes de las asambleas municipales del Poder Popular," *Granma,* January 12, 1993, p. 3.

20. Santana and Hernández, "El reto actual," p. 15.

21. Communist Party of Cuba, "Thesis: On the Full Exercise of Women's Equality," pp. 90–91.

22. *Directory of Officials of the Cuban Republic* (Washington, D.C.: Directorate of Intelligence, CIA, 1985), pp. 180–81.

23. *Europa World Book,* vol. 1, 1990, pp. 806–7.

24. Rosa Elvira Peláez, "Fidel Confers Félix Varela . . . ," *Granma Weekly Review,* October 31, 1982, p. 5; see also in the same issue "List of Recipients of Félix Varela order. . . ."

25. Georgina Jiménez, "Investigadores más destacados en 1989 en Educación Superior," *Granma,* February 20, 1990, p. 2; also "Investigadores más destacados . . . ," *Granma,* March 5, 1992, p. 1.

26. Mireya Castañeda, "Women in the Creative Work of the Revolution and in Its Defense," *Granma Weekly Review,* March 18, 1990, p. 12.

27. *CubaTimes,* July–August 1984, p. 8.

28. *Work Plan of the FMC,* p. 14.

29. FMC, *Memories, Second Congress,* p. 221.

30. "Lograr una base organizativa sólida," *Mujeres,* August 1970, pp. 88–89.

31. Heidi Steffins, "FMC at the Grass-roots," *Cuba Review* 4, no. 2 (1974): 25–26.

32. FMC, *Memories, Second Congress,* p. 127.

33. FMC, *Memorias, 1er Congreso,* p. 58.

34. "La mujer en la revolución," *Mujeres,* November 1974, pp. 11–14.

35. "Lograr una base," p. 89.

36. FMC, *Memories, Second Congress,* p. 126; Isabel Larguía and John Dumou-

lin, "Women's Equality and the Cuban Revolution," in *Women and Change in Latin America,* ed. June Nash and Helen Safa (South Hadley, Mass: Bergin and Garvey, 1986), p. 359.

37. FMC, *Memories, Second Congress,* p. 211.

38. Ibid., p. 87; Ricardo Villares and Janet Salvá, "La lucha por la igualdad y la integración plena de la mujer cubana," *Bohemia,* December 6, 1974, pp. 51–65.

39. The policy of disallowing housewives party membership was not changed until 1986.

40. Vilma Espín, "Final Declaration of the 4th FMC Congress," *Granma Weekly Review,* March 17, 1985, p. 5.

41. FMC, *Memorias, 1er Congreso,* pp. 6–7.

42. Ibid., p. 21.

43. FMC, *Memories, Second Congress,* p. 74.

44. Ibid., p. 190.

45. Villares and Salvá, "La lucha por la igualdad," p. 62.

46. *Boletín, 3rd Congreso de la FMC,* p. 8.

47. Ibid., p. 9.

48. Ibid.

49. FMC, *Memorias del 3er Congreso,* pp. 105–6.

50. Ibid.

51. Ibid., pp. 136–37.

52. *FMC IV Congreso: Recomendaciones* (Havana, 1985), pp. 3, 8–10, 17, 19.

53. Ibid., pp. 6, 27–28.

54. Diana Sosa, Juan Carlos Santos, and José A. de la Osa, "Aprobado por unanimidad el informe central al IV Congreso de la FMC," *Granma,* March 8, 1985, pp. 1, 3–4.

55. Arleen Rodríguez Derivet, "Viraje histórico en la organización feminina cubana," *Juventud Rebelde,* March 30, 1989, p. 10.

56. Mirta Rodríguez Calderón and Sonia Moro, "Cuéntame tu vida," *Bohemia,* March 2, 1990, pp. 4–7.

57. Frei Betto, interview with Fidel Castro, *Granma Weekly Review,* April 8, 1990, p. 9.

58. Castañeda, "Women in the Creative Work of the Revolution," p. 12.

59. "Noticias de Cuba," *Diario las Américas,* March 13, 1990, p. 7A.

60. Lois M. Smith, meeting with Esther Velis, FMC headquarters, Havana, January 1985.

61. The peasant markets were reopened in the fall of 1994.

62. *FMC IV Congreso: Informe central* (Havana, 1985), p. 55.

63. Rita Pereira, panel presentation at "Thirty Years of the Cuban Revolution: An Assessment," Halifax, Nova Scotia, October 25–28, 1989.

64. Pablo Alfonso, "Partido cubano se divorcia de Federación de Mujeres," *El Nuevo Herald,* October 18, 1991, pp. 1A, 4A.

Chapter 5

1. Fidel Castro, *History Will Absolve Me* (Havana: Editorial en Marcha, 1962), p. 32.

2. José A. de la Osa, "Día de la medicina latinoamericana," *Granma,* December 4, 1992, p. 1.

3. *Censos de población, viviendas y electoral,* pp. 204–5; "En la semana," *Bohemia,* March 13, 1992, p. 43.

4. *Censos de población, viviendas y electoral,* pp. 204–5; Vilma Espín, "Jamás seremos esclavas de una potencia extranjero de un patrón capitalista," *Granma,* March 7, 1990, p. 4; Sarah Santana and Carmen Hernández, "El reto actual: sobre la mujer y el hombre en Cuba," *Areito,* no. 5 (November 1990): 15.

5. Ross Danielson, *Cuban Medicine* (New Brunswick , N.J.: Transaction Books, 1979), pp. 32–63.

6. Ibid., p. 109.

7. Bernal Araújo and José Llorens Figueroa, *La lucha por la salud en Cuba* (Mexico City: Siglo Veintiuno Editores, 1985), p. 17.

8. Ibid., 16.

9. Danielson, *Cuban Medicine,* p. 207.

10. Ibid., p. 110.

11. Araújo and Llorens, *La lucha,* p. 18.

12. See José Seoane Gallo, *El foclor médico de Cuba* (Havana: Editorial de Ciencias Sociales, 1984); Lois M. Smith, "Progress, Science, and Myth: The Health Education of Cuban Women," *Cuban Studies* (Univ. of Pittsburgh) 19 (1989): 167–96.

13. Ibid.

14. Miriam Martínez, ed., *La mujer cubana y la salud pública* (Havana: Editorial Letras Cubanas, 1985).

15. Estimates of prerevolutionary infant mortality figures vary from sixty per thousand live births to more than eighty per thousand. Ibid.; Araújo and Llorens, *La lucha,* p. 20.

16. Ibid.

17. Isolina Triay, "Téstigo de excepción," *Mujeres,* December 1980, pp. 43–45.

18. Araújo and Llorens, *La lucha,* p. 47.

19. José A. de la Osa, "Un millonario de la salud pública cubana," *Granma,* December 31, 1988, p. 10.

20. Medea Benjamin, Joseph Collins, and Michael Scott, *No Free Lunch* (San Francisco: Institute for Food and Development, 1984), p. 99.

21. José M. Norniella, "Se elevó a 351,5 millones de pesos el subsidio estatal a los productos de primera necesidad," *Granma,* March 31, 1987, p. 1.

22. Eugenio R. Balari, "Improving Consumer Habits," *Granma Weekly Review,* September 20, 1987, p. 2.

23. Carmen Diana Deere, "Cuba's Struggle for Self-Sufficiency," *Monthly Review,* July–August 1991, pp. 55–73.

24. José A. de la Osa, "Con 10,2 en mortalidad infantil . . . ," *Granma,* January 5, 1993, p. 5; idem, "Births in Maternity Hospitals Rise to 99.8 Percent," *Granma Weekly Review,* April 19, 1992, p. 4.

25. Vilma Espín, "Jamás seremos esclavas a una potencia extranjera o de un patrón capitalista," *Granma,* March 7, 1990, p. 4.

26. *Work Plan of the Federation of Cuban Women,* p. 42; Gladys Castaño, "Siempre listas!" *Mujeres,* July 1976, p. 20.

27. Isolina Triay, "Brigadistas . . . ," *Mujeres,* September 1973, p. 7.

28. Lolangel Alvarez, "El valioso aporte de las brigadas sanitarias," *Mujeres,* April 1977, p. 50.

29. *Work Plan of the FMC,* p. 43.

30. Health Debate, "Disposición de residuales en zonas rurales," *Mujeres,* February 1967, p. 115; Health Debate, "Higiene de los alimentos," *Mujeres,* June 1967, pp. 92–93; Health Debate, "La Higiene," *Mujeres,* October 1966, pp. 120–21.

31. Health Debate, "La lactancia materna y su importancia," *Mujeres,* June 15, 1962, p. 64.

32. Araújo and Llorens, *La lucha,* p. 361.

33. Fidel Castro, "Analizan los problemas que afrontan la mujer en el aceso al trabajo y en su vida laboral," *Granma,* March 7, 1985, pp. 1–3.

34. Espín, "Jamás seremos esclavas," p. 4.

35. René Camacho Albert, "La lucha por preservar y mejorar la calidad de nuestras vidas," *Granma,* December 9, 1987, p. 3.

36. de la Osa, "Births in Maternity Hospitals Rise," p. 4.

37. Augustín Pérez Hechavarría, "Una doctora en la montaña," *Granma,* August 17, 1987, p. 2.

38. Benjamin, Collins, and Scott, *No Free Lunch,* p. 110.

39. José Norniella, "How the Average Cuban Lives," *Granma Weekly Review,* December 18, 1983, special supplement.

40. Cino Colina, "Will Cubans Die by the Mouth?," *Granma Weekly Review,* December 25, 1988, p. 3; Balari, "Improving Consumer Habits," p. 2.

41. Castro, "Analizan los problemas que afrontan la mujer," *Granma,* March 7, 1985, p. 3.

42. Benjamin, Collins, and Scott, *No Free Lunch,* p. 117.

43. See, for example, Martiza Cabrera, "Gymnasia feminina," *Mujeres,* September 1974, p. 43.

44. FMC, *Memorias del 3er Congreso,* (Havana, 1984), p. 119; Erick Romay, "Salud y estética," *Mujeres,* August 1977, pp. 74–75.

45. Gilberto Blanch, "Tres factores peligrosos," *Mujeres,* September 1981, pp. 12–13; Cino Colina, "Speaking from the Heart," *Granma Weekly Review,* October 22, 1989, p. 3; Araújo and Llorens, *La Lucha,* p. 320.

46. *Muchacha,* January 1986, inside back cover.

47. María Elena Zulueta, ed., *Manual de educación para la salud* (Havana: Editorial Científico-Técnica), p. 31. The presumption seemed to be that single women did not have regular sexual relations and thus were not in a higher-risk category until their thirtieth birthday. In fact, research in the United States has shown that women with multiple sexual partners are at slightly higher risk, regardless of marital status.

48. José A. de la Osa, "Tratamiento eficaz del cáncer uterino detectado precozmente," *Granma,* May 25, 1988, p. 2.

49. Dr. Pedro Rodríguez Domínguez, *Temas de salud sobre la mujer* (Havana: Editorial Científico-Técnica, 1985), p. 51; Orfilio Peláez, "Avanza introducción de la cirugía segmentaria en cáncer de mama," *Granma,* April 7, 1989, p. 2.

50. José A. de la Osa, "Comenzó programa de diagnóstico precoz del cancer de mama," *Granma,* October 9, 1989, p. 2.

51. José A. de la Osa, "Montarán en el Ameijeiras acelerador lineal de electrones," *Granma,* November 9, 1988, p. 1.

52. Peláez, "Avanza introducción de la cirugía segmentaria," p. 2.

53. See Jose A. de la Osa, "Día de la medicina latinoamericana," *Granma,* December 4, 1991, p. 1.

54. José A. de la Osa, "Realizan en Cuba primer trasplante de cerebro a cerebro,"*Granma,* January 30, 1988, p. 1.

55. Sally Quinn, "To Die Is Much Easier," *The Washington Post,* March 21, 1977, p. B5.

56. Paula E. Hollerbach and Sergio Díaz-Briquets, *Fertility Determinants in Cuba,* Committee on Population and Demography Report No. 26 (Washington, D.C.: National Academy Press, 1983), p. 138.

57. See, for example Alberto Salazar, "Hogar, dulce hogar?" *Bohemia,* January 18, 1991, pp. 10–12; Mirta Rodríguez Calderón, "Que nadie se entere," *Bohemia,* November 20, 1992, pp. B8–11.

58. See, for example, José Abrantes, "Nuestro pueblo puede tener la seguridad . . . ," *Granma,* September 21, 1988, p. 3.

59. Alfred Padula and Lois M. Smith, interview with Dr. Ada Ovies, Güines, Cuba, April 1986. In 1988, residents of Santiago de Cuba were engrossed in the televised trial of three men charged with the rape and murder of a female student. Two of the defendants were sentenced to die and a third received a thirty-year sentence. This rare public acknowledgment of the existence of rape in Cuba was part of a crackdown on crime that followed the implementation of a new penal code earlier in the year.

60. Rodríguez Calderón, "Que nadie se entere." At the Fifth International Interdisciplinary Congress on Women, held February 16–22, 1993, at the University of Costa Rica in San José, Ana Violeta Castañeda of the FMC publicly announced that "domestic violence is not a problem in Cuba." In a subsequent conversation with author Lois M. Smith she stated that she would be surprised if there were more than ten cases of rape nationally each year in Cuba. Both she and longtime FMC activist Carolina Aguilar expressed their opinion that denouncing violence against women was a North American agenda being imposed on Cuba by U.S. feminists. Furthermore, it was politically misguided. "The real issues of concern to women," said Aguilar, "are to have enough to eat, to have a job."

61. Luis Salas, *Social Control and Deviance in Cuba* (New York: Praeger, 1979), pp. 185, 187.

62. Comité Estatal de Estadísticas, *Anuario estadístico de Cuba* (Havana, 1980), p. 257.

63. Lorrin Philipson, "Suicides, Not Solidarity Under Castro," *The Wall Street Journal,* November 7, 1983, p. 34.

64. "El 28 de julio de 1980," *Casa de las Américas,* Mayo–June 1985, p. 13; Don Bohning, "Cuba Revolt Guerrilla Kills Herself," *The Miami Herald,* July 30, 1980.

65. Sarah Santana, "The Cuban Health Care System: Responsiveness to Changing Population Needs and Demands," *World Development,* no. 1 (1987): 116.

66. Rodríguez Domínguez, *Temas de salud,* p. 42; Araújo and Llorens, *La lucha,* p. 133.

67. Ministry of Public Health, "Información del Ministerio de Salud pública sobre el programa de lucha para la prevención del sindrome de inmunodeficiencia adquirida (SIDA) en Cuba," *Granma,* April 17, 1987, p. 3.

68. José A. de la Osa, "La forma más segura," *Granma,* October 21, 1987, p. 3.

69. "Estrategía cubana en la lucha contra el SIDA," *Granma,* June 18, 1988, p. 2.

70. Pablo Alfonso, "Cuba por dentro," *El Nuevo Herald,* May 9, 1992, p. 3A.

71. Sarah Santana, "Focus on: AIDS in Cuba," *Cuba Update,* Summer 1989, pp. 23–25.

72. José A. de la Osa, "El SIDA no se transmite . . . ," *Granma,* September 22, 1990, p. 2.

73. Carlos Cabrera, "On the Frontiers of AIDS," *Granma Weekly Review,* December 10, 1989, p. 12.

74. Victor F. Zonona, "Cuba's AIDS Quarantine Center Called 'Frightening,' " *The Los Angeles Times,* November 4, 1988, sec. 1, p. 1.

75. Santana, "AIDS in Cuba," p. 25.

76. *A Public Survey on the Quality of Health Care in the Province of Holguín, Cuba* (Havana: Communist Party of Cuba, 1988), pp. 4–5.

Chapter 6

1. Fidel Castro, speech at the close of the 2nd FMC Congress, in *Women and the Cuban Revolution,* ed. Elizabeth Stone (New York: Pathfinder Press, 1981), p. 68.

2. In Dr. Pedro Rodríguez Domínguez, *Temas de salud sobre la mujer* (Havana: Editorial Científico-Técnica, 1985), p. 7.

3. Monika Krause, ed., *Compilación de artículos sobre educación sexual para el médico de la familia* (Havana: Grupo Nacional de Trabajo sobre Educación Sexual, 1987), p. 3.

4. Mirta Rodríiguez Calderón, "Cuánto vale un aborto . . . ?" *Bohemia,* July 7, 1989, p. 14.

5. Mirta Rodríguez Calderón, "Con el indice en alto," *Bohemia,* September 8, 1989, p. 22.

6. José A. de la Osa, "Con 10,2 en mortalidad infantil . . . ," *Granma,* January 5, 1993, p. 5.

7. Rodríguez Domínguez, *Temas de salud,* p. 7.

8. Aldo Prieto Morales, *Lo circunstancia en la responsabilidad penal* (Havana: Editorial de Ciencias Sociales, 1983), p. 107.

9. Ibid., p. 108.

10. "Producir almohadas sanitarias en Bayamo," *Granma,* September 5, 1988, p. 2.

11. Alfred Padula and Lois M. Smith, interview with Monika Krause, Havana, April 1986.

12. Paula E. Hollerbach and Sergio Díaz-Briquets, *Fertility Determinants in Cuba,* Committee on Population and Demography Report No. 26 (Washington, D.C.: National Academy Press, 1983), p. 20.

13. Barent F. Landstreet, "Cuban Population Issues in Historical and Comparative Perspective" (Ph.D. diss., Cornell University, 1976), p. 199.

14. Elizabeth Fee, "Sex Education in Cuba: An Interview with Dr. Celestino Alvarez Lajonchere," *International Journal of Health Services* 18, no. 2 (1988): 345.

15. It is unclear why or how it was possible to offer tubal ligations but not abortions.

16. Lois M. Smith, interview with Monika Krause, Havana, January 1985.

17. Elizabeth Sutherland, *The Youngest Revolution: A Personal Report on Cuba* (London: Pittman Publishing, 1969), p. 178.

18. Health Debate, "El aborto," *Mujeres,* January 1978, p. 73.

19. Hollerbach and Díaz-Briquets, *Fertility Determinants,* p. 105; Padula and Smith, interview with Monika Krause.

20. José A. de la Osa, " Posible prevenir la hemofilia con diagnóstico prenatal . . . ," *Granma,* May 18, 1989, pp. 1–2. In 1988, panelists at a Havana seminar on family planning acknowledged that there were some "very rare" (left unspecified) potential side effects from IUD use. See de la Osa, "Debate en torna a métodos anticonceptivos," *Granma,* October 13, 1988, p. 2.

21. Rodríguez Domínguez, *Temas de salud,* pp. 68–69.

22. Rodríguez Calderón, "Cuánto vale un aborto?" p. 15.

23. Ibid., p. 20.

24. Krause, *Compilación de artículos,* p. 17.

25. Ibid., p. 9.

26. *Código de Defensa Social 1936,* vol. 10 (Havana: Manuales de Legislación y Jurisprudencia, 1953), pp. 152–53; Hollerbach and Díaz-Briquets, *Fertility Determinants,* p. 9.

27. Fee, "Sex Education," pp. 344–45; Seoane Gallo, *El foclor médico de Cuba* (Havana: Editorial dc Ciencias Sociales, 1984), pp. 798–802.

28. Oscar Lewis, Ruth M. Lewis, and Susan M. Rigdon, *Four Women* (Urbana: University of Illinois Press, 1977), p. 277.

29. Luisa Alvarez Vázquez, *La fecundidad en Cuba* (Havana: Editorial Ciencias Sociales, 1985), p. 30.

30. Krause, *Compilación de artículos,* p. 11.

31. Ibid., p. 12.

32. José Yglesias, *In the Fist of the Revolution* (New York: Vintage Books, 1969), p. 266.

33. Fee , "Sex Education," p. 346; Ross Danielson, *Cuban Medicine* (New Brunswick, N.J.: Transaction Books, 1979), p. 226.

34. Alvarez Vázquez, *La fecundidad,* p. 162.

35. *Ley del Código Penal,* Chapter VI, Law 21, Havana, February 15, 1979, pp. 157–59.

36. Hollerbach and Díaz-Briquets, *Fertility Determinants,* pp. 96, 115; Ministry of Public Health, *Programa Nacional de Atención Materno/Infantil* (Havana, 1983), p. 14; *Código Penal Ley 62* (Havana: Gaceta Oficial, 1987), pp. 88–89.

37. Rodríguez Calderón, "Cuánto vale un aborto?" pp. 14–15, 35; Fee, "Sex Education," p. 347; Pablo Alfonso, "Cuba por dentro," *El Nuevo Herald,* March 4, 1991, p. 3A.

38. Fidel Castro, "Este año ha sido importante . . . ," *Granma,* December 30, 1987, pp. 1–3; Krause, *Compilación de artículos,* pp. 9, 13.

39. Rodríguez Calderón, "Con el indice en alto," p. 22.

40. Krause, *Compilación de artículos,* pp. 13, 18; Lourdes Meluza, "Study: Cuban Religious Persecution Subtler Now, *The Miami Herald,* April 25, 1986, p. 6B.

41. Rodríguez Calderón, "Con el indice en alto," p. 23.

42. Rodríguez Calderón, "Cuánto vale un aborto?", p. 18.

43. Aloyma Ravelo, "Hablemos francamente: el aborto," *Muchacha,* March 1988, pp. 52–53.

44. Alvarez Vázquez, *La fecundidad,* pp. 26–28.

45. Monika Krause, *Algunos temas fundamentales sobre educación* (Havana: Editorial Científico-Técnica, 1985), pp. 14, 22; Marta Matamoros and María de los Angeles Rodríguez, "Embarazo en la adolescencia (1): Epidemia de alta frewencia," *Bohemia,* June 26, 1987, pp. 21–25; Fidel Castro, speech to the IV Congress of the Federation of Cuban Women, *Granma,* March 11, 1985, pp. 1–8.

46. José A. de la Osa, "Un aumento de los nacimientos ocurridos en 1982 corresponden a madres adolescentes," *Granma,* March 1, 1983, p. 3; Rodríguez Calderón, "Con el indice en alto," p. 25.

47. Ibid., p. 25.

48. Pablo Alfonso, "Cuba por dentro," *El Nuevo Herald,* March 4, 1991, p. 3A; Padula and Smith, interview with Monika Krause.

49. Padula and Smith, interview with Dr. Ada Ovies.

50. Padula and Smith, interview with Monika Krause.

51. Castro , "Este año ha sido importante.

52. Rodríguez Calderón, "Cuánto vale un aborto?" p. 15.

53. Isolina Triay, "La maternidad en Cuba," *Mujeres,* December 1973, pp. 56–59; Miriam Martínez, *La mujer cubana y la salud pública* (Havana: Editorial Letras Cubanas, 1985), p. 13.

54. Triay, "La maternidad en Cuba"; de la Osa, "Con 10,2 en mortalidad infantil."

55. "Hogares maternos," *Mujeres,* June 1971, pp. 42–45.

56. Isolina Triay, "Un hogar en la montaña," *Mujeres,* May 1983, pp. 6–7; Martínez, *La Mujer Cubana,* p. 13.

57. Padula and Smith, interview with Dr. Ada Ovies; José A. de la Osa, "Births in Maternity Hospitals Rise to 99.8 Percent," *Granma Weekly Review,* April 19, 1992, p. 4.

58. Rodríguez Domínguez, *Temas de salud,* pp. 57, 89, 90–93, 125. The authors have found no mention of information on postpartum depression in childbirth.

59. Mirta Rodríguez Calderón, "Papá en el parto!?" *Bohemia,* March 24, 1989, pp. 21–24; idem, "Vindicación de la ternura," *Bohemia,* June 16, 1989, pp. 21–25; idem, "Papi, te quiero . . . ," *Bohemia,* February 23, 1990, pp. 10–13.

60. Isolina Triay, "Antes de nacer," *Mujeres,* September 1975, pp. 50–51; Ministry of Public Health, *Programa Nacional de Atención Materno/Infantil* ; Isolina Triay, "Imágen transformada," *Mujeres,* December 1983, pp. 40–42.

61. Padula and Smith, interview with Dr. Ada Ovies; José A. de la Osa, "Dar seguridad y calidad a la vida," *Granma,* December 10, 1987, pp. 4–5; idem, "Montan técnica para el diagnóstico prenatal . . . ," *Granma,* May 6, 1987, p. 1; idem, "Ya han nacido en Cuba cuatro bebés in vitro . . . ," *Granma,* June 14, 1989, p. 2.

62. Fidel Castro, speech at the opening session of the Cuba 1984 Pediatric Congress (Havana , Editora Política, 1984), p. 20.

63. Padula and Smith, interview with Ada Ovies; Susana Lee, "Combatividad multiplicada contra lo mal hecho . . . ," *Granma,* September 27, 1987, p. 3.

64. Aldo Madruga, "El día que perdimos la bandera de Modelo," *Granma,* September 7, 1988, p. 4.

65. "Doctor díganos cómo explicar, curar or vencer la esterilidad," *Mujeres,* November 1966.

66. de la Osa, "Posible prevenir la hemofilia"; idem, "Ya han nacido en Cuba."

67. Rodríguez Domínguez, *Temas de salud*, pp. 28–31.

Chapter 7

1. "La FMC y la educación," *Mujeres*, August 1970, p. 21.

2. "Hacia el II Congreso Nacional de la FMC," *Mujeres*, August 1974, pp. 4–5.

3. Fidel Castro, speech of September 17, 1988, *Granma Weekly Review*, September 25, 1988, p. 12.

4. Georgina Jiménez, "Distinguia lo esencial de lo secundario," *Granma*, July 8, 1989, p. 2.

5. Jonathan Kozol, *Children of the Revolution* (New York: Delacorte Press, 1978), p. xii.

6. Vilma Espín, "Jamás seremos esclavas a una potencia estranjera o de un patrón capitalista," *Granma*, March 7, 1990, p. 4.

7. *Censos de población, viviendas y electoral*, p. 119; Luisa Eng, *La mujer cubana en la revolución educacional* (Havana: Editorial Letras Cubanas, 1985, pp. 26, 32.

8. Susan Schroeder, *Cuba: A Handbook of Historical Statistics* (Boston: G. K. Hall, 1982), p. 127.

9. Nikolai Kolesnikov, *Cuba: educación popular y preparación de los cuadros nacionales, 1959–1982* (Moscow: Editorial Progreso, 1983), p. 100.

10. Oscar Lewis, Ruth M. Lewis, and Susan M. Rigdon, *Four Women* (Urbana: University of Illinois Press, 1977), p. 66.

11. Ibid., p. 76.

12. Max Figueroa, Abel Prieto, and Raúl Gutiérrez, *The Basic Secondary School in the Country: An Educational Innovation in Cuba* (Paris: UNESCO Press, 1974), p. 4.

13. "Vamos a recoger café," *Mujeres*, September 15, 1962, pp. 15–16.

14. Eugene F. Provenzo and Concepción García, "Exiled Teachers and the Cuban Revolution," *Cuban Studies* 13, no. 1 (Winter 1983): 1–15.

15. Eng, *La mujer cubana*, p. 23.

16. Paula L. Pina, "Esta batalla requiere el concurso de todos," *Mujeres*, November 1976, p. 74.

17. Kolesnikov, *Cuba*, pp. 519–20.

18. Espín 1990, "Jamás seremos esclavas," p. 4.

19. "Aprobado el proyecto de código de vialidad y tránsito," *Granma*, September 29, 1987, pp. 1–4; "Santiago será la sede," *Granma*, April 30, 1988, pp. 1, 4.

20. Georgina Jiménez, "Crece la doble sesión en primaria," *Granma*, November 23, 1989, p. 4.

21. Nicolasa Díaz Chirolde, Nieve López López, and Magaly Egurrola Hernández, *Lectura 6 grado* (Havana: Editorial de Libros para la Educación, 1981).

22. Lourdes Díaz Canto, *Lectura 6 grado* (Havana: Editorial de Libros para la Educación, 1981), p. 157.

23. Martin Carnoy, "Educational Reform and Social Transformation in Cuba, 1959–1989," in *Education and Social Transformation in the Third World*, ed. Mar-

tin Carnoy and Joel Samoff (Princeton, N.J.: Princeton University Press, 1990), p. 185; Eng, *La mujer cubana,* p. 34.

24. Tim Coone, "Conquering the Citrus Markets," *Financial Times,* February 17, 1989.

25. Alfred Padula and Lois M. Smith, visit to "Battle of Jigüe" School, Havana Province, March 1986.

26. Manuel Sánchez Pérez, "La educación en Cuba," *Diario las Américas,* August 19, 1986, p. 5a.

27. Aloyma Ravelo, "Por qué las muchachas lavan la ropa a los varones?" *Muchacha,* December 1986, pp. 56–57.

28. Iraida Campo Nodal, "En la BECA hay monotonía," *Muchacha,* June 1988, pp. 6–8; Alfonso Chardy, "Quería irme antes del cataclismo," *El Nuevo Herald,* July 7, 1991, pp. 1D , 4D.

29. Alberto Salazar, "Renovar la Nueva Escuela," *Bohemia,* May 17, 1991, pp. 8–11.

30. *FMC IV Congreso: Draft Thesis,* pp. 43–44.

31. Alfred Padula and Lois M. Smith, visit to "Martyrs of Humboldt Seven" Polytechnical High School, Havana Province, March 1986.

32. Iraida Campo Nodal, "Títulos colgados en la pared?" *Muchacha,* June 1988, pp. 6–8.

33. Fidel Castro, speech on January 4, *Granma,* January 7, 1989, p. 3.

34. Castro, speech on September 17, 1988, p. 11.

35. Iraida Campo Nodal, "Necesidad ser útil," *Muchacha,* November 1987, p. 9; Marilys Suárez Moreno, "Esos Alumnos . . . Por qué abandonan el aula?" *Mujeres,* February 1987, pp. 8–9.

36. Mirta Rodríguez Calderón, "Acuerda SNTECD y MINED seleccionar a los maestros para escuelas de conducta," *Granma,* April 14, 1987, p. 2.

37. Espín, "Jamás seremos esclavas," p. 4.

38. *Censos de población, viviendas y electoral,* p. 119; María Dolores Ortíz, *La mujer cubana en la educación superior* (Havana: Editorial Letras Cubanas, 1985), pp. 20–21).

39. Mirta Rodríguez Calderón, "Soldados de la patria y de la salud del pueblo," *Mujeres,* February 1962, pp. 58–59.

40. "Geologas, geofísicas . . . ," *Mujeres,* November 1974, p. 23.

41. "Veterinarias . . . ," *Mujeres,* November 1974, p. 22.

42. Iris Davila, "La escalatina responde," *Mujeres,* March 1974, pp. 46–50, quote on p. 48.

43. James W. Wilkie, ed., *Statistical Abstract of Latin America,* vol. 26 (Los Angeles: UCLA Latin American Center, 1988), p. 170.

44. Oscar Rego, "Evaluación y vocación," *Bohemia,* June 19, 1987, p. 30.

45. José A. de la Osa, "Graduados por la Revolución más de 45,000 médicos," *Granma,* August 14, 1991, p. 1.

46. Castro, speech on September 17, 1988, p. 12.

47. Kolesnikov, *Cuba,* Table 6, p. 527.

48. Eusebio Mujal-León, *The Cuban University under the Revolution* (Washington, D.C.: Cuban American Foundation, 1988), p. 30; Georgina Jiménez, "Analizan esfuerzos por dar vuelco correcto a enseñanza universitaria," *Granma,* August 3, 1987, pp. 1, 3; Espín, "Jamás seremos esclavas," p. 4.

49. José Luis Llovio-Menéndez, *Insider: My Hidden Life as a Revolutionary in Cuba* (New York: Bantam Books, 1988), p. 308.

50. Comité Estatal de Estadísticas, *Anuario Estadístico de Cuba* (Havana, 1986), p. 203.

51. See Alfred Padula and Lois M. Smith, "The Revolutionary Transformation of Cuban Education, 1959–1987," in *Making the Future: Politics and Educational Reform in the United States, England, the Soviet Union, China, and Cuba,* ed. Edgar B. Gumbert (Atlanta: Center for Cross-Cultural Education, 1988), pp. 117–39; Marilys Suárez Moreno, "En busca de la semilla perdida," *Mujeres,* January 1987, pp. 12–13; "Fraude académico," *Somos Jóvenes,* September 1987, pp. 14–23; "Admite Fidel Castro que existe derrotismo en el pueblo cubano," *Diario las* February 8, 1987, p. 1a.

52. Castro, speech on September 17, 1988, p. 10.

53. Georgina Jiménez, "Can We Develop Without Manual Laborers?" *Granma Weekly Review,* June 23, 1991, p. 3.

54. Elsa Núñez, "Cómo son los escolares de 5to. y 6to. grados?" *Granma,* April 25, 1988, p. 3.

55. Isolina Triay, "Una educación igual," *Mujeres,* December 1988, pp. 4–7; Mirta Rodríguez Calderón, "Mamá de espaldas," *Bohemia,* April 28, 1989, pp. 21–27.

56. Katiuska Blanco and Luis Roger Ricardo, "Versión de las palabras de Carmen Rosa Báez," *Granma,* December 21, 1990, p. 5.

57. Katiuska Blanco, "Son tiempos de hacer y confiar," *Granma,* October 2, 1990, p. 2.

Chapter 8

1. Fidel Castro, speech at the close of the Fifth National Plenary of the FMC," in *Women and the Cuban Revolution* ed. Elizabeth Stone (New York: Pathfinder Press, 1981), p. 54.

2. Kathryn Lynn Stoner, *From the Houses to the Streets: The Cuban Woman's Movement for Legal Reform, 1898–1940* (Durham, N.C.: Duke University Press, 1991), p. 183.

3. *Censos de población, viviendas y electoral,* pp. 183, 204–5.

4. Isabel Larguía and John Dumoulin, "Women's Equality and the Cuban Revolution," in *Women and Change in Latin America,* ed. June Nash and Helen Safa (South Hadley, Mass.: Bergin & Garvey, 1986), pp. 345–46; Jean Stubbs and Mavis Alvarez, "Women on the Agenda: The Cooperative Movement in Rural Cuba," in *Rural Women and State Policy: Feminist Perspectives on Latin American Agricultural Development,* ed. Carmen Diana Deere and Magdalena León (Boulder, Colo.: Westview Press, 1987), p. 148.

5. "El socialismo es fuente de belleza," *Mujeres,* March 15, 1962, p. 1.

6. *Memories, Second Congress Cuban Women's Federation,* p. 95.

7. Ana Ramos, "La mujer y la revolución en Cuba," *Casa de las Américas,* March–June 1971, pp. 56–72; *Memories, Second Congress Cuban Women's Federation,* p. 99.

8. *Memoria, Primer Congreso de la FMC,* p. 28.

9. *Memories, Second Congress Cuban Women's Federation,* pp. 112–14.

10. Carmen Diana Deere, "Rural Women and Agrarian Reform in Peru, Chile, and Cuba," in *Women and Change in Latin America,* ed. Nash and Safa, p. 200.

11. Angela Soto, "1,000,000 mujeres en la producción = mil millones de pesos en valores creados," *Mujeres,* August 1966, pp. 4–9; Fidel Castro, Fifth National FMC Plenary, pp. 48–49.

12. Larguía and Dumoulin, "Women's Equality and the Cuban Revolution," in *Women and Change in Latin America,* ed. Nash and Safa, p. 349.

13. Geoffrey Fox, "Honor, Shame and Women's Liberation in Cuba: Views of Working Class Emigre Men," in *Female and Male in Latin America,* ed. Ann Pescatello (Pittsburgh: University of Pittsburgh Press, 1973), p. 275.

14. *Memories, Second Congress Cuban Women's Federation,* pp. 94–95.

15. Robert M. Bernardo, "Moral Stimulation and Labor Allocation in Cuba," in *Cuban Communism,* 4th ed., ed. Irving Horowitz (New Brunswick, N.J.: Transaction Books, 1981), pp. 185–218: 194.

16. Ramos, "La Mujer y la revolución," p. 71.

17. Augusto Martínez Sánchez, *Trabajo,* September 1964, p. 74.

18. Douglas Butterworth, *The People of Buenaventura* (Urbana: University of Illinois Press, 1980), p. 34.

19. This goal would not be achieved until 1984.

20. Angelina Chio Vidal, "Cuál es la tarea del Frente Feminina?" *Mujeres,* January 1971, pp. 56–60.

21. Ramos, "La Mujer y la revolución," p. 68.

22. *Memories, Second Congress Cuban Women's Federation,* p. 121.

23. Sara González and Angela Soto, "La mujer en la zafra gigante," *Mujeres,* August 1970, pp. 42–50, quote on p. 44.

24. Ramos, "La mujer y la revolución," p. 68.

25. Elizabeth Sutherland, *The Youngest Revolution: A Personal Report on Cuba* (London: Pittman Publishing, 1969), p. 179.

26. Ramos, "La mujer y la revolución," p. 68.

27. Rosario Fernández, "La mujer: fuerza decisiva en el desarollo económico," *Mujeres,* August 1971, pp. 90–91.

28. Ramos, "La mujer y la revolución," p. 68.

29. Carollee Bengelsdorf, "The Frente Feminino," *Cuba Review* 4, no. 2 (September 1974): 27–28. In the 1980s the Feminine Front was renamed the "Department of Women's Affairs," since the former title was considered "too confrontational." See Debra Evenson, "Women's Equality in Cuba: What Difference Does a Revolution Make?" *Law and Inequality* 4, no. 2 (Univ. of Minnesota Law School), July 1986; 302.

30. Jorge I. Domínguez, *Cuba: Order and Revolution* (Cambridge, Mass.: The Belknap Press of Harvard University Press, 1978), pp. 269–70.

31. Chio Vidal, "Cuál es la tarea," p. 56.

32. Ramos, "La mujer y la revolución," p. 68.

33. Fernández, "La mujer: fuerza decisiva," p. 91.

34. Claes Brundenius, *Revolutionary Cuba: The Challenge of Economic Growth with Equity* (Boulder, Colo.: Westview Press, 1983), p. 60.

35. Ibid., p. 70.

36. Janet Salvá, "En desarollo ascendente: industria ligera," *Bohemia,* March 11, 1975, p. 19.

37. Castro, speech at close of 2nd FMC Congress, p. 65.

38. *Memories, Third Congress of the FMC,* p. 71; Magaly Pérez and Noemí Pascual, *Estadísticas sobre la mujer cubana* (Havana: Editorial Letras Cubanes, 1985), p. 17.

39. Communist Party of Cuba, "Thesis: On the Full Exercise of Women's Equality," in *Women and the Cuban Revolution,* ed. Stone, p. 88.

40. *Memories, Second Congress of the FMC,* pp. 19, 278.

41. In 1975, 27 percent of women workers were categorized as "technicians," and women constituted 49 percent of Cuba's technicians. Over the next fifteen years the number of women technicians would grow by 124 percent. In 1989, 29 percent of women workers were technicians, and 58 percent of Cuba's technicians were women. *Memories, Third Congress of the FMC,* p. 71; Pérez and Pascual, *Estadísticas,* p. 17; "Thesis on Women's Equality," p. 88; *FMC V Congreso: Proyecto de informe central* (Havana, 1990), pp. 9, 15.

42. *Censos de población, viviendas y electoral,* p. 205; Janet Salvá, "De como Pinar del Río se anota una nueva victoria," *Bohemia,* May 9, 1975, pp. 16–21.

43. Max Azicri, "Women's Development Through Revolutionary Mobilization: A Study of the Federation of Cuban Women," in *Cuban Communism,* ed. Horowitz, p. 295.

44. Stubbs and Alvarez, "Women on the Agenda," p. 143.

45. Ibid., p. 148.

46. Ibid., p. 142.

47. Carmen Diana Deere, "The Latin American Agrarian Reform Experience," in *Rural Women and State Policy,* ed. Deere and León, p. 183; Deere, "Rural Women and Agrarian Reform," p. 201.

48. Jean Stubbs, "Gender Issues in Contemporary Cuban Tobacco Farming," *World Development* 15, no. 1 (1987): 56.

49. Elizabeth Croll, "Women in Rural Production and Reproduction in the Soviet Union, China, Cuba, and Tanzania: Case Studies," *Signs* 7, no. 2 (Winter 1981): 387; Deere, "Rural Women and Agrarian Reform," p. 202.

50. *Memories, Second Congress Cuban Women's Federation,* pp. 113, 195.

51. Janet Salvá, "Confecciones Alamar," *Bohemia,* August 22, 1975, pp. 4–6.

52. Carollee Bengelsdorf and Alice Hageman, "Emerging from Underdevelopment: Women and Work," *Cuba Review* 4, no. 2 (September 1974): 10.

53. *Memories, Second Congress Cuban Women's Federation,* p. 188.

54. Ibid., pp. 173–74.

55. Marta G. Sojo, "Trabajo para los que van a nacer," *Bohemia,* January 14, 1977, pp. 8–9.

56. *FMC IV Congreso: Draft Thesis,* p. 16.

57. Sally Quinn, "A Latino Is a Latino Is a Latino," *The Washington Post,* March 20, 1977, p. K3.

58. Marie Withers Osmond, "Women and Work in Cuba: Objective Conditions and Subjective Perceptions," Annual meeting of the American Sociological Association, August 26–30, 1985, Washington, D.C., pp. 32–33.

59. Domínguez, *Cuba,* p. 268.

60. Ibid., p. 184.

61. *Memories, Second Congress Cuban Women's Federation,* p. 189.

62. Ibid., p. 174; Muriel Nazzari, "The 'Woman Question' in Cuba: An Analysis of Material Constraints on Its Solution," *Signs,* no. 2 (Winter 1983); 246–63.

63. Communist Party of Cuba, "Thesis: On the Full Exercise of Women's Equality," pp. 74–105.

64. Ibid., p. 87.

65. Gladys Castaño, "La mujer y la seguridad social en Cuba," *Mujeres,* October 1979, pp. 56–57.

66. Raisa Pagés, "Debaten sobre factores que renan incorporación de la mujer a la CPA," *Granma,* November 12, 1988, p. 2. In 1985 the FMC requested that *cooperativistas* be allowed to retire at an earlier age because of the harder nature of rural work. It also requested that different agricultural production quotas be established for men and women. See *FMC IV Congreso: Recomendaciones* (Havana, 1990), pp. 5, 21.

67. Lazo González, "Con manos de mujer," *Bohemia,* June 17, 1977, pp. 30–33.

68. H. Núñez Lemus, "Electricistas mujeres . . . Por qué no?" *Bohemia,* October 10, 1975, pp. 60–61.

69. Lazo González, "Con manos de mujer," p. 32.

70. Solangel Alvarez, "En el mundo del acero," *Mujeres,* February 1979, pp. 7–9.

71. Lázaro Torres Hernández, "En Moa el heroismo se ha hecho cotidiano," *Bohemia,* January 14, 1977, p. 35.

72. Andres Rodríguez, "Una veterana del ICINAZ," *Bohemia,* March 11, p. 19.

73. Janet Salvá, "Mujeres de cascos," *Bohemia,* October 31, 1975, pp. 22–23.

74. Vilma Espín, "Constructoras," *Bohemia,* October 10, 1975, p. 55.

75. Janet Salvá, "Cuando Fidel dijo hay que incorporar mujeres a la construcción miles respondieron, 'Presente!' " *Bohemia,* December 12, 1975, pp. 32–34.

Chapter 9

1. Alfred Padula and Lois M. Smith, interview with Digna Cires, Havana, March 1986.

2. Raisa Pagés, "Las mujeres de Marimón," *Granma,* July 18, 1991, p. 6.

3. Pablo Alfonso, "Cuba por dentro: Jóvenes no quieren ser proletarios," *El Nuevo Herald,* March 13, 1991, p. 3A.

4. Raisa Pagés, "Conjuro de amores en El Sopapo," *Granma,* August 9, 1991, p. 2.

5. Cuban statistics categorize many employees of the health and education ministries not as service workers but as technicians. See, for example, *Memorias del 3er Congreso de la FMC,* p. 17.

6. Carmelo Mesa-Lago, "Economics: Realism and Rationality," in *Cuban Communism,* 4th ed., ed. Irving Horowitz (New Brunswick, N.J.: Transaction Books, 1981), pp. 11–46; idem, "The Economy: Caution, Frugality, and Resilient Ideology," in *Cuba: Internal and International Affairs,* ed. Jorge I. Domínguez (Beverly Hills, Cal.: Sage Publications, 1982), p. 136.

7. Fidel Castro, speech at the close of the 3rd FMC Congress, in *Women and the Cuban Revolution,* ed. Elizabeth Stone (New York: Pathfinder Press, 1981), p. 115.

8. Isabel Larguía and John Dumoulin, "Women's Equality and the Cuban Revolution," in *Women and Change in Latin America,* ed. June Nash and Helen Safa (South Hadley, Mass.: Bergin & Garvey, 1986), p. 352.

9. *V Congreso de la FMC: Proyecto de informe central* (Havana, 1990), p. 7.

10. Larguía and Dumoulin, "Women's Equality and the Cuban Revolution," p. 351.

11. *Proyecto de informe central,* p. 18.

12. *Memorias del 3er Congreso de la FMC,* p. 71; Magaly Pérez and Noemí Pascual, *Estadísticas sobre la mujer cubana* (Havana: Editorial Letras Cubanas, 1985), p. 17.

13. *IV FMC Congreso: Informe central,* p. 28.

14. Rhoda Pearl Rabkin, "Cuban Political Structure: Vanguard Party and the Masses," in *Cuba: Twenty-five Years of Revolution, 1959–1984* ed. Sandor Halebsky and John Kirk (New York: Praeger, 1985), pp. 251–69.

15. Jean Stubbs and Mavis Alvarez, "Women on the Agenda: The Cooperative Movement in Rural Cuba," in *Rural Women and the State Policy: Feminist Perspectives on Latin American Agricultural Development,* ed. Carmen Diana Deere and Magdalena León (Boulder, Colo.: Westview Press, 1987) p. 156.

16. *Proyecto de informe central,* p. 4.

17. Stubbs and Alvarez, "Women on the Agenda," p. 147.

18. *Latin America Press,* March 7, 1991, p. 6.

19. Jean Stubbs, "Gender Issues in Contemporary Cuban Tobacco Farming," *World Development* 15, no. 1 (1987): 56.

20. Carmen Diana Deere, "The Latin American Agrarian Reform Experience," in *Rural Women and State Policy,* ed. Deere and León, p. 185.

21. *Proyecto de Informe Central,* p. 9.

22. Ibid., pp. 18–19; Vilma Espín, "Jamás seremos esclavas a una potencia estranjera o de un patrón capitalista," *Granma,* March 7, 1990, p. 4.

23. Joaquín Oramas, "Nueva vía bordeará la bahía de Cienfuegos," *Granma,* January 23, 1989, p. 3.

24. Argelio Santiesteban, "Sin fiebre ni titulares," *Bohemia,* May 29, 1987, pp. 47–51, quote on p. 48.

25. Iraida Calzadilla Rodríguez, "Todo no brilla en el oro negro," *Muchacha,* October 1987, pp. 56–57.

26. "Ya se logró el primer 'chip' cubano," *Granma,* December 6, 1988, pp. 1–2; Robert Paneque Fonseca, "Esa gran fuerza," *Granma,* August 11, 1988, p. 3.

27. Fidel Castro, speech at the close of the 3rd FMC Congress, in *Women and the Cuban Revolution,* ed. Stone, p. 111.

28. José Gabriel Guma, "Inician internacionalistas cubanas tala de árboles en el extremo oriente soviético," *Granma,* September 22, 1987, p. 1.

29. Castro, speech at the close of the 3rd FMC Congress, p. 121.

30. Fonseca, "Esa gran fuerza," p. 3.

31. Mesa-Lago, "Economics," pp. 157–58.

32. Elsa M. Chaney, *Supermadre: Women in Politics in Latin America* (Austin: University of Texas Press, 1979), p. 64.

33. Muriel Nazzari, "The 'Woman Question' in Cuba: An Analysis of Material Constraints on Its Solution, *Signs,* no. 2 (Winter 1983): 246–63; Helen Icken Safa, "Women and Industrial Employment in Cuba," study prepared in collaboration with the Federation of Cuban Women, Kellogg Center, University of Notre Dame, 1989.

34. Fidel Castro, speech at the close of the 3rd FMC Congress, p. 119.

35. *Directory of Officials of the Cuban Republic, 1989,* p. 109.

36. Safa, "Women and Industrial Employment," p. 16.

37. Marta Núñez Sarmiento, *Mujeres en empleos no tradicionales* (Havana: Editorial de Ciencias Sociales, 1991), p. 22.

38. Marie Withers Osmond, "Women and Work in Cuba: Objective Condi-

tions and Subjective Perceptions," revised version of a paper presented at the Annual Meeting of the American Sociological Association, Washington, D.C., August 26–30, 1985.

39. Linda Fuller, *Work and Democracy in Socialist Cuba* (Philadelphia: Temple University Press, 1992), p. 32.

40. Ibid., pp. 32, 155.

41. "Mujer trabajadora, familia y defensa de la patria socialista," *Granma,* January 25, 1990, p. 2.

42. *Memories, Second Congress Cuban Women's Federation,* pp. 19, 278; Max Azicri, "Women's Development Through Revolutionary Mobilization: A Study of the Federation of Cuban Women," in *Cuban Communism,* ed. Horowitz, p. 295; *Proyecto de informe central,* p. 4.

43. For example, in 1989 women constituted 66 percent of the workers and 31 percent of the leaders in the Ministry of Education. In the Ministry of Public Health women represented 70 percent of workers and only 22 percent of leaders. Only as directors of polyclinics (47 percent) did women achieve parity. *Proyecto de informe central,* pp. 4, 18.

44. Federation of Cuban Women, *FMC IV Congreso: Informe Central,* p. 4.

45. Marilys Suárez Moreno and Iraida Rodríguez Pérez, "Luz verde para dirigir," *Mujeres,* March 1988, p. 5.

46. Marisol Ramírez, "Mujeres dirigentes; tema para controversia," *Mujeres,* April 1987, p. 8.

47. Larguía and Dumoulin, "Women's Equality and the Cuban Revolution," p. 351.

48. Communist Party of Cuba, "Thesis: On the Full Exercise of Women's Equality," in *Women and the Cuban Revolution,* ed. Stone, p. 90.

49. Núñez Sarmiento, *Mujeres en empleos,* p. 7.

50. Lisanka, "Te gusta tu oficio?" *Bohemia,* February 3, 1989, pp. 25–32.

51. Núñez Sarmiento, *Mujeres en empleos,* p. 19.

52. Safa, "Women and Industrial Employment," pp. 9–10.

53. Calzadilla, "Todo no brilla en el oro negro," p. 11; Federation of Cuban Women, *FMC IV Congreso: Recomendaciones a la tesis,* p. 7.

54. *Directory of Officials of the Cuban Republic, 1989,* pp. 51–52.

55. Janet Salvá, "Aquí si hay igualdad . . . ," *Bohemia,* March 1, 1985, pp. 42–45.

56. Núñez Sarmiento, *Mujeres en empleos,* p. 5.

57. Orlando Gómez, "Una mujer fuera de serie," *Granma,* July 5, 1988, p. 2.

58. Claes Brundenius, *Revolutionary Cuba: The Challenge of Economic Growth with Equity* (Boulder, Colo.: Westview Press, 1983), pp. 127–28, 196; Mesa-Lago, "Economics," pp. 136–37.

59. *FMC IV Congreso: Draft Thesis,* p. 18; *FMC IV Congreso: Recomendaciones a la tesis,* p. 9.

60. "Vías para gestionar empleo," *Mujeres,* January 1983, p. 44.

61. Lisanka, "Te gusta tu oficio?" p. 30.

62. Andrés Gómez, "Una lucha que tenemos que librar todos," *Areíto* 2, no. 8 (November 1990): 8.

63. Georgina Jiménez, "Can We Develop Without Manual Laborers?" *Granma Weekly Review,* June 23, 1991, p. 3.

64. Lisanka, "Te gusta tu oficio?" p. 28.

65. Ibid., p. 30.

66. Ibid., p. 32.

67. Fidel Castro, speech at the meeting of the PCC of Havana Province, *Granma Weekly Review,* January 25, 1987, p. 2; *Latin American Weekly Report,* December 11, 1986, p. 3; Fidel Castro, *Granma,* November 30, 1987, pp. 1–3, quote on p. 3; Fernando Davalos, "Nadie en desamparo," *Bohemia,* April 3, 1992, pp. 30–33.

68. *FMC IV Congreso: Draft Thesis,* p. 16.

69. Gardenia Miralles, "Enseñar la cultura del trabajo," *Granma,* November 28, 1987, p. 3.

70. Raisa Pagés, "El trabajo directo con hombre," *Granma,* December 17, 1987, p. 3.

71. "Más de 33 mil trabajadores incorporados a contingentes," *Granma,* December 23, 1989, p. 2; "60 contingentes constituidos," *Granma,* August 12, 1989, p. 3; *Granma Weekly Review,* December 15, 1987.

72. Fidel Castro, speech at the closing of the meeting of the Central Committee of Havana Province, *Granma,* December 2, 1987, p. 4.

73. "Aquí todos los días" *Granma,*

74. Sara Más, "A la distancia de un año," *Granma,* March 12, 1992, p. 4.

75. Alfred Padula, visit to Cuba, May 1992.

76. "Cuban Women Help to Overcome Crisis," *Latin American Press* 23, no. 25 (July 4, 1991): 2.

77. Alfred Padula, visit to Cuba, May 1992.

78. Francisco Linares Calvo, "Dicta Resolución el CETSS referida a la protección de la madre trabajadora," *Granma,* July 19, 1991, p. 2.

Chapter 10

1. Fidel Castro, speech at the close of the 2nd FMC Congress, p. 68.

2. Gilberto Blanch, "Para que no se alborote el corral," *Mujeres,* April 1983, pp. 40–41.

3. Vilma Espín, "La batalla por el ejercicio pleno de la igualdad de la mujer: acción de los comunistas," *Cuba Socialista,* no. 2 (March–April 1986), p. 36.

4. Lazo González, "Con manos de mujer," *Bohemia,* June 17, 1977, p. 30.

5. Karen Offen, "Feminism and Sexual Difference in Historical Perspective," in *Theoretical Perspectives on Sexual Difference,* ed. Deborah L. Rode (New Haven, Conn: Yale University Press, 1992), pp. 13–20.

6. Vicente Arruzazabala, "El trabajo de la mujer," *Trabajo,* October 1964, pp. 64–65.

7. Ibid., p. 65.

8. Margaret Randall, *Women in Cuba: Twenty Years Later* (New York: Smyrna Press, 1981), p. 28.

9. Georgina Duvallon, "Para proteger a la mujer," *Mujeres,* May 1968, p. 13.

10. Max Azicri, "Women's Development through Revolutionary Mobilization: A Study of the Federation of Cuban Women," in *Cuban Communism,* 4th ed., ed. Irving Horowitz (New Brunswick, N.J.: Transaction Books, 1981), p. 297.

11. *Memorias del 3er Congreso,* p. 78.

12. Espín, "La batalla," p. 39.

13. *Proyecto de informe central,* p. 28.

14. Gladys Castaño, "Usted tiene el deber de protegerla," *Mujeres,* May 1982, pp. 10–11.

15. Ibid., p. 11.

16. *Constitución de la República de Cuba, 1976,* p. 23.

17. *Constitución de la República de Cuba, 1992.*

18. Espín, "La batalla," pp. 39–40.

19. Fidel Castro, speech at the close of the Fifth National Plenary of the FMC, p. 50.

20. Inger Holt-Seeland, *Women of Cuba* (Westport, Conn.: Lawrence Hill, 1982), p. 5.

21. Marta Rojas, *La cueva del muerto* (Havana: Union of Cuban Artists and Writers, 1983), p. 97.

22. Joe Nicholson, Jr., *Inside Cuba* (New York: Sheed and Ward, 1974), p. 97.

23. Ibid., p. 98. When a labor shortage emerged a few years later in the construction sector, the government decided that construction work was indeed appropriate for women. A massive campaign was launched to encourage women to enter the field (see chapter 8).

24. *IV Congreso: Informe Central,* pp. 37–39.

25. Alfred Padula and Lois M. Smith, interview with Digna Cires, April 1986.

26. Espín, "La batalla," pp. 38–39.

27. José Ramón Fernández, speech to the National Seminar of the Secretariat of Education and the FMC, *Bohemia,* June 27, 1975, pp. 51–52.

28. Daisy Martin, "Como trabajamos," *Mujeres,* April 1987, p. 48.

29. Marta Núñez Sarmiento, *Mujeres en empleos no tradicionales* (Havana: Editorial de Ciencias Sociales, 1991), pp. 12–15.

30. Isabel Moya, "Sin movil aparente?" *Mujeres,* August–September 1991, pp. 2–3.

31. Núñez Sarmiento, *Mujeres en empleos,* p. 21.

32. Espín, "La batalla," pp. 41, 44.

33. Mirta Rodríguez Calderón, "Mantener a los hijos es un deber . . . ," *Granma,* November 2, 1987, p. 7.

34. *FMC IV Congreso: Draft Thesis,* pp. 15–16.

35. Andrés Gómez, "Una lucha que tenemos que librar todos," *Areito* 2, no. 8 (November 1990): 7.

36. Heidy González Cabrera, "Un peldaño más hacia la victoria," *Mujeres,* July 1984, pp. 11–13, quote on p. 13.

37. Mirta Rodríguez Calderón, "Cómo lo ven ellos?" *Granma,* March 18, 1987, p. 3.

38. Espín, "La batalla," p. 42.

39. Ibid., p. 40.

40. Ibid., pp. 34, 40.

41. Ibid., p. 44.

42. Communist Party of Cuba, "Thesis: On the Full Exercise of Women's Equality," in *Women and the Cuban Revolution,* ed. Elizabeth Stone (New York: Pathfinder Press, 1981), p. 101.

43. Espín, "La batalla," p. 57.

44. Ibid., p. 40.

45. Sarah M. Santana and Carmen Hernández, "El reto actual," *Areito* 8 (November 1990): 15.

46. Espín, "La batalla," p. 34. Many Cuban women continue to feel more comfortable with men in leadership roles. For example, a debate over the promotion of women at a textile plant in Pinar del Río prompted one woman worker to comment that "management requires authority, which comes naturally to men. Managers have to think of the plant above everything, and women are incapable of this." See Marisol Ramírez, "Mujeres dirigentes: tema para controversia," *Mujeres,* April 1987, pp. 8–9.

47. Rodríguez Calderón, "Cómo lo ven ellos?" p. 3.

48. Espín, "La batalla," p. 44.

49. *IV Congreso: Informe Central,* p. 43; Núñez Sarmiento, *Mujeres en empleos.*

Chapter 11

1. Justina Alvarez, "Ayudarán a liberar a la mujer," *Trabajo,* March 1962, p. 57.

2. Fidel Castro, speech at the close of the Fifth National Plenary of the FMC, p. 53.

3. Fidel Castro, speech at the closing of the Central Committee of Havana Province, p. 4.

4. Castro, speech at the close of the Fifth National Plenary of the FMC, p. 53.

5. FMC, *Memoria: Primer Congreso* (Havana, 1962), p. 70.

6. Ibid., p. 63.

7. Alvarez, "Ayudarán a liberar a la mujer."

8. Jorge I. Domínguez, *Cuba: Order and Revolution* (Cambridge, Mass.: The Belknap Press of Harvard University Press, 1978), p. 267.

9. "El pago de los padres por círculo infantil solo sufraga parte de los gastos," *Trabajadores,* March 3, 1989, p. 9.

10. Marta Núñez Sarmiento, *Mujeres en empleos no tradionales* (Havana: Editorial de Ciencias Sociales, 1991), p. 16.

11. Sandra Malmquist, "Cuban Infant and Toddler Daycare: Socialization in a Revolutionary Society" (Master's thesis, Wesleyan University, 1984), p. 30.

12. Lois M. Smith, interview with day care official, Havana, January 1985.

13. *Granma,* "Junto al pueblo . . . ," December 11, 1987, p. 1.

14. Malmquist, "Cuban Infant and Toddler Daycare," p. 129.

15. "Vigoroso respaldo femenino a las tareas de la revolución," *Granma,* March 7, 1990, pp. 1–3.

16. Susana Lee, "Quién puede cerrar un círculo infantil?" *Granma,* May 20, 1988, p. 2.

17. Orlando Gómez, "A plena capacidad . . . ," *Granma,* June 8, 1988, p. 2.

18. *FMC IV Congreso, Recomendaciones a la tesis,* p. 20.

19. *FMC IV Congreso, Draft Thesis,* p. 38.

20. Janet Salvá, "La igualdad plena de la mujer," *Bohemia,* August 22, 1975, pp. 46–47.

21. Espín, "La batalla por el ejercicio pleno de la igualdad de la mujer: acción de los comunistas," *Cuba Socialista,* no. 2 (March–April 1986): 42.

22. Diana Sosa and José A. de la Osa and Juan Carlos Santos, "Analizan los problemas que afronta la mujer en el acceso al trabajo y en su vida laboral," *Granma,* March 7, 1985, pp. 1–3.

23. Germaine Greer, "Politics—Cuba," in *Women: A World Report* (New York: Oxford University Press, 1985), p. 273.

24. *FMC IV Congreso, Recomendaciones a la tesis,* pp. 15, 19.

25. Lisanka, "Te gusta tu oficio?" *Bohemia,* February 3, 1989, p. 27.

26. *FMC IV Congreso, Recomendaciones a la tesis,* p. 14.

27. Fidel Castro, speech at the closing of the Central Committee of Havana Province, p. 4.

28. Raisa Pagés, "Debates sobre factores que frenan la incorporación de la mujer a la CPA," *Granma,* November 12, 1988, p. 2.

29. "Vigoroso respaldo femenino a las tareas de la revolución," *Granma,* p. 3.

30. *Memories, Second Congress Cuban Women's Federation,* p. 178.

31. Carollee Bengelsdorf, "On the Problem of Studying Women in Cuba," in *Cuban Political Economy: Controversies in Cubanology,* ed. Andrew Zimbalist (Boulder, Colo.: Westview Press, 1988), p. 134.

32. Abel Sardiña, "The Ration Book, An Economic Achilles' Heel?" *Granma Weekly Review,* March 5, 1989, p. 3.

33. Gladys Hernández, "Nuevo reglamento para distribuir artículos electro-domésticos," *Granma,* April 1, 1988, p. 2. In 1991 women sugar workers complained to a visiting journalist from the FMC's *Mujeres* magazine that they were being denied access to appliances distributed through the union at their mill. The journalist criticized the union and called the practice "not only profoundly unjust but also arbitrary and illegal." See Isabel Moya, "Sin movil aparente?" *Mujeres,* August–September 1991, pp. 2–3.

34. *FMC IV Congreso: Draft Thesis,* p. 36.

35. *Memories, Third Congress of the FMC,* p. 90.

36. After years of looking the other way, the government began to arrest professional *coleros* in 1990.

37. Gladys Castaño, "Nuevo horario para la trabajadora," *Mujeres,* October 1980, pp. 7–9; *Memories, Third Congress of the FMC,* p. 93; *FMC IV Congreso: Informe Central,* pp. 54–55.

38. Alfred Padula, visit to Cuba, May 1992.

39. Sally Quinn, "Wilma *[sic]* Espín: The First Lady of the Revolution," *The Washington Post,* March 26, 1977, p. B3.

40. *Memories, Third Congress of the FMC,* p. 92.

41. Daisy Martín, "Necesita ayuda en su hogar?" *Mujeres,* November 1980, pp. 10–11.

42. *FMC IV Congreso: Draft Thesis,* p. 37.

43. Daisy Martín, "Artesanas camajuanis," *Mujeres,* February 1983, pp. 16–17.

44. Daisy Martín, "Sin salir de casa," *Mujeres,* May 1983, p. 21.

45. *FMC V Congreso: Proyecto de Informe Central,* p. 10; *FMC IV Congreso: Informe Central,* p. 19.

46. Isabel Larguía and John Dumoulin, *Hacia una concepción científica de la emancipación de la mujer* (Havana: Editorial de Ciencias Sociales, 1983), p. 7; Bengelsdorf, "On the Problem of Studying Women in Cuba," p. 124.

47. Sheila Rowbotham, *Women, Resistance, and Revolution* (New York: Pantheon Books, 1972), p. 27.

48. Larguía and Dumoulin, *Hacia una concepción científica,* p. 60.

49. Margaret Randall, *Women in Cuba: Twenty Years Later,* (New York: Smyrna Press, 1981), p. 10.

50. Ibid., p. 40.

51. Margaret Randall, *Gathering Rage* (New York: Monthly Review Press, 1992).

52. Susan Kaufman Purcell, "Modernizing Women for a Modern Society: The Cuban Case," in Female and Male in Latin America, ed. Ann Pescatello (Pittsburg: University of Pittsburgh Press, 1973), p. 258.

53. Max Azicri, "Women's Development through Revolutionary Mobilization: A Study of the Federation of Cuban Women," in *Cuban Communism,* 4th ed., ed. Irving Louis Horowitz (New Brunswick, N.J.: Transaction Books, 1981), p. 295.

54. Domínguez, *Cuba: Order and Revolution,* pp. 498–500.

55. Bengelsdorf, "On the Problem of Studying Women in Cuba," pp. 123–24.

56. Ibid., p. 129.

57. Larguía and Dumoulin, *Hacia una concepción científica,* p. 102.

58. Ibid., pp. 57, 80.

59. Ibid., p. 57.

60. Marisela González López and Gisela Pérez Fuentes, "La situación legal de la mujer," *Revista Cubana de Derecho,* 1987: 3–26, esp. p. 16.

61. Carmen Diana Deere, "The Latin American Agrarian Reform Experience," in *Rural Women and State Policy: Feminist Perspectives on Latin American Agricultural Development,* ed. Carmen Diana Deere and Magdalena León (Boulder, Colo.: Westview Press, 1987), p. 185; idem, "Rural Women and Agrarian Reform in Peru, Chile, and Cuba," in *Women and Change in Latin America,* ed. June Nash and Helen Safa (South Hadley, Mass.: Bergin & Garvey, 1986), p. 202.

62. Debra Evenson, "Women's Equality in Cuba: What Difference Does a Revolution Make?" *Law and Inequality* (Univ. of Minnesota Law School), no. 2 (July 1986): 309.

63. Bengelsdorf, "On the Problem of Studying Women in Cuba," p. 129.

64. Muriel Nazzari, "The Woman Question in Cuba: An Analysis of Material Constraints on Its Solution," *Signs,* no. 2 (Winter 1983): 246–63.

65. Helen Icken Safa, "Women and Industrial Employment in Cuba," study prepared in collaboration with the Federation of Cuban Women, Kellogg Center, University of Notre Dame, 1989, p. 6; Eugenio R. Balari et al., *La mujer cubana: el camino hacia su emancipación* (Havana: Instituto Cubano de Investigaciones y Orientaciones de la Demanda Internal, 1980).

66. Marie Withers Osmond, "Women and Work in Cuba: Objective Conditions and Subjective Perceptions," revised version of a paper presented at the annual meeting of the American Sociological Association, Washington, D.C., August 26–30, 1985), p. 9.

67. Ibid., pp. 10, 28.

68. Ibid., p. 24.

69. Ibid., pp. 27–28.

70. Safa, "Women and Industrial Employment in Cuba," p. 15.

Chapter 12

1. Katia Valdés and Lisanka, "No solo cariño y protección," *Bohemia,* August 28, 1987, p. 26.

2. Marilys Suárez and Isolina Triay, "No hay recetas . . . pero reciben igual educación?" *Mujeres,* November 1988, pp. 4–9.

3. Carollee Bengelsdorf, "On the Problem of Studying Women in Cuba," in *Cuban Political Economy: Controversies in Cubanology,* ed. Andrew Zimbalist (Boulder, Colo.: Westview Press, 1988), p. 121.

4. Margaret Randall, *La mujer cubana ahora* (Havana: Editorial de Ciencias Sociales, 1972), p. 13.

5. Martínez-Alier, Verena, *Marriage, Class and Colour in Nineteenth-Century Cuba* (London: Cambridge University Press), p. 141.

6. Gunnel Granlid and Goran Palm, quoted in *Voices of National Liberation,* ed. Irwin Silber (New York: Central Book Company, 1970), p. 157.

7. Isabel Larguía and John Dumoulin, *Hacia una concepción científica de la emancipación de la mujer* (Havana: Editorial de Ciencias Sociales, 1983), p. 7.

8. Ibid., pp. 10, 53, 55, 56.

9. Laura Gotkowitz and Richard Turits, "Socialist Morality: Sexual Preference, Family, and State Intervention in Cuba," *Socialism and Democracy* (1988): 9.

10. George Miller Stabler, "Bejucal: Social Values and Changes in Agricultural Practices in a Cuban Urban Community" (Ph.D. diss., Michigan State University, 1958).

11. Bengelsdorf, "On the Problem of Studying Women in Cuba," p. 122.

12. Suzanne Garment, "Cuban Politics: Living with the Lies," *The Wall Street Journal,* April 19, 1985, p. 29.

13. Lois Smith and Alfred Padula, "Sex, Socialism and Soap Opera: Cuba's 'La Delegada,'" in *Consumable Goods II,* ed. Mary Louise Quinn and Eugene P. A. Schleh (Orono, Me.: National Poetry Foundation, 1988), pp. 77–85.

14. Alfred Padula, "Cuba Comes Home," *The Times of the Americas,* February 21, 1990.

15. Alex Larzelere, *The 1980 Cuban Boatlift: Castro's Ploy—America's Dilemma* (Washington, D.C.: National Defense University Press, 1988), p. 222.

16. Bryan O. Walsh, "Cuban Refugee Children," *Journal of Inter-American Studies and World Affairs,* nos. 3–4 (July–October 1971), pp. 378–415.

17. Vivian Crucet, "Rinden homenaje a Polita Grau . . . ," *Diario las Américas,* October 7, 1989, p. 3B.

18. Fidel Castro, *History Will Absolve Me* (Havana: Editorial en Marcha, 1962), p. 31.

19. Ibid., pp. 34–35.

20. Douglas Butterworth, *The People of Buena Ventura* (Urbana: University of Illinois Press, 1980), pp. 27, 49.

21. *Anuario estadístico 1980,* p. 129.

22. "Dos muertos y dos desaparecidos en La Habana al derrumbarse un edificio," *Diario las Américas,* July 3, 1987, p. 15A.

23. Jill Hamberg, "Cuba," in *The International Handbook of Housing Policies and Practices* (Westport, Conn.: Greenwood Press, 1990), p. 382.

24. Victor Ego Ducrot, "Main Demand of Cuban Workers is Housing," *Granma Weekly Review,* May 17, 1987, p. 3.

25. Nelson Valdés, presentation to South Eastern Conference of Latin Americanists, Ibor City, Tampa, Florida, 1981. See also "Crean albergues para el amor en La Habana por la falta de viviendas," *Diario las Américas,* August 25, 1987, p. 1.

26. Jill Hamberg, *Under Construction: Housing Policy in Revolutionary Cuba* (New York: Center for Cuban Studies, 1985), p. 9.

27. Hamberg, "Cuba," p. 382.

28. Rafael Calcines, "A Development Challenge," *Granma Weekly Review,* May 3, 1987, p. 2.

29. Juan Jesús Aznarez, "Cuba necesitará un millón de viviendas en el año 2 mil," *Granma,* March 3, 1987, p. 1.

30. Paula E. Hollerbach and Sergio Díaz-Briquets, *Fertility Determinants in Cuba,* Committee on Population and Demography Report No. 26 (Washington, D.C.: National Academy Press, 1983), p. 98.

31. Ibid., p. 37.

Chapter 13

1. Mónica Sorín Zocolsky, *Padres e hijos: Amigos o adversarios?* (Havana: Editorial de Ciencias Sociales, 1990), p. 13.

2. Tania, "El paraíso perdido," *Somos Jóvenes,* December 1988, pp. 44–50, esp. p. 44.

3. Mirta Rodríguez Calderón, "Madres solteras: salto a la angustia," *Bohemia,* August 11, 1989, p. 21.

4. Patricia Arés Muzio, *Mi familia es así* (Havana: Editorial de Ciencias Sociales, 1990), p. 129.

5. Daniel A. Peral Collado, "El proyecto del código de la familia," *Revista Cubana del Derecho,* June–December 1974), p. 32.

6. Raúl Gómez Treto, "New Family Code in Cuba," LADOC 7 (1979): 18.

7. *Family Code, 1975,* Law No. 1289 (Havana: Editorial Orbe, 1980), p. 6.

8. Ibid., pp. 9–10.

9. Ibid., pp. 18, 33.

10. Ibid., p. 20.

11. Fred Ward, *Inside Cuba Today* (New York: Crown Publishers, 1978), pp. 34–35; Elizabeth Sutherland, *The Youngest Revolution: A Personal Report on Cuba* (London: Pittman Publishing, 1969), p. 168.

12. Raimundo Rodríguez, "Marriage and Divorce Among Cuban Youth," *Granma Weekly Review,* November 17, 1991, p. 2.

13. Marguerite G. Rosenthal, "Single Mothers in Cuba: Social Policy for an Emerging Problem," presented at conference on the Cuban revolution, Halifax, Nova Scotia, November 1–4, 1989, p. 28.

14. "Elevada tasa de divorcios en Cuba," *Diario las Américas,* June 29, 1988, p 3A; Rodríguez, "Marriage and Divorce Among Cuban Youth," p. 2; Claribel Terre and Juan Carlos Rivero, "Salvarnos de nosotros mismos," *Bohemia,* August 21, 1992, p. 9.

15. George Gedda, "Fidel at Sixty," *Maine Sunday Telegram,* July 27, 1986, p. 29A.

16. Jack Anderson, "Cuban Defector Tells Tale on CIA," *Portland Evening Express,* March 21, 1988, p. 12.

17. Georgie Ann Geyer, *Guerrilla Prince: The Untold Story of Fidel Castro* (Boston: Little Brown, 1991), p. 334.

18. Anne-Marie O'Connor, "Fidel's Last Resort," *Esquire,* March 1992, p. 156.

19. Anne Louise Bardach, "Conversations with Castro," *Vanity Fair,* March 1994, p. 133.

20. Geyer, *Guerillo Prince,* p. 390.

21. Ibid., p. 14.

22. Agustín Tamargo, "El amor y el coca-cola," *El Nuevo Herald,* August 11, 1991, p. 16A.

23. Nilda Cepero-Llevada, "La mujer y el matrimonio," *El Nuevo Herald,* August 22, 1991, p. 12A.

24. Kathryn Lynn Stoner, *From the House to the Streets: The Cuban Woman's Movement for Legal Reform, 1898–1940* (Durham, N.C.: Duke University Press, 1991), pp. 51–52.

25. Ibid., pp. 158–59.

26. *The Family Code, 1975,* p. 29.

27. Ibid., pp. 30–31, 40–41.

28. Jorge Hernández et al., "Estudio sobre el divorcio," *Humanidades,* no. 3 (Univ. of Havana Center for Scientific and Technical Information) (January 1973), pp. 20, 60.

29. Mario López Cepero and Ernesto Chávez Alvarez, *Características de la divorcialidad cubana* (Havana: Editorial de Ciencias Sociales, 1976), Appendix, Table 12.

30. Hernández et al., "Estudio sobre el divorcio," p. 69.

31. Lois M. Smith, "Teenage Pregnancy and Sex Education in Cuba," paper presented at the Latin American Studies Association Meeting, New Orleans, April 1988.

32. Jotape, "Los jóvenes no esperan," *Bohemia,* July 1, 1988, pp. 26–27.

33. Terre and Rivera, "Salvarnos de nosotros mismos," p. B9.

34. Tania, "El paraíso perdido."

35. Marguerite G. Rosenthal, "The Problems of Single Motherhood in Cuba," in *Cuba in Transition,* ed. Sandor Halebsky et al. (Boulder, Colo.: Westview Press, 1992), p. 166.

36. López Cepero and Chávez Alvarez, *Características,* pp. 22, 73.

37. Mirta Rodríguez Calderón, "Entretelas del presente," *Bohemia,* October 30, 1992, p. 4.

38. Ibid., p. 6.

39. Hernández et al., "Estudio sobre el divorcio," p. 2.

40. Mirta Rodríguez Calderón, "Cuántos hay como Domingo y Rebeca?" *Granma,* May 13, 1987, p. 3.

41. López Cepero and Chávez Alvarez, *Características,* p. 43.

42. Inger Holt-Seeland, *Women of Cuba* (Westport, Conn.: Lawrence Hill, 1982), p. 10.

43. Hernández et al., "Estudio sobre el divorcio," p. 51.

44. Mirta Rodríguez Calderón, "Mamá de espaldas," *Bohemia,* April 28, 1989, p. 27.

45. Arés Muzio, *Mi familia es así,* pp. 49–51.

46. Ibid., p. 128.

47. Cino Colina, "Speaking from the Heart," *Granma Weekly Review,* October 22, 1989, p. 3.

48. Arés Muzio, *Mi familia es así,* pp. 152, 159.

49. Ibid., pp. 125–26.

50. Safa, "Women and Industrial Employment," pp. 5–6.

51. Arés Muzio, *Mi familia es así,* p. 65.

52. Max Azicri, "Women's Development through Revolutionary Mobilization: A Study of the Federation of Cuban Women," in *Cuban Communism,* 4th ed., ed. Irving Horowitz (New Brunswick, N.J.: Transaction Books, 1981) , p. 291; Eugenio R. Balari et al. *La mujer cubana: el camino hacia su emancipación* (Havana: Instituto Cubano de Investigaciones y Orientaciones de la Demanda Internal, 1980), pp. 00–00.

53. Arés Muzio, *Mi familia es así,* pp. 126–27.

54. Ibid., p. 127.

55. Ibid., p. 160.

56. Rodríguez Calderón, "Madres solteras," p. 26; idem, "Cuánto vale . . . ?" *Bohemia,* November 16, 1990, pp. 12–15; idem, "Matrimonios sin papeles," *Bohemia,* May 31, 1991, pp. 4–9, quote on p. 5.

57. Mirta Rodríguez Calderón, "Informa de nuevas tareas para una nueva etapa," *Granma,* October 17, 1987, p. 1.

58. Rosenthal, "The Problems of Single Motherhood," p. 166.

59. Orfilio Peláez, "Young Single Mothers in Cuba," *Granma Weekly Review,* May 29, 1988, p. 2.

60. Ibid.

61. Mirta Rodríguez Calderón, "Por qué, papi, por qué?" *Bohemia,* February 23, 1990, pp. 4–9, esp. p. 6.

62. Peláez, "Young Single Mothers in Cuba," p. 2.

63. Deborah Schnookal, ed., *Cuban Women Confront the Future* (Melbourne: Ocean Press, 1991), pp. 71–72.

64. Marta Gómez Ferrals, "Madres de primera o de segunda?" *Cuba Internacional,* November 1989, pp. 38–42, esp. p. 42.

65. Rodríguez Calderón, "Madres solteras," p. 23.

66. Rodríguez Calderón, "Por qué, papi?" p. 6.

67. Rodríguez Calderón, "Cuánto vale . . . ?" p. 6.

68. Fidel Castro, interviewed by Frei Betto, *Granma Weekly Review,* April 8, 1990, p. 9.

69. Rosenthal, "The Problems of Single Motherhood," p. 170.

70. Rodríguez Calderón, "Madres solteras," p. 24.

71. Ibid., p. 25.

72. Rodríguez Calderón, "Por qué, papi?" p. 7.

73. Rodríguez Calderón, "Madres solteras," p. 23.

74. Ibid.

75. "El mejor solución será el trabajo," *Granma,* October 29, 1987, p. 5.

76. Mimi Whitefield, *The Miami Herald,* June 30, 1991, p. 16A.

77. Rodríguez Calderón, "Madres solteras," pp. 23–24.

78. Heidy González Cabrera and Marilys Suárez Moreno, "Padres superocupados, fenómeno de nuestros días, *Mujeres,* July 1988, pp. 4–7; quote on p. 6.

79. Arés Muzio, *Mi familia es así,* pp. 84–86.

80. Ibid., p. 106.

81. Ibid., pp. 3, 46–47, 128–29, 147.

82. Sorín Zocolsky, *Padres e hijos,* p. 74.

83. Luis Salas, *Social Control and Deviance in Cuba* (New York: Praeger, 1979), pp. 14–15.

84. Ibid., p. 23.

85. González Cabrera and Suárez Moreno, "Padres Superocupados," p. 7.

86. Mirta Rodríguez Calderón, "Quiérame, mami . . . ," *Bohemia,* December 20, 1991, pp. 4–7, esp. p. 5; idem, "Restaurar sonrisas," *Bohemia,* August 7, 1992, pp. 19–21.

87. González Cabrera and Suárez Moreno, "Padres Superocupados," p. 5.

88. Rodríguez Calderón, "Madres solteras," p. 24.

89. Sorín Zocolsky, *Padres e hijos,* pp. 5, 94.

90. Marilys Suárez Moreno, "Fenómeno de nuestros días," *Mujeres,* June 1988, pp. 4–7.

91. Arés Muzio, *Mi familia es así,* p. 163.

92. Ibid., p. 16.

Chapter 14

1. Diana Martínez, "The First Time I Heard About Sex," *Granma Weekly Review,* January 21, 1990, p. 8.

2. Marta Matamoros and María de los Angeles Rodríguez, "Embarazo en la adolescencia (part 1): Epidemia de alta frecuencia," *Bohemia,* June 26, 1987, p. 21.

3. Heidi González Cabrera, "Para aprender . . . el amor," *Mujeres,* August 1989, p. 13.

4. Monika Krause, ed., *Compilación de artículos* (Havana: Grupo Nacional de Trabajo sobre Educación Sexual, 1987), p. 25.

5. Pedro Juan Gutiérrez, "Se acabó el querer?" *Bohemia,* August 24, 1990, p. 5.

6. Anna Thompson, "Eros and Chaos," *Lears,* January 1993, p. 67.

7. Ibid., p. 68.

8. Mirta de la Torre Mulhare, "Sexual Ideology in Pre-Castro Cuba: A Cultural Analysis," (Ph.D. diss., University of Pittsburgh, 1969), p. 275.

9. Oscar Lewis, Ruth M. Lewis, and Susan M. Rigdon, *Four Women* (Urbana: University of Illinois Press, 1977), p. 336.

10. Enrique Fernández, "Love in the Time of AIDS," *The Village Voice,* August 22, 1989, p. 46.

11. Carlos Paz Pérez, *De lo popular y lo vulgar en el habla cubana* (Havana: Editorial de Ciencias Sociales, 1988).

12. Lewis, Lewis, and Rigdon, *Four Women,* p. 278.

13. Mulhare, "Sexual Ideology in pre-Castro Cuba," p. 187.

14. Ibid., p. 269.

15. Margaret Randall, *Gathering Rage: The Failure of the Twentieth Century Revolutions to Develop a Feminist Agenda* (New York: Monthly Review Press, 1992), pp. 130–31; Thompson, "Eros and Chaos," p. 67.

16. Lewis, Lewis, and Rigdon, *Four Women,* pp. 67–68.

17. Ibid., p. 68.

18. Samuel Feijoó, "Revolución y vicios," *El Mundo,* April 15, 1965, p. 5.

19. See, for example, Allen Young, *Gays Under the Cuban Revolution* (New York: Vintage Books, 1981); Marvin Leiner, *Sexual Politics in Cuba: Machismo, Homosexuality, and AIDS* (Boulder, Colo.: Westview Press, 1994); Nestor Almendros and Orlando Jiménez-Leal, *Conducta impropia* (Madrid: Biblioteca Cubana Contemporanea, 1984), Salas, *Social Control.*

20. "Los cubanos y el homosexualismo," *Mariel,* Spring 1984, p. 8.

21. Lois M. Smith, meeting of the FMC local delegation, Cienfuegos, January 1985.

22. Ministerio de Justicia, *Ley No. 62, Código Penal,* Havana, pp. 141–42.

23. Fidel Castro, "Un grano de maíz," *Bohemia,* November 27, 1992, pp. 23–25.

24. Center for Cuban Studies, "Gay Organization in Support of Cuba," *CCS Newsletter,* November 1992, p. 12.

25. Claribel Terre Morell, "Ojo, que viene el coco," *Bohemia,* December 13, 1991, pp. 11–13.

26. Erena Hernández, personal correspondence with Lois M. Smith, July 27, 1994.

27. *Granma,* April 10, 1967

28. Communist Party of Cuba, "Thesis: On the Full Exercise of Women's Equality," p. 101.

29. Ibid.

30. The first, entitled *Sexuality, Personality, and Education,* was written for teachers by psychologists Alicia González and Beatriz Castellanos. The second, *Human Sexuality,* is a collection of works written by teachers for educators and parents. See Sara Mas, "Neither a Dilemma nor a Sport," *Granma Weekly Review,* January 27, 1991, p. 3.

31. See Lois M. Smith, "Sexual Messages in Revolutionary Cuba," paper presented at a conference on the Cuban Revolution, Halifax, Nova Scotia, October 25–28, 1989; Idem, "Sexuality and Socialism in Cuba," in *Cuba in Transition,* ed. Halebsky et al. (Boulder, Colo.: Westview Press, 1992), pp. 177–91.

32. Dr. Siegfried Schnabl, *En defensa del amor* (Havana: Editorial Científico-Técnica, 1985), p. 51.

33. See, for example, Heidy González Cabrera, "Para aprender . . . el amor (part 2)," *Mujeres,* September 1989, pp. 12–13.

34. Ibid., p. 13.

35. Sylvia Orans, "Cuban Women Move out from Sexism's Shadow," *The Guardian,* February 11, 1987, p. 11.

36. Heidy González Cabrera, "Camino a la felicidad," *Mujeres,* July 1989, p. 13.

37. González Cabrera, "Para aprender . . . el amor (part 2)," p. 13.

38. Carlos Cabrera and Cino Colina, "Why Blush?" *Granma Weekly Review,* May 14, 1989, p. 3.

39. Gladys Egües and Reina Santana, "Tirar la casa por la ventana," *Mujeres,* June 1991, pp. 44–47.

40. Aloyma Ravelo, "Hablemos francamente," *Muchacha,* November 1987, p. 52.

41. María del Carmen Mestas and Aloyma Ravelo, "Libertad o libertinaje?" *Muchacha,* January 1987, p. 29.

42. Waldo González López, "Crisis en la narrativa del amor?" *Muchacha,* September 1989, pp. 6–7.

43. Ilsa Bulit, "No matemos al amor," *Bohemia,* April 3, 1987, p. 3.

44. Matamoros and Rodríguez, "Embarazo en la adolescencia (part I)," p. 25.

45. See Monika Krause, "La televisión y el sexo," *Bohemia,* July 24, 1987, p. 84.

46. Natividad Guerrero, *La educación sexual en la joven generación* (Havana: Editorial Política, 1985), pp. 25–27.

47. Schnabl, *En defensa del amor,* p. 55.

48. Krause, *Compilación de artículos.*

49. See Smith, "Sexuality and Socialism in Cuba."

50. Ilsa Bulit, "Solo el amor," *Bohemia,* August 5, 1988, p. 30.

51. Guerrero, *La educación sexual,* p. 81.

52. Mirta Rodríguez Calderón, "Consideran urgente propiciar diálogos sobre sexualidad," *Granma,* May 27, 1987, p. 2.

53. Iraida Campo, "No decir adiós a la infancia," *Muchacha,* September 1989, p. 52.

54. Cary Carrobello, Neysa Ramón, and Ariel Terrero, "La gente va llegando al baile," *Bohemia,* August 9, 1991, pp. 4–9.

55. "To Dance or Not to Dance?" *Granma Weekly Review,* September 15, 1991, p. 3.

56. Alfred Padula, visit to Varadero, Cuba, May 1994.

57. Luis Manuel, "El caso de Sandra," *Somos Jóvenes,* September 1987, pp. 68–81.

58. "Crean 'albergues' para el amor en la Habana por la falta de viviendas," *Diario las Américas,* August 25, 1987, pp. 1, 5.

59. Orlans, "Cuban Women Move Out," p. 10.

60. González Cabrera, "Camino a la felicidad," p. 13.

61. José Luis Llovio-Menéndez, *Insider: My Hidden Life as a Revolutionary in Cuba* (New York: Bantam Books, 1988), p. 128.

62. Lois M. Smith, interview with Monika Krause, Havana, January 1985.

Conclusion

1. Mirta Rodríguez Calderón, "Entretelas del presente," *Bohemia,* October 30, 1992, p. 4.

2. Personal correspondence to Lois M. Smith, July 27, 1994.

3. Hortensia Torres, "Otorgada la distinción 23 de agosto . . . ," *Granma,* August 24, 1994, p. 1.

4. Mirta Rodríguez Calderón and Sonia Moro, "Cuéntame tu vida," *Bohemia,* March 2, 1990, p. 5.

5. Ana Santiago, *Granma,* January 3, 1992.

6. Nancy Saporta Sternbach, Marysa Navarro-Aranguren, Patricia Chuchryk, and Sonia E. Alvarez, *Feminisms in Latin America: Identity, Strategy, and Democracy* (Boulder, Colo.: Westview Press, 1992), p. 218.

7. Ileana Fuentes, *Cuba sin caudillos: Un enfoque feminista para el siglo XXI* (Princeton, N.J.: Linden Lane Press, 1994), p. 33.

8. Uva de Aragón Clavijo, *El caimán ante el espejo* (Miami: Ediciones Universal, 1993), pp. 37–41.

9. Mirta Rodríguez Calderón, "Sin tiempo para el desaliento," *Bohemia,* March 6, 1992, pp. 38–43.

10. Alfred Padula, visit to Cuba, May 1992.

11. Jeff Cohen, "Cuba Libre," *Playboy,* March 1991, pp. 69–74, 157–58.

12. Lois M. Smith, conversation with Carolina Aguilar, San José, Costa Rica, February 1993.

13. Alfred Padula, visit to Cuba, May 1994.

14. Ileana Fuentes-Pérez, "El machismo y los destinos de Cuba," *El Nuevo Herald,* April 3, 1990, p. 5A.

Bibliography

Aguirre, Benigno E. "Women in the Cuban Bureaucracy, 1968–1974." *Journal of Comparative Family Studies* 1 (Spring 1976): 23–40.

Aguirre, Mirta. *Influencia de la mujer en Iberoamérica*. Havana: Imprenta P. Fernández, 1947.

Almendros, Nestor, and Orlando Jiménez-Leal. *Conducta impropia*. Madrid: Biblioteca Cubana Contemporánea, 1984.

Alvarez Vázquez, Luisa. *La fecundidad en Cuba*. Havana: Editorial Ciencias Sociales, 1985.

Araújo, Bernal, and José Llorens Figueroa. *La lucha por la salud en Cuba*. Mexico City: Siglo Veintiuno Editores, 1985.

Arguelles, Lourdes, and B. Ruby Rich. "Notes Toward an Understanding of the Cuban Lesbian and Gay Male Experience." *Signs* 4 (1984): 683–99.

———. "Homosexuality, Homophobia and Revolution: Notes Toward an Understanding of the Cuban Lesbian and Gay Male Experience, Part II." *Signs* 1 (1985): 120–36.

Arnaz, Desi. *A Book*. New York: William Morrow, 1976.

Azicri, Max. "Women's Development Through Revolutionary Mobilization: A Study of the Federation of Cuban Women." In *Cuban Communism*, edited by Irving Louis Horowitz, pp. 276–308. New Brunswick, N.J.: Transaction Books, 1981.

Balari, Eugenio R., Violeta Chang Banos, Ana González Mora, and Elena Ortero de Armas. *La mujer cubana: el camino hacia su emancipación*. Havana: Instituto Cubano de Investigaciones y Orientación de la Demanda Internal, 1980.

Bengelsdorf, Carollee. "The Frente Feminino." *Cuba Review* 2 (1974): 27–28.

———. "On the Problem of Studying Women in Cuba." *Race & Class* 2 (1985): 35–50.

————. "On the Problem of Studying Women in Cuba." In *Cuban Political Economy: Controversies in Cubanology,* edited by Andrew Zimbalist, pp. 119–36. Boulder, Colo.: Westview Press, 1988.

Bengelsdorf, Carollee, and Alice Hageman. "Emerging from Underdevelopment: Women and Work." *Cuba Review* 2 (1974): 3–12.

Benjamin, Medea, Joseph Collins, and Michael Scott. *No Free Lunch.* San Francisco: Institute for Food and Development, 1984.

Bonachea, Rolando, and Marta San Martín. *The Cuban Insurrection, 1952–1959.* New Brunswick, N.J.: Transaction Books, 1974.

Bonachea, Rolando, and Nelson Valdés, eds. *Cuba in Revolution.* Garden City, N.Y.: Anchor Books, 1972.

Bourne, Peter. *Fidel: A Biography of Fidel Castro.* New York: Dodd, Mead, 1986.

Brückner, Heinrich. *Antes de que nazca un niño.* Havana: Editorial Gente Nueva, 1985.

————. *Piensas ya en el amor?* Havana: Editorial Gente Nueva, 1981.

Brundenius, Claes. *Revolutionary Cuba: The Challenge of Economic Growth with Equity.* Boulder, Colo.: Westview Press, 1983.

Bunck, Julie Marie. "The Cuban Revolution and Women's Rights." In *Cuban Communism,* edited by Irving Louis Horowitz, pp. 443–64. New Brunswick, N.J.: Transaction Books, 1989.

Butterworth, Douglas. *The People of Buena Ventura: Relocation of Slum Dwellers in Postrevolutionary Cuba.* Urbana: University of Illinois Press, 1980.

Caballero, Armando O. *La mujer en el 95.* Havana: Editorial Nueva Gente, 1982.

Cardenal, Ernesto. *In Cuba.* New York: New Directions, 1972.

Carnoy, Martin. "Educational Reform and Social Transformation in Cuba, 1959–1989." In *Education and Social Transformation in the Third World,* edited by Martin Carnoy and Joel Samoff, pp. 153–208. Princeton, N.J.: Princeton University Press, 1990.

Casal, Lourdes. "Revolution and *Conciencia:* Women in Cuba." In *Women, War and Revolution,* edited by Carol R. Berkin and Clara M. Lovett, pp. 183–206. New York: Holmes & Meier, 1980.

Castro, Fidel. *History Will Absolve Me.* Havana: Editorial en Marcha, 1962.

Casuso, Teresa. *Cuba and Castro.* New York: Random House, 1961.

de Céspedes, Benjamin. *La prostitución en la ciudad de la Habana.* Havana: O'Reilly, 1883.

Chaney, Elsa M. *Supermadre: Women in Politics in Latin America.* Austin: University of Texas Press, 1979.

Chevigny, Bell Gale. "Running the Blockade: Six Cuban Writers." *Socialist Review,* September–October 1981, pp. 83–112.

Clavijo, Uva de Aragón. *El caimán ante el espejo.* Miami: Ediciones Universal, 1993.

Collazo, Bobby. *La última noche que pasé contigo: 49 años de la farándula cubana.* San Juan, P.R.: Editorial Cubanacán, 1987.

Comité Estatal de Estadísticas. *Censo de población y de viviendas, 1981.* Vol. 3. Havana.

————. *Anuario Estadístico de Cuba.* Havana, 1986.

Constitución de la República de Cuba, 1976. Havana: Editorial de Ciencias Sociales, 1985.

Constitución de la República de Cuba, 1992. Granma, September 22, 1992, pp. 3–10.

Croll, Elisabeth J. "Women in Rural Production and Reproduction in the Soviet Union, China, Cuba, and Tanzania: Case Studies." *Signs* 7, no. 2 (Winter 1981): 375–99.

Cuban Communist Party. *A Public Survey on the Quality of Health Care in the Province of Holguín, Cuba.* 1988.

Danielson, Ross. *Cuban Medicine.* New Brunswick, N.J.: Transaction Books, 1979.

Deere, Carmen Diana. "Cuba's Struggle for Self-Sufficiency." *Monthly Review,* July–August 1991, pp. 55–73.

———. "The Latin American Agrarian Reform Experience." In *Rural Women and State Policy: Feminist Perspectives on Latin American Agricultural Development,* edited by Carmen Diana Deere and Magdalena León, pp. 165–90. Boulder, Colo.: Westview Press, 1987.

———. "Rural Women and Agrarian Reform in Peru, Chile, and Cuba." In *Women and Change in Latin America,* edited by June Nash and Helen Safa, pp. 189–207. South Hadley, Mass.: Bergin & Garvey, 1986.

del Aguila, Juan M. *Cuba: Dilemmas of a Revolution.* Boulder, Colo.: Westview Press, 1984.

Díaz-Briquets, Sergio, and Lisandro Pérez. "Fertility Decline in Cuba: A Socioeconomic Interpretation." *Population and Development Review* 8, no. 3 (September 1982): 513–37.

Díaz González, Elena. "La mujer y las necesidades humanas básicas." *Economía y desarollo* September–October 1981, 211–24.

Directory of Officials of the Cuban Republic. Washington, D.C.: Directorate of Intelligence, Central Intelligence Agency, 1985.

Directory of Officials of the Cuban Republic. Washington, D.C.: Directorate of Intelligence, Central Intelligence Agency, 1989.

Dolz, María. *La liberación de la mujer cubana por la educación.* Havana: Oficina del Historiador de la Ciudad, 1955.

Domínguez, Jorge I. *Cuba: Order and Revolution.* Cambridge, Mass.: The Belknap Press, 1978.

Doran, Terry, Janet Satterfield, and Chris Stade. *A Road Well Traveled: Three Generations of Cuban American Women.* Fort Wayne, Ind.: Latin American Educational Center, 1988.

Eckstein, Susan. "The Impact of the Cuban Revolution: A Comparative Perspective." *Comparative Studies in Society and History* 3 (1976): 502–33.

Eng, Luisa. *La mujer cubana en la revolución educacional.* Havana: Editorial Letras Cubanas, 1985.

Engels, Federico. *El órigen de la familia, la propiedad privada y el estado.* Havana: Instituto Cubano del Libro, 1972.

Escobar, Froylan, and Félix Guerra. *El Che en la Sierra Maestra.* Mexico City: Editorial Diogenes, 1973.

Espín, Oliva M. "Cultural and Historical Influences on Sexuality in Hispanic/Latin Women." In *All American Women,* edited by Johnnetta B. Cole. London: The Free Press, 1986.

Espín Guillois, Vilma. *Cuban Women Confront the Future.* Melbourne, Australia: Ocean Press, 1991.

———. "Deborah." *Revista de la Universidad de Oriente,* March 1975, pp. 57–96.

———. "La batalla por el ejercicio pleno de la igualdad de la mujer: acción de los comunistas." *Cuba Socialista* 2 (March–April 1986): 27–68.

————. *La mujer en Cuba: Historia.* Havana: Editorial de la Mujer, 1990.

Europa Yearbook: A World Survey. Vol. 2. London: Europa Publications, 1984, pp. 1469–1476.

Europa Yearbook: A World Survey. Vol. 1. London: Europa Publications, 1990, pp. 796–811.

Evenson, Debra. "Women's Equality in Cuba: What Difference Does a Revolution Make?" *Law and Inequality* 2 (July 1986): 295–326.

Federation of Cuban Women. *Memoria, Primer Congreso de la FMC.* Havana, 1962.

————. *Political Orientation Guide.* Havana, 1973.

————. *Memories, Second Congress Cuban Women's Federation.* Havana: Editorial Orbe, 1975.

————. *Work Plan of the FMC.* Havana: Editorial Orbe, 1975.

————. *Mujeres ejemplares.* Havana: Editorial Orbe, 1977.

————. *Boletín, 3er Congreso de la FMC.* Havana, 1980.

————. *Tercer boletín.* Havana, 1982.

————. *Boletín especial.* Havana, 1983.

————. *Memorias del 3er Congreso de la Federación de Mujeres Cubanas.* Havana: Editorial de Ciencias Sociales, 1984.

————. "La eliminación de todas las formas de discriminación contra la mujer en Cuba." *Boletín especial.* Havana, 1984.

————. *FMC IV Congreso: Recomendaciones a la tesis.* Havana, 1985.

————. *IV Congreso de la FMC: Informe Central.* Havana, 1985.

————. *IV Congreso: Draft Thesis, Cuban Women, 25 Years of Revolution.* Havana, 1985.

————. *III Encuentro Continental de Mujeres.* Havana, 1988.

————. *Estatutos.* Havana, 1990.

————. *V FMC Congreso: Proyecto de Informe Central.* Havana, 1990.

Fee, Elizabeth. "Sex Education in Cuba: An Interview with Dr. Celestino Alvarez Lajonchere." *International Journal of Health Services* 18, no. 2 (1988): 343–56.

Fernández, Gastón A. "The Freedom Flotilla, A Legitimate Crisis of Cuban Socialism?" *Journal of Interamerican Studies and World Affairs* 2 (May 1982): 183–209.

Fernández Pereira, Rosario, et al. *La batalla por el sexto grado.* Havana: Editorial Pueblo y Educación, 1985.

Figueroa, Max, Abel Prieto, and Raúl Gutiérrez. *The Basic Secondary School in the Country: An Educational Innovation in Cuba.* Paris: UNESCO Press, 1974.

Fox, Geoffrey E. "Honor, Shame and Women's Liberation in Cuba: Views of Working-Class Emigré Men." In *Female and Male in Latin America,* edited by Ann Pescatello, pp. 273–90. Pittsburgh: University of Pittsburgh Press, 1973.

Fuentes, Ileana. *Cuba sin caudillos: Un enfoque feminista para el siglo XXI.* Princeton, N.J.: Linden Lane Press, 1994.

Fuller, Linda. *Work and Democracy in Socialist Cuba.* Philadelphia: Temple University Press, 1992.

Gadea, Hilda. *Ernesto, A Memoir of Che Guevara.* Garden City, N.Y.: Doubleday, 1972.

García Llanes, Marisel, and Marcia Alonso Martínez. "Algunas consideraciones martianas sobre la mujer." *Islas* 75 (May–August): 160–73, University of Las Villas.

García Tuduri, Mercedes. "Resumen de la historia de la educación en Cuba: su evaluación, problemas y soluciones del futuro." *Temática Cubana: Primera reunión de Estudios Cubanos (Revista Exilio)*, Winter 1969–Spring 1970, pp. 108–42.

Geyer, Georgie Anne. *Guerrilla Prince: The Untold Story of Fidel Castro*. Boston: Little Brown, 1991.

Gilpin, Margaret. "Health and the Right to Health Care: The Cuban Experience." *Cuba Update* 5 (Fall 1984): 13–18.

Gómez, Andrés. "Una lucha que tenemos que librar todos." *Areito* 8 (November 1990): 5–12.

Gómez, Liliana, ed. *Primer libro de la Orden Ana Betancourt*. Havana: Editorial Orbe, 1974.

Gómez Treto, Raúl. "New Family Code in Cuba." *LADOC* 7 (1979): 18–25.

Gongora Echenque, Manuel. *Lo que he visto en Cuba*. Madrid: Imprenta Gongora, 1929.

González López, Marisela, and Gisela Pérez Fuentes. "La situación legal de la mujer." *Revista Cubana de Derecho*, 1987, pp. 3–26.

Gotkowitz, Laura, and Richard Turits. "Socialist Morality: Sexual Preference, Family, and State Intervention in Cuba." *Socialism and Democracy*, 1988, pp. 7–29.

Granlid, Gunnel, and Goran Palm. "The More Men and Women of the Working Class Dedicate Themselves to Family Life the More They Get Mutilated and Corrupted." In *Socialism and Democracy*, edited by Irwin Silber, pp. 157–61. New York: Central Book Company, 1970.

Greer, Germaine. "Politics—Cuba." In *Women: A World Report*, pp. 271 91. New York: Oxford University Press, 1985.

Guerrero, María Luisa. *Elena Mederos: Una mujer con perfil para la historia*. Miami: Ediciones Universal, 1991.

Guerrero, Natividad. *La educación sexual en la joven generación*. Havana: Editorial Politica, 1985.

Hamberg, Jill. "Cuba." In *The International Handbook of Housing Policies and Practices*. Westport, Conn.: Greenwood Press, 1990.

———. *Under Construction: Housing Policy in Revolutionary Cuba*. New York: Center for Cuban Studies, 1985.

Harter, Hugh A. "Gertrudis Gómez de Avellaneda." In *Spanish American Women Writers*, edited by Diane E. Marting, pp. 210–25. Westport, Conn.: Greenwood Press, 1990.

Hernández, Jorge, et al. "Estudio sobre el divorcio." *Humanidades*, January 1973, Universidad de la Habana, Centro de Información Científica y Técnica.

Hollerbach, Paula E., and Sergio Díaz-Briquets. *Fertility Determinants in Cuba*. Committee on Population and Demography Report No. 26. Washington, D.C.: National Academy Press, 1983.

Holt-Seeland, Inger. *Women of Cuba*. Westport, Conn.: Lawrence Hill, 1982.

Kolesnikov, Nikolai. *Cuba: Educación popular y preparación de los cuadros nacionales, 1959–1982*. Moscow: Editorial Progreso, 1983.

Kozol, Jonathan. *Children of the Revolution*. New York: Delacorte Press, 1978.

Krause, Monika. *Algunos temas fundamentales sobre educación sexual.* Havana: Editorial Científico-Técnica, 1985.

Krause, Monika, ed. *Compilación de artículos sobre educación sexual para el médico de la familia.* Havana: Grupo Nacional de Trabajo sobre Educación Sexual, 1987.

Larguía, Isabel, and John Dumoulin. "Women's Equality and the Cuban Revolution." In *Women and Change in Latin America,* edited by June Nash and Helen Safa, pp. 344–66. South Hadley, Mass.: Bergin & Garvey, 1986.

———. *Hacia una concepción científica de la emancipación de la mujer.* Havana: Editorial de Ciencias Sociales, 1983.

Larzelere, Alex. *The 1980 Cuban Boatlift: Castro's Ploy—America's Dilemma.* Washington, D.C.: National Defense University Press, 1988.

Lavrin, Asunción. "Female, Feminine and Feminist: Key Concepts in Understanding Women's History in Twentieth Century Latin America." *University of Bristol, Occasional Lecture Series,* no. 4 (November 1988), 1–17.

Leiner, Marvin. *Sexual Politics in Cuba: Machismo, Homosexuality, and AIDS.* Boulder, Colo.: Westview Press, 1994.

Lerner, Gerda. *The Creation of Patriarchy.* New York: Oxford University Press, 1986.

Lewis, Oscar, Ruth M. Lewis, and Susan M. Rigdon. *Four Women.* Urbana: University of Illinois Press, 1977.

Lewis, William. "Cirilio Villaverde." In *Latin American Writers,* edited by Carlos A. Sole, pp. 169–74. New York: Scribners, 1989.

Llanes, Julio M. *Celia nuestra y de las flores.* Havana: Editorial Gente Nueva, 1985.

Llovio-Menéndez, José Luis. *Insider: My Hidden Life as a Revolutionary in Cuba.* New York: Bantam, 1988.

Lockwood, Lee. *Castro's Cuba; Cuba's Fidel.* New York: Vantage Press, 1969.

López Cepero, Mario, and Ernesto Chávez Alvarez. *Características de la divorcialidad cubana.* Havana: Editorial de Ciencias Sociales, 1976.

Malmquist, Sandra Elizabeth. "Cuban Infant and Toddler Daycare: Socialization in a Revolutionary Society." Master's thesis, Wesleyan University, 1984.

Martínez-Alier, Verena. *Marriage, Class and Colour in Nineteenth-Century Cuba.* London: Cambridge University Press, 1974.

Martínez Guayanes, María A. "La situación de la mujer en Cuba en 1953." *Santiago* (Univ. of Oriente), September 1974, pp. 195–226.

Martínez, Miriam, ed. *La mujer cubana y la salud pública.* Havana: Editorial Letras Cubanas, 1985.

Matthews, Herbert. *The Cuban Story.* New York: Braziller, 1961.

de Merlin, Condesa. *Viaje a la Havana.* Havana: Editorial de Arte y Literatura, 1974.

Mesa-Lago, Carmelo. "Economics: Realism and Rationality." In *Cuban Communism,* 4th ed., edited by Irving Louis Horowitz, pp. 11–46. New Brunswick, N.J.: Transaction Books, 1981.

Mesa-Lago, Carmelo, ed. *Revolutionary Change in Cuba.* Pittsburgh: University of Pittsburgh Press, 1971.

Ministry of Education. *Manual de educación formal.* Havana, 1983.

Ministry of Public Health. *Programa nacional de atención materno/infantil,* 1983.

Montejo, Esteban. *Autobiography of a Runaway Slave.* New York: Vintage Books, 1968.

Moore, Carlos. *Castro, the Blacks and Africa*. Los Angeles: University of California Press, 1988.

Mora Morales, Esther Pilar. *The Truth About the Political Imprisonment of Women in Castro's Cuba*. Miami: Revista Ideal, 1986.

Moreno Fraginals, Manuel. *El Ingenio*. Vol. 2. Havana: Editorial Ciencias Sociales, 1978.

Moreno, José A. "From Traditional to Modern Values." In *Revolutionary Change in Cuba*, edited by Carmelo Mesa-Lago, pp. 471–97. Pittsburgh: University of Pittsburgh Press, 1971.

Morgan, Robin, ed. *Sisterhood Is Global*. Garden City, N.Y.: Anchor Books, 1984.

Mota, Francisco G. *Por primera vez en Cuba*. Havana: Editorial Gente Nueva, 1982.

Muguercia, Alberto, and Ezequiel Rodríguez. *Rita Montaner*. Havana: Editorial Letras Cubanas, 1984.

Mujal-León, Eusebio. *The Cuban University Under the Revolution*. Washington, D.C.: Cuban American Foundation, 1988.

Mulhare, Mirta de la Torre. "Sexual Ideology in Pre-Castro Cuba: A Cultural Analysis." Ph.D. dissertation, University of Pittsburgh, 1969.

Murray, Nicola. "Socialism and Feminism: Women and the Cuban Revolution, Part 1." *Feminist Review* 2 (1979): 57–71.

———. "Socialism and Feminism: Women and the Cuban Revolution, Part 2." *Feminist Review* 3 (1979): 99–108.

Nazzari, Muriel. "The 'Woman Question' in Cuba: An Analysis of Material Constraints on Its Solution." *Signs* 2 (Winter 1983): 246–63.

Nicholson, Jr., Joe. *Inside Cuba*. New York: Sheed and Ward, 1974.

Noa, Frederick. "The Condition of Women in Cuba." *Outlook Magazine*, March 16, 1905, pp. 642–47.

Núñez Jiménez, Antonio. *La abuela*. Lima, Peru: Campodonico-ediciones S.A., 1973.

Núñez Machín, Ana. *Mujeres en el periodismo cubano*. Santiago de Cuba: Editorial Oriente, 1989.

Núñez Sarmiento, Marta. *Mujeres en empleos no tradicionales*. Havana: Editorial de Ciencias Sociales, 1991.

Oficina Nacional de los Censos Demográfico y Electoral, *Censos de Población, Viviendas y Electoral*. Havana, 1953.

Olesen, Virginia. "Confluences in Social Change: Cuban Women and Health Care." *Journal of Interamerican Studies and World Affairs* 4 (November 1975): 398–411.

Ortiz, María Dolores. *La mujer cubana en la educación superior*. Havana: Editorial Letras, 1985.

Ortuzar-Young, Ada. "Lydia Cabrera." In *Spanish American Women Writers*, edited by Diane E. Marting, pp. 105–14. Westport, Conn.: Greenwood Press, 1990.

Osmond, Marie Withers. "Women and Work in Cuba: Objective Conditions and Subjective Perceptions." Revised version of paper presented at the annual meeting of the American Sociological Association, August 26–30, 1985, Washington, D.C.

Padula, Alfred. "Cuba: The Fall of the Bourgeoisie, 1959–1961." Ph.D. dissertation, University of New Mexico, 1974.

Padula, Alfred, and Lois M. Smith. "The Revolutionary Transformation of Cuban Education, 1959–1987." In *Making the Future: Politics and Educational Reform in the United States, England, the Soviet Union, China and Cuba,* edited by Edgar B. Gumbert, pp. 117–39. Atlanta, Ga.: Center for Cross-Cultural Education, 1988.

———. "Women in Socialist Cuba, 1959–1984." In *Cuba: Twenty-five Years of Revolution, 1959–1984,* edited by Sandor Halebsky and John M. Kirk, pp. 79–91. New York: Praeger, 1985.

Paulston, Roland G. "Cambios en la educación cubana." *Aportes* 21 (July 1971): 60–83.

Pavón González, Ramiro. *El empleo femenino en Cuba.* Havana: Editorial de Ciencias Sociales, 1977.

Paz Pérez, Carlos. *De lo popular y lo vulgar en el habla cubana.* Havana: Editorial de Ciencias Sociales, 1988.

Peral Collado, Daniel A. "El Proyecto del Código de la Familia." *Revista Cubana del Derecho,* June–December 1974, pp. 31–58.

Pérez, Louis A. *Cuba: Reform or Revolution.* New York: Oxford University Press, 1989.

Pérez, Magaly, and Noemí Pascual. *Estadísticas sobre la mujer cubana.* Havana: Editorial Letras Cubanas, 1985.

Prieto Morales, Aldo. *Lo circunstancia en la responsibilidad penal.* Havana: Editorial de Ciencias Sociales, 1983.

Provenzo, Eugene F., and Concepción García. "Exiled Teachers and the Cuban Revolution." *Cuban Studies* 1 (Winter 1983): 1–15.

Purcell, Susan Kaufman. "Modernizing Women for a Modern Society: The Cuban Case." In *Female and Male in Latin America,* edited by Ann Pescatello, pp. 257–71. Pittsburgh: University of Pittsburgh Press, 1973.

Ramos, Ana. "La mujer y la revolución en Cuba." *Casa de las Américas* March–June 1971, pp. 56–72.

Randall, Margaret. *Gathering Rage: The Failure of the Twentieth Century Revolutions to Develop a Feminist Agenda* New York: Monthly Review Press, 1992.

———. *La mujer cubana ahora.* Havana: Editorial de Ciencias Sociales, 1972.

———. *Women in Cuba: Twenty Years Later.* Brooklyn, N.Y.: Smyrna Press, 1981.

Rodríguez Calderón, Mirta. *Dígame usted!* Havana: Editorial Pablo de la Torriente Brau, 1989.

Rodríguez Domínguez, Dr. Pedro. *Temas de salud sobre la mujer.* Havana: Editorial Científico-Técnica, 1985.

Rojas, Marta. *La cueva del muerto.* Havana: Union of Cuban Artists and Writers, 1983.

Romeu, Raquel. *La mujer y el esclavo en la Cuba de 1840.* Montevideo, Uruguay: Asociación de literatura hispánica, 1987.

Rosenthal, Marguerite G. "The Problems of Single Motherhood in Cuba." In *Cuba in Transition,* edited by Sandor Halebsky et al., pp. 161–76. Boulder, Colo.: Westview Press, 1992.

Rowbotham, Sheila. *Women, Resistance and Revolution.* New York: Pantheon Books, 1972.

Sabás Alomá, Mariblanca. *Feminismo: cuestiones sociales-crítica literaria.* Havana: Editorial Hermes, 1930.

Safa, Helen Icken. "Women and Industrial Employment in Cuba." Study prepared in collaboration with the Federation of Cuban Women. Kellogg Center, University of Notre Dame, 1989.

Salas, Luis. *Social Control and Deviance in Cuba*. New York: Praeger, 1979.

Santamaría Haydée. *Moncada*. Secaucus, N.J.: Lyle Stuart, 1980.

Santana, Sarah M. "The Cuban Health Care System: Responsiveness to Changing Population Needs and Demands." *World Development*, no. 1 (1987): 113–25.

———. "Focus on: AIDS in Cuba." *Cuba Update* Summer 1989, pp. 23–25.

Santana, Sarah M., and Carmen Hernández. "El reto actual." *Areito* 8 (November 1990): 13–16.

Schnabl, Dr. Siegfried. *En defensa del amor*. Havana: Editorial Científico-Técnica, 1985.

Schnookal, Deborah, ed. *Cuban Women Confront the Future*. Melbourne, Australia: Ocean Press, 1991.

Schroeder, Susan. *Cuba: A Handbook of Historical Statistics*. Boston: G. K. Hall, 1982.

Segura Bustamante, Inés. *Cuba siglo XX y la generación de 1930*. Miami: Ediciones Universal, 1986.

Séjourné, Laurette. *La mujer cubana en el quehacer de la historia*. Mexico City: Siglo Veintiuno, 1980.

Scoane Gallo, José. *El folclor médico de Cuba*. Havana: Editorial de Ciencias Sociales, 1984.

Silber, Irwin, ed. *The Revolutionary Ideology of the "Third World" as Expressed by Intellectuals and Artists at the Cultural Congress of Havana, January 1968*. New York: Central Book Company, 1970.

Smith, Lois M. "Progress, Science and Myth: The Health Education of Cuban Women." In *Cuban Studies* (Univ. of Pittsburgh) 19 (1989): 167–96.

———. "Sexuality and Socialism in Cuba." In *Cuba in Transition*, edited by Sandor Halebsky et al., pp. 177–91. Boulder, Colo.: Westview Press, 1992.

———. "Teenage Pregnancy and Sex Education in Cuba." Paper presented at the Latin American Studies Association, New Orleans, La., March 1988.

Smith, Lois M., and Padula, Alfred. "Twenty Questions on Sex and Gender in Revolutionary Cuba." In *Cuban Studies* (Univ. of Pittsburgh) 18 (1988): 149–58.

Sternbach Saporta, Nancy, Marysa Navarro-Aranguren, Patricia Chuchryk, and Sonia E. Alvarez. *Feminisms in Latin America: Identity, Strategy, and Democracy*. Boulder, Colo.: Westview Press, 1992.

Stone, Elizabeth, ed. *Women and the Cuban Revolution*. New York: Pathfinder Press, 1980.

Stoner, Kathryn Lynn. *From the House to the Streets: The Cuban Woman's Movement for Legal Reform 1898–1940*. Durham, N.C.: Duke University Press, 1991.

———. "Ofelia Domínguez Navarro: The Making of a Cuban Socialist Feminist." In *The Human Tradition in Latin America*, edited by William H. Beezley and Judith Ewell, pp. 119–40. Wilmington, Del.: Scholarly Resources, 1988.

Stubbs, Jean. "Gender Issues in Contemporary Cuban Tobacco Farming." *World Development* 1 (1987): 41–65.

———. *Tobacco on the Periphery: A Case Study in Cuban History*. London: Cambridge University Press, 1985.

Stubbs, Jean, and Mavis Alvarez. "Women on the Agenda: The Cooperative Movement in Rural Cuba." In *Rural Women and State Policy,* edited by Carmen Diana Deere and Magdalena Leon, pp. 142–61. Boulder, Colo.: Westview Press, 1987.

Sutherland, Elizabeth. *The Youngest Revolution: A Personal Report on Cuba.* London: Pittman Publishing, 1969.

Szulc, Tad. *Fidel, A Critical Portrait.* New York: Avon Books, 1986.

de la Torriente, Lolo. "La mujer como factor de progreso en la vida cubana." In *Libro de Cuba: Edición conmemorativa del cincuentenario de la independencia, 1902–1952.* Havana: n.p., 1954, p. 180.

Valdés, Nelson P. "A Bibliography of Cuban Women in the Twentieth Century." *Cuban Studies Newsletter* 4 (June 1974): 1–31.

Valdés, Nelson P., and Nana Elsasser. "La Cachita y El Che: Patron Saints of Revolutionary Cuba." *Encounters* (Univ. of New Mexico) Winter 1989, pp. 30–34.

Walsh, Bryan O. "Cuban Refugee Children." *Journal of Inter-American Studies and World Affairs* 3–4 (July–October 1971): 378–415.

Ward, Fred. *Inside Cuba Today.* New York: Crown Publishers, 1978.

Werner, David. "Health Care in Cuba Today: A Model Service or a Means of Social Control—or Both." The Hesperian Foundation, n.d.

Wilkie, James W., ed. *Statistical Abstract of Latin America.* Vol. 26. Los Angeles: University of California, Los Angeles Latin American Center, 1988.

Yglesias, José. *In the Fist of the Revolution.* New York: Vintage Books, 1969.

Young, Allen. *Gays Under the Cuban Revolution.* San Francisco: Grey Fox Press, 1981.

Zulueta, María Elena, ed. *Manual de educación para la salud.* Havana: Editorial Científico-Técnica, 1985.

Index

and abortion law, 73–74
and emotion, 70
and laws governing prostitution, 40
Lenin, Vladimir, 5, 41
Lesbians, 170, 173
Levda, Marta, 119
Life expectancy, 59, 61
Literacy campaign, 37, 83–84, 172
de Llovio-Menéndez, José Luis and
    Maggie, 91
Lorenzo, Orestes, 148
Love, 147, 177

Maceo, Antonio, 11
Machado, Gerardo, 18–19, 26
Machismo, 76, 168, 176, 184, 185. *See*
    also Gender; Men: resistance to
    change of; Sexual discrimination
Maids, 137, 140, 151, 170, 187. *See*
    also Domestic service; United
    Family Services
Male irresponsibility, 166. *See also*
    Fathers: absentee; Fathers:
    delinquent
Mariana Grajales brigade, 30–31
Mariel exodus, 181
Marinello, Juan, 89
Marrero, Yolanda, 82
Marriage, 88, 104, 145, 154–57,
    160, 165
  in colonial era, 9, 18, 26
  common-law, 145
  and consensual unions, 155, 156
  decreasing importance of, 160
  early, 157
  and "marriage palaces," 155
  and remarriage, 157
  sex in, 169, 174, 200 n. 47
Martí, José, 12, 27, 31, 83
Martínez, Diana, 168
Martínez-Alier, Verena, 145
Martínez Sánchez, Agosto, 99
Marxism, 4, 52, 95, 131, 139, 145,
    172
Masturbation, 170
Material incentives, 99, 101, 142
Maternal mortality, 59, 69, 77
Maternity homes, 77
Maternity law (1974), 19, 96, 104,
    105
Maternity leave, 126, 127
Matthews, Herbert, 27
Mechanization, 125, 186
Mederos, Elena, 17, 35, 90

Media, 54
Medical school enrollment, 73
Medicine. *See* Health care system
Men
  avoidance of "women's" work by,
    129
  and day care, 54
  and exile, 148
  and family leave, 127
  and family responsibilities, 141
  and gender roles, 160
  and housework, 147
  loss of power of, 147, 150, 166
  opposition to Family Code, 105
  resistance to change of, 37, 98,
    100, 107, 110, 158
  sexual behavior of, 66, 179
  and sharing of child care, 104, 133
Menopause, 70
Menstruation, 38, 62, 70, 122
Mesa, Liliam, 27
Mesa-Lago, Carmelo, 113
Microbrigades, 119, 135
Middle-class women, 10, 20, 37–39,
    58, 132, 148, 151, 152
Militarism, 11, 54, 93, 182, 184–85
  and the FMC, 50
Military, 49, 52, 83, 148, 182, 185
  and combat, 13, 24, 27, 30–31
Mistresses, 24, 171
Modernization, 139, 140
Molina Morejón, Hilda, 65
Moncada attack, 23–24
Montejo, Esteban, 9
Moral double standard, 76, 128–29,
    177, 179, 185
Moral incentives, 99, 142
Mosquera, Josefina, 20
Mother companions, 62
Motherhood, 121, 122, 140, 166,
    171. *See also* Childbirth; Gender:
    traditional roles and attitudes
    toward; ideals; Parenting; Single
    mothers
  and moral agency, 16
  and nationhood, 184
  and sexuality, 171
Muchacha (magazine), 36, 60, 143
Mujeres (magazine)
  ceases publication, 143
  criticized as boring, 52
  as educational tool of FMC, 36
  investigative reporting in, 127
  letters-to-the-editor column, 117